Embodying Honor

WOMEN IN AFRICA AND
THE DIASPORA

Series Editors

STANLIE JAMES
AILI MARI TRIPP

Embodying Honor

Fertility, Foreignness, and
Regeneration in Eastern Sudan

Amal Hassan Fadlalla

The University of Wisconsin Press

This book was published with the support of

the OFFICE OF THE VICE PRESIDENT FOR RESEARCH
and
the WOMEN'S STUDIES PROGRAM
at the University of Michigan

and

the ANONYMOUS FUND OF THE COLLEGE
OF LETTERS AND SCIENCES
at the University of Wisconsin–Madison.

The University of Wisconsin Press
1930 Monroe Street, 3rd Floor
Madison, Wisconsin 53711-2059

www.wisc.edu/wisconsinpress/

3 Henrietta Street
London WC2E 8LU, England

Library of Congress Cataloging-in-Publication Data
Fadlalla, Amal Hassan.
Embodying honor: fertility, foreignness, and regeneration
in eastern Sudan / Amal Hassan Fadlalla.
p.   cm. — (Women in Africa and the diaspora)
Includes bibliographical references and index.
ISBN 0-299-22380-9 (cloth: alk. paper)
1. Fertility, Human—Social aspects—Sudan.   2. Sex role—Sudan.
3. Women—Sudan—Social conditions.
4. Hadendowa (African people)—Sexual behavior.
I. Title.   II. Series.
HQ766.5.S76F33   2007
306.874′309624—dc22   2007011785

In memory of
HASSAN FADLALLA
(father and friend)

❧

In memory of
MARYAM ʿUMAR

❧

To
my MOTHER

❧

To
the HADENDOWA WOMEN FOR A JUST FUTURE

Walls, town,
And port,
Refuge of death,
Gray sea
Where the wind crashes;
Everything sleeps.
. . . .
It's the swarm of jinn passing by,
Whirling and whistling.
. . . .
O Prophet, if your hand saves me
From these foul evening demons,
Then I'll prostrate my bare forehead
Before your sacred incense burners.
. . . .
Strange sounds
Still come to us.
Thus from the Arabs
When the horn sounds
A song from the shore
For the moment arises,
And the child who dreams
Dreams dreams of gold.
The mournful jinn,
Sons of misdeeds,
In the darkness
Hasten their steps.
Their swarm rumbles.
Thus, deeply, murmurs
A wave that one sees not
This vague sound
Which falls asleep
Is the wave
On the shore.
It is the plaintive prayer
Almost suppressed,
Of a holy woman
For a soul deceased.
One has doubts about the nights
I listen:
All flees,
All passes on;
Space wipes out the noise.

      Victor Hugo, "Les Djinns"

Contents

Contents

Illustrations

Figures

Map

Tables

Color insert following page 106

Acknowledgments

Many individuals and institutions contributed to the birth of this project. Particular thanks are due colleagues, friends, and staff at the Department of Anthropology and the Program of African Studies at Northwestern University, the Department of Anthropology and the Red Sea Area Project at the University of Khartoum (Sudan), the Center for Population and Development Studies at Harvard University, and the Women's Studies Program and the Center for Afroamerican and African Studies (CAAS) at the University of Michigan for their invaluable academic support.

At Northwestern, I wish to thank professors Tim Earle, Helen Schwartzman, Gil Stein, Mary Weismantel, Karen Hansen, Bill Murphy, Robert Launay, Jane Guyer, Akbar Virmani, Bashir Diagne, and Mohamed Mahmoud. I am deeply indebted to Caroline Bledsoe, Micaela di Leonardo, and Jane Guyer, who meticulously supervised the dissertation version of this project. My interactions with them as committee members have broadened my intellectual horizons and extended beyond to touch my personal life. Special thanks are due Professor John Hunwick for his translation of Victor Hugo's poem "Les Djinns." My thanks are also extended to Elise Levine and Jennifer Johnson-Kuhn and to Mette Shayne and David Easterbrook at the Africana Library.

My dissertation fieldwork and its subsequent analysis were made possible by the generous support of the Rockefeller Foundation, the Population Council, and the Center for Development Studies, Bergen University (Norway). I owe particular thanks to Professor Leif Manger at the University of Bergen. At the University of Khartoum, professors Salah al-Shadhali, Fahima Zahir, Idris Salim, Hassan Mohamed Salih, and Hassan Abdel-Ati offered invaluable academic support.

My tenure at Harvard and the University of Michigan has helped shape the final stages of this project. At Harvard, Michael Reich, Alan Hill, Alaka Basu, the Bell Fellows, and the staff at the Center for Population and Development Studies deserve special thanks for their assistance. At Michigan, professors James Jackson, Pamela Reid, Valerie Turab, Kevin Gains, Abby Stewart, Mamadou Diouf, Frieda Ekotto, Naome Andre, Ann Larimore, David Cohen, Elizabeth Cole, Elisha Rene, Kelly Askew, Marcia Inhorn, Rae Silverman, Julius Scott, Aferworki Paulos, Nesha Hanif, Lori Brooks, and the staff at both Women's Studies and CAAS are due particular thanks for their support. I would also like to thank David Peck, Dottie Riemenschneider, and Karl Longstreth at the University of Michigan Library and Christiane Anderson at the University of Michigan Herbarium for their assistance.

In Sinkat town, where I did my fieldwork, I was surrounded by the care and kindness of many people to whom I will always be indebted. I am grateful to the Hadendowa women who opened their homes and hearts for me during my stay among them and treated me like one of their own. My knowledge of their worldviews and struggles would not have been possible without their warm acceptance and hospitality. I would particularly like to acknowledge the invaluable help and support of the late Maryam 'Umar, who treated me like a member of her family, introducing me to many of her relatives and friends. Her untimely death was a severe shock to me.

Other individuals in Sinkat share credit for helping me bring this project to fruition. 'Umada Sharif, Haj Alsafi, Abu Amna, and the late Shaikh Abu Hadiyya and his family were especially supportive during the difficult circumstances of fieldwork. I would also like to thank the doctors, the staff, and health visitor Khadija 'Uthman at Sinkat Hospital, the Red Crescent staff, the judge and staff of the Sinkat court, and the staff at the local police station. My gratitude extends to my field assistants Asha Ahmad, Halima Salih, Miriam Khaurshid, Amna Ahmad, and 'Aisa Aljailani for facilitating and conducting interviews during my fieldwork. My thanks are also due their families, who kindly embraced me and provided me with supportive company. I am grateful to Balait and Asha for their generosity and support. I am also indebted to the late Mohamed Al-Madani Hajar (a relative and a grandfather) and his family for hosting me during the first months of my fieldwork. I am grateful to the staff of the United Nations program in Sinkat, whose support and friendship helped facilitate my research. In Port Sudan, special thanks are due my friend Salwa 'Abd Allah and her family, who accommodated me during my short visits to the town. I would also like to thank Sayyid Dabalaub at the Ministry of Agriculture and the staff of Oxfam for providing me with helpful data.

I extend my gratitude to many of my Hadendowa colleagues and friends in the diaspora who helped in various ways, especially with Tu-Badawie terminologies. Thanks to Musa Kilai, Musa Sidi, Mohamed Adraub, Mohamed Babikir, Abd al-Rahman Bakash, and Mahmoud Karar.

I am fortunate to have the support, love, kindness, and generosity of many special friends and colleagues. Micaela di Leonardo, Heather McClure, Nasrin Qadir, Mary Ebling, Akbar Virmani, Giulia Barerra, Nadia Muhammad Khair, Anwar Elhaj, Sondra Hale, Bill Schiller, Nadine Naber, Atef Said, Thomas Abowd, Jati Lal, Miriam Tiktin, Patrick Dodd, and Dario Gaggio have earned my unending gratitude.

I will forever be indebted to my family, whose constant support and encouragement over the distance has been a source of immense motivation and fortitude during some of the hardest times in my life. My gratitude to my mother, Umm Sitrain Yasin; my brothers, Badr al-Din and Muhammad; my sisters, Amira, Ni'mat, and Ihasn; my nieces, Shirin and Shahad; and my twin nephews, Hassan and Ghassan. The support of the various members of my extended families is deeply appreciated. My utmost gratitude is due my friend, husband, and soul mate Shafei Dafalla, whose companionship and support has brought tremendous joy and strength into my life. I am particularly indebted to Shafei for designing the Sudan map and for his artistic vision, which helped improve the quality of my photographic work.

Finally, I am grateful to the editors of *Identities: Global Studies in Culture and Power* for publishing "Modest Women, Deceptive *Jinn*: Identity, Alterity, and Disease in Eastern Sudan," my first article from this project, which appears in revised form as chapter 2 of this book.

Embodying Honor

Writing in margins of anthropologist's notebook

Introduction

Weaving the Web of Regeneration

But your kind of weaving is lucrative; mine isn't.

Fatima

At sunset some of my Hadendowa female friends and I sat, our bodies wrapped in *fautas* (body wraps), at the edge of the *khaur* (dry stream) that divides displaced Hadendowa shanty settlements from the town center, or *alhishan*. *Alhishan* is where most non-Hadendowa reside (northern Sudanese, Kurds, Ashraf, and few Beja elite), and it is where the central government of Khartoum runs the Sinkat district of the Red Sea province. The court, the police station, the hospital, the schools, the market, and the famous tomb of Alsharifa Maryam (a renowned non-Hadendowa female saint) are all at the center beyond the *khaur*. At this hour, many poor Hadendowa women who work in the *hishan* as maids cross the *khaur* back to their families. Veiled, they must keep an upright posture, look straight ahead, and avoid talking with strange men, laughing, or chatting loudly in the street. This is how a woman of *durarit* (honor) is expected to carry herself outside her immediate familial boundaries. As we were sitting on the bank of the *khaur*, a woman in an old yellow *fauta* changed her direction

3

and came toward us. One of my friends said, "This is Halima." I responded, "How could you know? She is all covered up." Surprised, my friend looked at me and retorted, "By the way she walks!" I felt embarrassed, for I had known Halima for several months and yet was unable to identify her in the street. Halima was one of the women I was trying to interview, but her hectic work schedule had delayed our meeting. This time, however, when she set foot on the other side of the *khaur*, I was able to successfully arrange a meeting.

When we met, Halima, who is in her early to midthirties, talked about the suffering and misfortune that she had experienced "through her body" since puberty.

> I was a child. I got married when I was around fourteen and wanted to get pregnant soon after and have a son. But probably because I was very young, I did not give birth as soon as I expected. I waited seven years and almost lost hope of becoming a mother. Although my relatives were supportive, I noticed how their tones would change when they talked about reproductive matters in my presence. Everybody would suddenly emphasize that I was still very young.
>
> Finally, I got pregnant, but I miscarried when I was seven months pregnant. It was a boy. My emotional pain was overwhelming: How could I wait that long and then have my son die? He was fine—no ulcers, no defects, and no sickness. What had gone wrong? I did not understand. It was a bad omen to begin my life like that. I was miserable. My family, especially my husband, worried. This is when we began to consult *fuqara* [religious people] in the area. We were in the rural area then. After that, I lost three children the same way (two girls and a boy), all within a two-year birth interval. After each pregnancy we would consult a new *faqir*. My husband went as far as Sawakin and Kassala to consult religious people recommended by our distant relatives because it was not good for me to travel.
>
> When we lost our animals due to drought, we moved to Sinkat. Here we consulted a renowned female healer, who checked my body and told me that there was nothing wrong with me but an evil eye. My husband and I made a *nadur* [promise to God] that we would fast fifteen days during the summer if I would give birth to a living son. I gave birth to Ali in Sinkat, and we fulfilled our *nadur*. But after Ali, the cycle of misfortune continued, and again I lost three children the same old way (two girls and a boy). I did not check with a doctor. It is not something we normally do. I checked with a midwife at the health center, and she said I had "poisoning of the umbilical cord." I did not understand and continued with the healers.
>
> My husband then died of malaria. He was young, and he died unexpectedly. He had a fever, and everybody suspected it was malaria. We did not check with the doctor, but relied only on our way of healing. I do not have many relatives left. They all died young because of famines, because of diseases, or maybe, I guess, because of God's will.

Ali is the one I care about the most. I work as a maid: I clean houses and wash clothes in the town center. I work hard until my whole body hurts, just for a little money to keep us alive. I try to protect Ali so much, and sometimes it irritates him. He is a grown up now, but because of my overwhelming care he has not contracted *hisba* [measles] or *katkauta* [whooping cough] yet. If there is a disease outbreak where we live, I travel with him to wherever we have relatives so that he won't get sick. It is like a *halafa* [reverse logic] that wherever there is danger, you do the opposite to avert it. When Ali was born, we performed a series of *halafa* rituals for him. For instance, we did not do the *tamnai aurauk* [the ritual of celebrating the birth of a male child and his mother's safety] immediately. We waited fourteen days and then performed the ritual but without the dancing that characterizes it as a form of *halafa*. We just slaughtered a sheep to ward off evil and diseases. Ali is about twelve now. He went to school, but he quit because he insisted that he work to help me. He is my back support, the joy of the family and his father's wish. I want him to live longer.

Halima's story captures the plight of many poor Hadendowa women who attempt to manage their reproductive suffering in a patrilineal society where collective identity, marital security, and social status hinge on a woman's ability to regenerate the patrilineage. This cultural dynamic unravels multilayered meanings of gender and fertility that are experienced through the body in various ways that are significant to our anthropological understanding of health and reproduction. This ethnography examines in particular a predominant discourse about the feminization of social vulnerability that women express through their reproductive health narratives and ritual practices. Through these discursive practices, women of different fertility situations, most of whom do not use contraceptives, and for whom biological fate can be capricious in their impoverished settings, manage their reproductive misfortunes, emotional suffering, and conjugal lives in order to become responsible mothers. The focus on the feminization of social vulnerability shifts attention from anthropology's symbolic emphasis on gendered meanings of fertility to a conception of ritual symbolism and practices as diagnostics of historical relationships of power, marginality, and social conflict.

In such discursive practices, the female body, as a spatial metaphor, becomes the locus of anxieties about foreign dangers and diseases that are perceived to disrupt reproduction, morality, identity, and social well-being. In this context the very concept of fertility describes a precarious trajectory (a threatened corporeal capacity) that women monitor continuously to achieve fertility possibly resulting in more sons than daughters. For Hadendowa women childbearing and child rearing are intertwined concepts, central to notions of "proper" fertility and motherhood. These concepts include both the physical aspect of investing in the pre- and postnatal health of both mothers and infants and the social aspect of transmitting knowledge of gender propriety from generation to generation. Although childbearing is a central theme in anthropological studies of reproduction (e.g., Delany 1991; Sobo 1993a, 1993b, Abu-Lughod 1993; Inhorn 1994; Bledsoe 2002), socialization and child rearing are usually classified as relevant topics for psychological anthropology or culture-and-personality studies (e.g., Riesman 1986, 1992). The conceptualization of child rearing as closely tied to ideas of reproductive well-being and social status is not fully integrated into anthropological studies of fertility and reproduction. Fertility, however, can be a useful analytical category that extends the meanings of "healthy reproductive bodies" beyond the anthropological emphasis on childbearing to incorporate the meanings of raising children well.

Fertility outcomes are also gendered, reflecting how cultural meanings attributed to having sons and daughters are anchored in a plethora of ritual practices and historical narratives that substantiate a couple's fertility decisions. Unlike interpretive anthropologists, demographers have paid close attention to gender preference, its influence on fertility outcomes, and its impact on the number of "missing girls," especially in Asia. In Asia son preference is so strong that it is reflected in differential healthcare practices for children, leading in some cases to higher mortality rates for girls (Levine 1987; Das Gupta 1987; Pong 1994; Croll 2000; Sen 2001). Africa presents a stark contrast to the Asian pattern. Son preference is extremely widespread, yet since girls are not unwanted, the ideology produces no obvious difference in the mortality rate of male and female children (Cain 1983, 1991; Gadalla, McCarthy, and Campbell 1985; Obermeyer 1995, 1996).[1] Like many African examples, the case of the Hadendowa of eastern Sudan presents a strong ideology of son preference even though there are no distorted sex ratios and differential mortality rates between male and female children in the region (*Sudan Demographic and Health Survey* 1991). This is because fertile women are seen as central to the process of regeneration, whereas preference for sons can be explained usually according to the sociohistorical responsibilities of defending the patrimony and generating the patriline.

Thus mothers of sons are more revered than childless and "son-infertile" women and are often referred to as *masait* (blessed) to mark their particular status. This singular status is historically grounded in the narrative of Hadat (the lioness), the mother of the founders of the seven existing Hadendowa lineages. The name of the group, Hadendowa, itself derives from the composite term Hadat-indiwab (meaning "Hadat's family").

---

1. An exception is the child mortality rates among the matrilineal Tonga of southern Zambia, which seem to indicate a preference for daughters (Clark et al. 1995).

Women depict Hadat as a virtuous wife and a responsible mother who breast-fed her seven sons and raised them well, thereby imparting the meanings of honor, courage, and responsibility. Against this glorious history of mothering, reproductive mishaps such as infertility, infant mortality, successive miscarriages, and children's sickness have a negative impact on women's ability to achieve the status of "proper" fertility and motherhood. Women such as Halima, who experienced multiple reproductive traumas, are seen as women whose fertility has gone awry and are thus perceived as more threatening to the collective well-being than are infertile women. Their plight is attributed to a host of diseases related to the evil eye and other ailments associated with dangerous external forces that invade their bodies and render them socially marginal.

Such pervasive ideas about threatened fertility and well-being underlie women's perceptions of birth control methods as foreign devices that tamper with their reproductive potential and thus prevent them from achieving a desired fertility path that may result in a preferable number of sons and daughters. While sons are strongly preferred, daughters are indispensable, and in any household their absence is equated with social barrenness. Indeed, values attributed to having sons and daughters transcend the cost-benefit calculations of their upbringing to encompass other meanings of affection and togetherness (see Saghayroun 1983; Khalifa 1984; Abu-Lughod 1993). A woman may decide to continue or stop childbearing based on the gender, survivorship, and health of her children regardless of her reproductive age (see Bledsoe 2002). This does not imply an unintentional effort by women to regulate their fertility; on the contrary, since fertility revolves around healthy childbearing and child rearing, becoming a responsible mother entails diligent investment in mothers' and infants' health through diet, herbal medicine, rest, prolonged breast-feeding, and performance of certain rituals to invigorate the body during the different stages of the life cycle.

Meanings attributed to sons and daughters also highlight the social obligation of motherhood: the commitment to raising children well, which means raising them to become "true" Hadendowa who will, in turn, fulfill their obligations toward their parents even after their parents' death. During my fieldwork, Nisa, a divorced, childless woman of about fifty, died alone in her home. Her relatives gathered during her funeral to mourn her loss. Although both her female and male relatives took care of preparing her body for burial according to Islamic conventions, the presence of a daughter or a son during these preparation rituals marks the social status of the deceased and the continuation of his or her legacy after death. Nisa's childless situation augmented her kin's sadness over her loss as expressed through this mourning lyric:

Taauti bawamamaita.	No daughters to mourn your loss [to receive our condolences].
Taauri bawamamaita.	No sons to mourn your loss [to receive our condolences].
Imbasau difaiau aisimianaita.	On the day you died, the door to your house was closed.
Adawai badawni nishayaita.	[No daughter shedding tears] near your funeral bed.
Titkauwai bititkauwaina lihidayait.	No son to put you down in your grave.

The death of a childless woman marks the "social death" of her tent cluster. After a women's death, her female relatives dismantle the tent, the symbol of fertility and group regeneration, and her corpse is handed to her male relatives, who march with it to the graveyard outside the women's compound. The tent cluster thus cycles through the reproductive histories of the mother and her female offspring. Women's central position in the process of regeneration evokes feminists' concerns about power, agency, and consent (e.g., Abu-Lughod 1986, 1990; Morgan 1994; Greenhalgh 1994). Within the limits of this constructed vision of fertility and womanhood, responsible mothering becomes a vital source for acquiring honor and social status. Women, however, present themselves as consenting agents (although resistance occurs) who actively attempt to influence their reproductive well-being and to adjust their own fertility practices to achieve respect and social security. Halima's detailed ethnography of pregnancies and births summarized earlier is an example of how women demonstrate their agency by investing financially (with the help of their families) and through various health practices to protect their fertility and their children's future productive and reproductive careers.

Although demographic perspectives on fertility and gender preference draw attention to broader patterns on both the macro level of population structures and on a micro level of family strategies to achieve desired fertility outcomes, explanations of fertility decisions and gender preference often do not explore their complexity and their embeddedness in corporeal experiences and practices. Anthropologists are increasingly directing attention to the significance of situating fertility and demographic phenomena in a web of interrelated social relationships that involve parents, children, and kin (Greenhalgh 1995; Carter 1995; Kertzer and Fricke 1997; Skinner 1997, Basu and Aaby 1998). Fertility is seen as a social institution embedded in political histories and kinship processes (Yanagisako and Collier 1994; Handwerker 1990; Rapp 1991; Ginsburg and Rapp 1995; Strathern 1992) and in gender praxis and systems of power and knowledge that socialize and recruit individuals and groups for certain social positions and functions

(Guyer 1995). Individuals themselves become valuable through their social location in knowledge processes and not merely by virtue of their productive and reproductive capacities. Accordingly children are "produced and treated as 'wealth,' in a qualitative, career building sense" (Guyer 1996, 13), and their potentialities are thus harnessed to maintain and reproduce existing relations of power and systems of knowledge.

The Hadendowa emphasis on gender preference and reproductive well-being therefore presents a stark contrast to the Asian example and shifts the focus to a new level of intragender asymmetries wherein women themselves are differentiated by virtue of their physical well-being and their ability or inability to bear and raise healthy, successful children, especially sons. Missing from our ethnographic accounts in both interpretative and medical anthropology is how women's personal experiences of childbearing and child rearing are closely linked to gender preference, to situations of poverty and suffering (see Kleinman and Kleinman 1991), and to constructions of identity and success in health and social life

Situating fertility in the Hadendowa's cosmic understanding produces a multitude of interrelated meanings about gender, kinship, health, and "embodied spatiality." When women are seen as key figures in the process of regeneration and socialization, they are also regarded as "honorable subordinates" whose sexuality and reproductive abilities are endowed with contradictory meanings of blessing and danger. Such ideas are explained according to the moral definition of men's and women's bodies and their spatial situation within and without the boundaries of the domestic social space. The domestic social space is the locus of power, morality, fertility, and well-being. It is where children are born, nourished, and socialized and where kinship relations are fostered and maintained. Outside this space reside other people, spirits, and certain plants whose encounters are suffused with dangerous powers that threaten regenerative identities.

The inner social space is organized according to matrilocal rules, in which the tent of the mother is set at the center of each compound surrounded by those of her married daughters and granddaughters. Like a fertile womb that links men with their forefathers, the tent occupies the center of the domestic social space. It is also associated with feminine sexuality and emotional vulnerability that men must transcend to gain physical and moral control and to assert their ability to defend the ancestral land. Just as men assert their *durarit* by securing the livelihood of their families and protecting the ancestral land and bloodlines, vested in women's regenerative power, women enhance their *durarit* and social security through modesty (the protection of the potent female body) and the successful bearing and rearing of children, especially sons. Unlike the West, where fertility is usually perceived according to "time in the body" (see Martin 1987; Bledsoe

2002), among the Hadendowa meanings of childbearing and child rearing are learned through spatially embodied social experiences grounded in notions of reproductive and social wellness.

Fertility is thus not about time as much as it is about dangerous influences that transgress Hadendowa physical and social boundaries through mobility and foreign interactions to target people's regenerative capacities. That investment in health is so crucial to the Hadendowa construction of fertility and social wellness, in a society that has been plagued by successive famines, dire poverty, and high malnutrition and mortality rates for most of its history of dislocation, is instructive. The Hadendowa (Kipling's unruly "Fuzzy-Wuzzy"), who are characterized in the scant historical literature as bellicose, aloof, and resistant to change, are yet to be fully incorporated into the postcolonial literature on the histories, cultures, and struggles of African pastoralists. Contending with the meager resources of pastoralism and its often devastating consequences, the Hadendowa, like many pastoral groups in the country, have occupied a marginal position in the political economy of the Sudan since the colonial era. Not surprisingly, these realities of poverty and marginalization are mapped onto the Hadendowa landscape and woven into their discourses of sickness and suffering. They are also embodied in their practices of fertility and infertility and their perception of foreignness as it enters the gendered social space and endanger collective well-being.

Such anxieties regarding threatened fertility and well-being, anthropologists posit, can no longer be seen as indigenous isolates; their interpretations are embedded in local and global processes and relations of power and inequalities that shape and reinforce their practical meanings (e.g., Morsy 1990; Farmer 1992). Within these fields of power, the body's state of health and sickness signifies other social, political, and spatial relations (Douglas 1966, 1970; Foucault 1977, 1980; Lock and Scheper-Hughes 1990; see also Asad 1973, 1993). Perceptions of healthy bodies are gendered and contrasted with ideas of sickness, hostilities, and social death (e.g., Kopytoff 1991; Farmer 1992, 1996). Scholarly emphasis on the body and its function and well-being have also brought into focus the central role that representations of gendered identities and women's social place play in constructions of fertility, procreation, and reproductive health (e.g., Delaney 1991; Inhorn 1994; Bledsoe 2002). Women's bodies, as the loci of fertile wombs and of political struggles, become sites for symbolic rituals and polyvocal discourses describing gender asymmetries and powerful others (Boddy 1989). This ethnography engages these anthropological perspectives and further extends notions of social boundaries and gender asymmetries to incorporate local and global configurations of power and their manifestation in the realities of poverty, disease, and underdevelopment. It highlights the ways in which constructions of gender, fertility, and well-being denote meanings of identity, regeneration, and honor in the face of increasing mobility, marginality, and external influence. These analytical extensions take into consideration how meanings of body space are embedded in historical relations of conflicts and in exchanges of commodities and ideas that challenge existing social orders and are thus received with both resistance and accommodation (e.g., Helms 1988; Stoler 1991; Keesing 1992; Stoller 1995).

The fertility histories elicited during interviews also demonstrate how women's fertility strategies and decision-making are shaped not only by cultural constructions but also by their contingent life events, reproductive histories, and social positions in particular conjugal relations (see chapters 4 and 5). They also illustrate how fertility traumas such as miscarriages and children's prolonged sickness and death are perceived as missed reproductive opportunities that depreciate women's reproductive potential and emotional well-being and deprive them of social status (see Bledsoe, Banja, and Hill 1998). In poor economies, successful bearing and rearing of children, especially sons, are not regarded as random occurrences; rather high rates of fertility and child survival are viewed as complex achievements.

According to Halima, "death strikes from time to time and when God wills," but when death strikes repeatedly, especially when babies and women's reproductivity are at stake, the causes of death are investigated beyond their natural instances. What is "natural" is in accord with God's orderly creation; however, there are dangerous forces that seek to tamper with this creation in order to inflict harm on humans, especially Muslims. Such explanations also prevail when droughts, poverty, and external danger are linked and questioned. During such crises, families hang the *sunkab* (a bundle of dried dom-tree fronds, used as a symbol of fertility) inside the tents to ward off external danger and to guard the fertility of both women and the land.[2]

Thus, in accounting for her reproductive trauma, Halima consistently integrated her fertility history with the situation of poverty in which the majority of her people live. Poverty is an externally impelled danger that she battles every day to ensure her survival and the survival of her only son. The moment she conveyed to us that "her whole body hurts" after a long working day in the *hishan*, we were obliged to cut short our *sakanab* (exchange of information, as she calls it) and to question the ethics of doing politically inactive anthropology in such poor settings. In a later interview, Halima responded to one of my questions with an accusative tone: "Suffering is part of our lives. We say that the Hadendowa in the *khala* [rural area] are closer

2. Henceforth, I will use "foreignness" and "otherness" interchangeably to denote Hadendowa conceptualizations of external danger.

to death than they are to life and you ask me about these issues of child-bearing and sons! It is true that we like to have as many sons as God permits, many children. But how could we in this hardship: the famine, poverty, and the hot sun above."

The prevalent theme of social vulnerability that emerged throughout the women's stories describes how external danger invades the land and women's wombs through the mobility of the evil eye, immoral spirits, mysterious diseases (e.g., syphilis), and the consumption of foreign commodities that affect both reproductive health and render people socially inept. The representation of woman as threatened land (see Bourdieu 1990) that links men with their ancestors is the locus of explaining kinship relations and states of reproductive bodies under assault. Although men's bodies are susceptible to invading sicknesses, their ailments are often explained as inherited from their mothers, via the womb and particularly through the mixing of men's and women's substances (milk/semen and blood) during intercourse and gestation. By using foreignness as a double-edged category of power and danger, this ethnography offers a "local" reading of political economy grounded in experiences of poverty and suffering and articulated through the conceptualization and production of social difference.

For most Hadendowa what is proximate is endowed with the power to heal and regenerate and belongs to the realm of *auslif* (the familiar and habitual) as learned and experienced through the legacy of the ancestors and the power of the Qur'an, hadith (the Prophet's sayings), and the baraka of religious saints and healers. *Auslif* also derives its power from the Hadendowa's identification with a glorious past set forth by their ancestors, who defeated many invading forces and established their power over vast territories in eastern Sudan. Thus meanings of *auslif* are anchored in notions of both land and blood, which generate a common sense of *durarit* and unite members of the same group. In contrast, what is deemed distant and foreign is endowed with subversive power and must be scrutinized and closely filtered through local logics and practices. This social dichotomy, however, is a fuzzy construct because the boundaries between the proximate and the distant shift in time, allowing for appropriation, negotiation, and resistance to cultural hegemonies. In new contexts of urban marginality, for instance, where many displaced Hadendowa have left their rural areas because of droughts and famines, *auslif* confronts novel definitions of power, religion, and modernity reinforced by urban non-Hadendowa residents and by the current Islamist government of the Sudan. These encounters are woven into women's and men's narratives as they attempt to navigate the constraints of urban life, comment on "political Islam," and negotiate new ideas pertinent to gender, *durarit*, and reproductive health.

The discursive theme of foreignness that pervades women's fertility healing rituals emphasizes the dichotomy between a Hadendowa identity, founded on *auslif*, purity, and honor, and its negation, which is grounded in immorality, deception, and corruption. In practice, however, these dichotomies fuse through the *halafa* logic, which Halima briefly described. Through *halafa*, foreign commodities, objects, and substances associated with otherness are made proximate and counteracted with powerful domestic substances (such as milk, blood, and amulets, all of which are endowed with blessing) to eliminate external danger and to empower the very bodies they afflict. Foreign spirits and substances are seen as powerfully dangerous because of their ability to traverse space and time, to invade Hadendowa social and physical boundaries, and to endanger fertility during the different life-cycle transitions (e.g., circumcision, marriage, pregnancy, delivery, breast-feeding, and child development). *Halafa*, however, works forward and backward in time, protecting against future ills and bringing sick persons back into "the rite time," that is, the moment of their alien attack, in order to normalize their health. *Halafa* as a logic of appropriation and resistance also offers a glimpse into how processes of negotiation, incorporation, and social change take place. For during this process, foreign ideas may withstand the test of practice and be incorporated or rejected, all in the name of maintaining *auslif* and the legacy of the ancestors.

In this sense *halafa* enables women such as Halima to attempt more than one medical practice to heal their fertility traumas. Some women we interviewed went as far as consulting doctors, sometimes against their elders' will yet in the name *halafa*. If these new paths are deemed fruitful, the women may even claim their ownership. Halima, who came to Sinkat after the drought of the 1980s that devastated the economies of many Hadendowa families in the hills, consulted the health visitor (senior midwife) at the hospital. The hospital, as a foreign institution associated with death and with both Western and northern Sudanese hegemonies and healing practices, is seriously debated in daily conversations. Halima consulted the senior midwife, however, because her "familiar paths" managed by herbalists, religious healers, and spirit-possession specialists had not yet resolved her problem. She seemed puzzled when she remarked that her children had continued to die despite her serious attempts to protect her pregnancy through dietary medicine. But her hope for a cure through the midwife faced another obstacle: she had to follow up with a specialist in Port Sudan (a larger city, approximately 120 kilometers from Sinkat) since the hospital in Sinkat was not fully equipped to evaluate her case. Halima's choice to continue with her healers, however, was motivated not only by her inability to take the expensive trip to Port Sudan but also by her reaction to the midwife's diagnosis. "I was baffled, scared, and skeptical," she said, because "the midwife told me that I had poisoning of the umbilical cord." Poisoning for Halima meant digestion of substances that could have put her life at risk but most importantly could have shown on her children's skin. On the contrary, she related that her children "were delivered with no scratches or deformities on their skin." This is plausible, for most cases of repeated miscarriages and children's deaths are attributed to the mysterious disease *tisaramt* (syphilis), which, according to women, leaves its marks on children's skin. When she returned to the healers, Halima said that she was certain that the causes of her trauma lay within the realm of the unfamiliar, which is infested with dangerous forces, beyond the proximate network of her close kin and material culture that are endowed with the power to heal and regenerate.

Thus, when Halima's body failed and was perceived as "abnormal," a whole world and its material production were to be blamed. Women's narratives about external danger and social vulnerability speak to this worldly accusation. During healing practices, women negotiate their gender predicament by lifting the blame from their own bodies to the powerful level of the body politic, within which both men and women are rendered marginal and threatened. Women's fertility healing practices, therefore, are not mere performances for enacting gender asymmetries; rather they are sites of action and empowerment (Comaroff and Comaroff 1993) through which they strive to change their predicaments. Whyte is right in urging anthropologists to situate their fascination with rituals: "We skip quickly over morbidity and mortality figures, if we have them at all. We describe healing rituals, and the effectiveness of symbols, without going back three weeks later to learn how the patient is doing. We are entranced by the logic of ritual, the form, the assertions, but we tend to ignore the logic of affliction when it resists efforts to shape it" (1997, 21).

Understanding the logic of affliction also calls for grasping the logic of certainty (see Lambek 1990; James 1995) in people's description and management of their suffering and misfortune as experienced through historical realities of poverty and marginalization. For Hadendowa women, both *auslif* and *halafa* provide the ritual space and moments of certitude through which they comment on their predicament, evaluate its causes, and meet dangerous spirits on "*halafa* turf" to avert disempowerment and restore the power of their familiar world. In situations of poverty and global inequalities, where the poor are denied access to the advances of modernity, these ritual practices also offer venues for negotiations, agency, and resistance.

The Hadendowa-Beja and the Research Site

The Hadendowa are one of the predominately pastoral Beja groups that inhabit the Red Sea area in the northeastern quadrant of the Sudan. This area extends from the Sudanese-Egyptian borders in the north to the Sudanese-Ethiopian-Eritrean frontiers in the southeast, and from the Atbara River in the west to the Red Sea coastal plains in the east. The Beja confederation

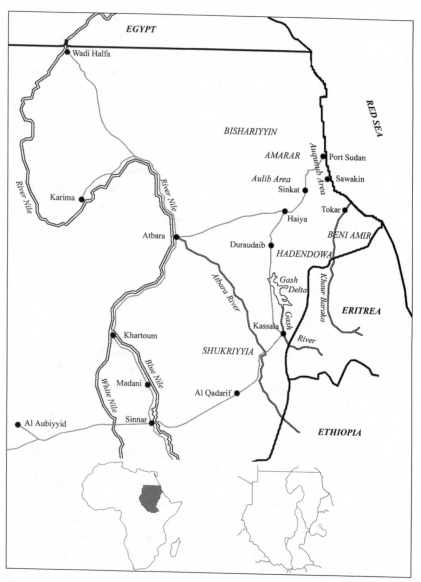

Hadendowa territory and that of neighboring Beja groups *(map courtesy of Shafei Dafalla)*

comprises ten to fourteen groups, which include the major "tribes" of the Bishariyyin in the north, the Amarar in the Port Sudan district, the Hadendowa in Sinkat and in the area south of the Gash Delta, and the Beni Amir near the southeastern borders. Living in the area are also non-Beja groups such as the pastoral Rashida, who migrated from Arabia during the nineteenth century (see Young 1996), and other Sudanese groups, mainly from northern and western Sudan. The latter constitute the majority of urban dwellers in the eastern region. Except for the Beni Amir, who are Tigray speakers, all other Beja speak Tu-Badawie (a Cushitic language). Formally educated Hadendowa and some urban residents speak Arabic as well as Tu-Badawie. Arabic is the official language of the Muslim north and its educated elite, who have held power since the country's independence in 1956.

The region covers one-tenth of the country's total area, approximately 219,920 square kilometers (El Nour 1991). Its dominant geographical features are rocky hills and mountains abutted by seasonal watercourses and streams. Due to the area's geographical location within the semiarid zone, the annual rainfall fluctuates between four hundred and one hundred millimeters and decreases toward the north. Generally, 98 percent of the entire area receives less than two hundred millimeters of rain annually (El Harbi and Ziad 1990). The region is divided into two rainfall zones: the coastal plain area (auqunub), which receives rain from November to February, and the hinterland area (aulib), which receives rain from July to October. These two rainfall zones determine the nomadic movements of most rural Beja groups, whose lives depend on the availability of water and pastures.

Despite its rich economic potential, Sudan is one of the poorest nations in the world, owing to decades of colonial and postcolonial policies that have deepened ethnic and class divisions and resulted in the destitution of large sections of the population. The Beja are among the most impoverished groups in the country, due to the paucity of both national and international development projects in the region, resulting in successive droughts and famines—"structural violence" (Farmer 1996)—against which the Beja must struggle. For decades the intricate histories of ethnic and racial conflict in the Sudan have been overshadowed by the north-south civil war, whose toll has been the loss of millions of lives and a depleted national economy. Representations of Sudan's ethnic conflict in the Western popular media often conform to the simplistic categorization of "Arab-Muslim" aggressors vis-à-vis "black Christian/Muslim" victims. Such representations give slight attention to Sudan's political history, which produced and continues to generate ethnic and racial divisions, sectarianism, poverty, the commodification of weapons, and the emergence of armed oppositional groups fighting for inclusion and equal distribution of power and resources. These dichotomies also ignore the plight of other minorities in the country, including Muslims and other religious ethnicities. Thus it is not surprising that at the historical juncture of the Sudanese government's signing a peace agreement with the southern opposition, an unprecedented escalation of violence and atrocities has occurred in the Darfur region of western Sudan. The Beja elite, who have also been struggling for political inclusion (through one of their political organizations, the Beja Congress), are warning of similar consequences if the government does not take their political grievances seriously. The Beja demonstration in January 2005 in Port Sudan against Beja exclusion from the north-south wealth-sharing agreement, and the police brutality that led to the killing, injuries, and detention of many Beja activists and civilians, portend an escalation of violence in the eastern region if the Beja demands are not included in an encompassing national peace agreement.

During my fieldwork in 1998, the government accused the exiled northern Sudanese opposition, including the Beja Congress, of launching attacks on the Beja villages along the Sudanese-Ethiopian-Eritrean borders. None of the women and men interviewed, however, cited these sporadic attacks as a reason for their migration to Sinkat town, as many of these villages were depopulated due to famines and long histories of economic injustice.

Statistical data on the demography of eastern Sudan as well as its rural and urban population are not current. According to the most recent census data of 1990, 60 percent of the region's population is nomadic, while 40 percent live in urban areas. The Hadendowa are one of the largest Beja groups, although no recent statistical data are available on their total numbers. The group's kinship structure follows a segmentary system, with fourteen *adats* (maximal lineages), each of which occupies an independent territory within what is known as the Hadendowa collective land. Members of each lineage trace their descent seven generations back to Barakawin, the ancestral forefather, through his seven sons and grandsons. These lineages further subdivide into *diwabs* (minimal lineages) that constitute the tent clusters of several families. Each *diwab* occupies a distinct territory within the lineage boundaries.

At the level of political administration, all Hadendowa lineages are headed by a *nazir*, a leadership role that has long been assigned to the Wililiab lineage. Each lineage is led by an *aumda*, who communicates with the *nazir* and *shaikhs*, leaders of *diwabs*, on land-tenure issues and tribal conflicts. This tribal structure was instituted during British colonial rule and has carried over into the postindependence system of governance to facilitate the link between Beja groups and local and central governments (Dirar 1992).

Muslim Hadendowa employ both customary and Islamic regulations in matters concerning tribal conflicts and personal affairs. The grass-roots political organization at the *diwab* level is the *qalad*, a council of *aumkir* (consultation) that includes the *shaikh* and other male elders whose role is the observance of *auslif* regulations. The *nazir* and the *aumda*, in coordination with government apparatuses in towns, often intervene in lineage conflicts

Qalad meeting outside courthouse in Sinkat town

over land ownership and boundaries. Pastoral Hadendowa, like other Beja groups, rely on meager economic resources, mainly animal herding and cultivation of small sorghum fields during rainy seasons. The rainfall shortage in the area since the 1980s threatens this economic foundation. Many Hadendowa now depend on donations from relief organizations and on petty jobs in towns. As an economic strategy, men leave their families behind to migrate in search of seasonal jobs as dock laborers in Port Sudan or as workers in the agricultural projects of Toker, Gash, and Qadarif in the east. Non-Arabic-speaking Hadendowa are among the least privileged groups in the country in terms of education, economic status, and the small number of their elite who advance to higher political offices.

My research in eastern Sudan was conducted in two different phases: The first phase was during 1989–91, when I was a master's student at the University of Khartoum working under the umbrella of the Red Sea Area Project (RESAP), a joint project initiated by scholars from the University of Khartoum and the University of Bergen, Norway, to direct the attention of governments and policymakers to the urgency of scholarly and humanitarian intervention in eastern Sudan. The second phase was conducted from

November 1997 to December 1998 as part of my dissertation fieldwork. During these two phases, I worked primarily with displaced Hadendowa women in the shanty settlements of Sinkat town.

Sinkat town is the capital of the Sinkat district, which includes the small towns and rural areas of Qabait, Arkawit, Haiya, Tahamiam, and Duraudaib. Because of its proximity to the country's two old ports of Sawakin and Port Sudan and its moderate climate, it is a significant administrative center and a summer resort. The town market is a hub for nomadic groups who trade their livestock products for other consumer goods. Historically, Sinkat was a small trading center along the caravan routes that connected northern Sudan with Sawakin in the nineteenth century (H. A. Ahmed 1974). Not much, however, has been written about the town's growth before the Turco-Egyptian occupation of the Sudan (1820–81), during which Sinkat was a military post and a battlefield for the anticolonial resistance movement led by Osman Digna, a Beja leader, during the Mahadist revolution (1881–98; see Daly 1991). During the colonial and postindependence periods, the town's administrative role increased due to the construction of the Khartoum–Port Sudan railway in 1927 and a highway in the 1980s. Hassan Abdel-Ati (1990) also attributes the growth of the small town to the abundance of water resulting from the many seasonal valleys and streams, which make possible year-round use of surface wells, whereas water shortage is a major problem in the arid Red Sea area. Moreover, Sinkat is a religious center for the prominent Khatmiyya sect, a Sufi order whose members assume descent from the Prophet Muhammad. Many Khatmiyya religious leaders, *ashraf* (honorable), are buried in Sinkat, and special attention is drawn to the popular Alsharifa Maryam, the granddaughter of the founder of the sect. According to the Sinkat council's statistical data (1993) the population of the district is forty-eight thousand; that of the town is ten thousand.

There were seven shanty settlements around Sinkat town during my fieldwork. Although I interviewed people from different residential areas, I focused on one that included both old and recent Hadendowa migrants. Whereas each Hadendowa *diwab* occupies a distinct territory in rural areas, the *diwab* dissolves in town, and members of different lineages live near one another. The focus settlement, which I will refer to as Nasib (not its real name), has an approximate population of two thousand, of whom 20 percent (ca. four hundred) are women of reproductive age. Most women interviewed spoke Tu-Badawie. Those who had lived longer in Sinkat town also spoke Arabic, and in such cases I conducted the interviews myself. Since my spoken Tu-Badawie is moderate, I enlisted the aid of four Hadendowa female assistants, who helped conduct, transcribe, and interpret interviews during the different phases of the project. These assistants were born and raised in Sinkat town and had completed secondary or high school and worked on and off with governmental and nongovernmental organizations in town. The residence of these assistants in Sinkat and their acquaintance with different Hadendowa women in the area facilitated the interview process, especially with women who had misgivings about my position as a northern Sudanese interested in documenting their personal and familial histories.

Although my interviews were mainly with women, I also interviewed a few Hadendowa men, some of whom were related to my female interviewees, and others who were *aumdas*, *shaikhs*, or government employees. Their insights provided valuable additions to the women's narratives about the politics and culture of reproduction. During my stay in Sinkat, I visited Aukar, the original Hadendowa homeland, where Hadat and Barakawin, the ancestral mother and father, and their seven sons were buried. I also visited other rural areas. The interviews I conducted with a few men and women in these areas substantiated the historical narratives related by the Hadendowa in town.

Encountering Foreignness

Late one evening, at the beginning of my fieldwork, a female friend and I were returning home after a RESAP meeting. We were chatting loudly, and due to the dim light of the crescent moon, we did not notice that we were crossing through a Hadendowa tent cluster. Suddenly an old woman began to chase after us, threatening that she would discipline us with her cane. Since our spoken Tu-Badawie was moderate and we were taken by surprise, the only thought that came to my mind was that the woman might have mistaken us for Hadendowa girls, for whom it was inappropriate to wander around at that hour of the evening. With this in mind, we stopped, and I responded loudly, "We are *balawait*." The woman immediately turned her back to us and silently returned to her compound.

Like the colonial British and the Turks, Arabic-speaking northern Sudanese, who have held power since the country's independence, are perceived as *balawait* ("foreigners" and "intruders" in the Tu-Badawie language), who possess dangerous morality. Some Hadendowa friends jokingly explained to me that it also means *bala*, Arabic for misfortune or catastrophe. *Balawait* stands in opposition to Badawait (Bedou or Arabs), which the Hadendowa use to identify themselves. It indicates both a nomadic lifestyle and a distinct code of honor that set them apart from other non-Beja groups (see chapter 2).

Although the voices of a few Hadendowa men are represented, this ethnography's main focus is women's narratives. This strategy is influenced by the misrepresentation of Hadendowa women in the scant available literature and by my own position as a northern Sudanese cast as foreign in her own native country. The *balawait*/Badawait distinction is at the heart of understanding my own position as a researcher coming from the northern Sudanese elite, whose historical association with both Arab and Western hegemonies is unequivocal. *Balawait* women in particular are perceived as sexually lax in their relationship with men, a perception I attempted to avert by working mostly with women. Thus by denouncing us as *balawait*, whose behavior is seen as a moral violation of Hadendowa propriety codes, the elder woman reacted to my response in a way that was both disciplinary and exclusionary. This dilemma of being a *balawait* who also lives in the West emerges throughout my discussions and conversations with women and men. Thus, although I was there to write about the Hadendowa ways, my actions were continuously observed and commented on. This fact also shifted my attention to my own feminism as an elite northern Sudanese woman. Sudanese women's feminism (or womanism) has so far functioned within the umbrella of party and state politics, and feminist agendas for social change have served the interest of specific classes of women (see Hale 1996). Although Sudanese feminists attempt to distance themselves from Western feminism by constructing a nationalist discourse about an ideal Sudanese woman citizen, Hadendowa women in the east associated me with both Western and northern Sudanese hegemonies. Even the current discourse about Islamic feminism was constantly criticized as a personal attack on the Hadendowa's understanding of Islam and womanhood.

For Hadendowa women who are living different realities, it was not surprising that their critique of my position was woven into their own narratives about poverty, suffering, and marginalization and their understanding of histories of colonialism and dominance, including that of the northern Sudanese elite. Thus my research questions related to fertility, sexuality, and rituals were mocked at times as being irrelevant to the Hadendowa predicaments of poverty and poor health and were often interrupted by provocative questions such as, "What is in your research for us?" or "Is your research going to get us more *iqatha* [relief] food?" Such questions drew my attention not only to my own feminism but also to my training in anthropology, a discipline that has long been implicated in hegemonic relations of power and accused of cultural relativism that shies away from politicizing people's social realities (see di Leonardo 1998).

Giving voice to Hadendowa women and contextualizing their stories in their attempts to manage their suffering and to protect their well-being is not an exercise in "compassionate liberalism" but a hard-learned lesson from the women's own explanation of their plight and their demand for my reflexivity as well as my constant revisions and reexaminations of my field

Weaving

methodologies and questions. Haisha, a senior Hadendowa woman, never stopped reminding me that writing notes in their presence represents "bragging about my writing ability" and does not reflect a genuine interest on my part to listen to and memorize their stories. Fatima, who spent most of her days weaving mats from dry palm fronds to sell for pennies, responded to my genuine interest to learn how to weave by saying, "But you weave." When I insisted that I didn't know how to weave, she remarked, "You write, but your kind of weaving is lucrative; mine isn't." I nodded and said, "I will try to weave fairly." The question thus remains, Can these critiques help us examine our own academic and feminist practices to envision a link between academia, activism, and advocacy for marginalized groups?

This pressing question motivated me to personally intervene in situations where I was able to influence the outcome. Creating viable connections among hospital staff and some of the Hadendowa women and men who find the hospital inaccessible proved to be feasible at times. Working with various nongovernmental organizations (NGOs) in the area and linking their project planning and available resources with community needs and people's perceptions of development was also a useful feat. But how

Balawait (*saulit* hairstyle)

can these circumstantial efforts and our attempts to write from the margins enhance a global movement to end poverty and social injustice?

My decision to braid my hair and wear a *fauta* was significant in bringing me closer to the women interviewed and was a source of jokes and laughter. This did not completely erase my *"balawaitness,"* however. The majority of women who agreed to be interviewed insisted that I use pseudonyms, which they chose themselves, when weaving their stories.

This introduction interlaces the theoretical and ethnographical threads through which women's stories, such as that of Halima, guide the theme of this book. In chapter 1, I begin by situating the Hadendowa's state of poverty and marginalization in their historical struggles with multiple droughts and famines that attest to the failures of both colonial and postcolonial governments in attending to the welfare of the poor. Despite the paucity of their economic resources, the Hadendowa ground their identities in an imagined resourceful land that has fostered their historical ties with the ancestors. The chapter examines how constructions of identity and honor and of gender and regeneration are learned and transformed through kinship relations, lineage politics, conflict over land ownership, and foreign interactions.

Chapter 2 extends the aforementioned threads of gender, honor, and political economy to describe a moral spatiality within which Hadendowa women see foreignness and boundary crossing as threatening to fertility, health, and regeneration. The chapter situates these perceptions of danger and disease in the Hadendowa's colonial and postcolonial histories of marginalization and their cultural interactions with different ethnic groups. Within this political economy of honor, Hadendowa women embody cultural meanings of affinity, modesty, and responsible motherhood that can be threatened by the perceived deceptiveness of an unbound foreign world. Through the social scaling of honor and the *halafa* mimetic logic of reversing danger, distant powers are made proximate to substantiate the mastery of the power within and to normalize reproductive health and collective well-being.

The themes of foreignness and social vulnerability span chapter 3 to show how gendered identities are constructed and experienced through connected notions of body space. The asymmetrical constructions of men's and women's honor and social place through the different life-cycle events are unified in ritual practices of marriage, socialization, and fertility to emphasize meanings of collective identity and regeneration. Although these unified "di-visions" (Bourdieu 1990) guide social experiences, they also identify an exterior domain of foreignness that informs social discourses and fertility praxis. The chapter also examines the limits of power and resistance pertinent to spatially embodied gender arrangements.

Chapter 4 sets the ritual stage for a sociohistoric reading of fertility that not only differentiates children by gender but also classifies women according to their physical and moral abilities to undertake the task of childbearing and child rearing. The chapter examines the various strategies and healing practices that women of different fertility statuses employ in their quest to gain propriety and responsible motherhood. In this context, *auslif* is negotiated through the *halafa* logic and its capacity to incorporate processes of social change and familiarize the dangerous effect of foreign influences. Through women's different voices, the chapter examines the tensions inherent in an ideal fertility and its practices as manifest in the meanings attributed to sons and daughters, to polygyny and adoption, and to the power and danger of the spirit world.

Chapter 5 further extends the notions of fertility, foreignness, and gendered identities to introduce women's concepts of healthy reproductive trajectories, wherein both childbearing and child rearing are seen as intertwined aspects of fertility and regeneration. Contrary to Western medical and demographic constructions of fertility as a linear trajectory determined by the logic of biological time, Hadendowa women see fertility as a spatially threatened bodily investment whose successful outcomes lead to honor and social well-being. Through the voices, narratives, and detailed fertility histories of several women, the chapter sheds light on women's reproductive trajectories, their management of suffering and fertility traumas, and the specificity and precariousness of the life events that shape their conjugal relations, fertility decisions, and social statuses.

While the Hadendowa are generally misrepresented in the available texts, Hadendowa women are seen as circumscribed by a strict code of shame that denies their agency (e.g., Paul 1954; Mohamed Salih 1976). This ethnography proves otherwise: Hadendowa women present, through their own voices and actions, their families' struggles for survival and their attempts to contest and negotiate their gender constraints. Their stories further deconstruct the stereotypical representation of Muslim-African and Middle Eastern women as passive victims of the institutions of patrilineality, veiling, polygyny, reproduction, motherhood, and honor.

Lila Abu-Lughod (1986) has denounced the objectification of women under the undifferentiated categories of honor and shame and the universalization of what Pitt-Rivers (1977) calls "the politics of sex," which preoccupied Middle Eastern and Mediterranean scholars for two decades (see also Herzfeld 1980; Gilmore 1987). Although the Hadendowa construct of *durarit* is an overarching concept that guides social experience, its meanings merge, according to social contexts, with other concepts and logics of practice to highlight questions of marginality, identity, and women's social place. By writing "against power," I attempt to do justice to the Hadendowa women and men and to incorporate their voices into the national political map. A growing number of gender studies in the Sudan focus on the experiences of northern Sudanese women (e.g., Boddy 1989; Kenyon 1995; Hale 1997; Gruenbaum 1982, 2001); this ethnography opens the door for integrating minority women's voices into the ongoing research on gender in the Sudan.

Chapter 1

Famished Land

Gender, Identity, and Place

Starvation is the characteristic of some people not having
enough to eat. It is not the characteristic of there being
not enough food to eat.

Amartya Sen, *Poverty and Famines*

Historically, the Hadendowa have claimed ownership of a large portion of
the eastern Sudan. This expansive, hilly land, with its seasonal water valleys
and scattered dry scrub, is often described as the endowment for which
Hadendowa ancestors fought invading powers to establish the notion of a
homeland and a united community, rooted in common blood and a sentiment of *durarit*. Meanings of *durarit* are anchored in this construct of
an ancestral land that has for centuries sustained Hadendowa pastoral ways
of life and cradled the fragmented market economy at the core of its few
flourishing urban centers. Urban centers, however, which are geared toward
benefiting specific economic sectors and classes, cut off the pastoral economy of the region, preventing nomads from receiving their equal share in
aid, health services, and development programs. The centralization of resources, combined with droughts and famines over the years, have heightened Hadendowa marginalization. In response the Hadendowa have employed multiple strategies to sustain their vulnerable subsistence economy.

Selling firewood

Door of *bukar* made of USAID oil cans

Scholars no longer attribute poverty, starvation, and famines to the availability of food and commodities; rather their causes are sought in the socioeconomic and political mechanisms that determine the ownership of such commodities as well as the control over their distribution, prices, and supply (Sen 1981). Just as people in urban areas, especially the upper classes, are less vulnerable to famines, the majority of pastoralists, peasants, and those who are out of government "sight" are the ones who bear the brunt of poverty and starvation. The history of poverty and famine in eastern Sudan is thus embedded in a sociopolitical structure within which certain classes are doomed to suffer (Edkins 2000).

Population at Risk

In Sudan droughts and famines have been attributed to a process of environmental degradation exacerbated by both colonial and postcolonial agricultural policies. The Sudan's mandatory subscription to IMF policies and its structural adjustment programs, under the pretext of accelerating development through liberalizing local economies, led to the worst humanitarian crises during the 1980s and 1990s. These policies have created tremendous food shortages and laid the foundation for the isolation of many agro-pastoralists and people in rural communities through neoliberal export-oriented economies (O'Brien 1985; Abdel-Ati 1988; see also Deng and Minear 1992). Malpractice in the agrarian sector, as exemplified in land erosion and the removal of vast vegetation covers for mechanized farms, contributed to the process of desertification and rain failure that culminated in the devastating famine of 1982–84, which affected the rural economies of many areas in the Sudan, including the Red Sea province. During this drought many vulnerable groups were trapped in a vicious cycle. The shortage of rainfall meant lack of work for most agro-pastoralists, who faced the failure of their crops, the scarcity of seeds for future seasons, the high prices of seeds and cereals, the death of their animals, and the resulting starvation, high mortality rates, and displacement.

This cycle of destitution manifested itself in different facets of the country's economic performance that relied heavily on both agriculture and animal husbandry. As a result of the devastating drought of the 1980s, production from rain-irrigated agriculture fell by 58 percent, leading to a 25 percent decline in the country's agricultural production between 1981 and 1985 (Umbada 1989). Such decline instigated the movement of many starving and malnourished nomads and agro-pastoralists, especially from western Sudan, to the capital city. Images of the displaced, hungry population storming the suburbs of Khartoum produced the fixed imagery of the "famished African child" and the "helpless refugee" (cf. Malkki 1996) widely consumed by Western media, and revealed both the government's failure to treat its citizens as equal subjects, and the limits of humanitarianism's capacity to analyze and respond to global inequalities and man-made disasters. Famine, as a violent manifestation of starvation causing havoc and death (Sen 1981), claimed the lives of a great number of the country's productive population. The United Nations reported that about one million people were displaced from their homelands, and 150 people died daily of starvation during the famine of the 1980s (Abdel-Ati 1988).

The movement of pastoralists to towns also negatively affected the country's exports. Nomads, who represented 40 percent of the country's population and owned 90 percent of all domestic animals, contributed significantly to the government's revenue. An estimated 65 percent of the country's livestock, or thirty-three million animals, died in the famine of the 1980s (Umbada 1989). This loss depleted the food sources of many vulnerable groups, leading to the use of wild plants as an alternative food source (De Waal 1989).

Faced with the influx of a displaced population and international reports on famine conditions in the country, Gaafar Mohammed Numeri's government (1969–85) declared a state of emergency and attributed the causes of famine to droughts and other climatic changes to save its political image. Ironically, the country's exports of sorghum, the major food staple for the majority of the population, continued even during the famine's climax. The amount of grain exported between 1980 and 1982 was estimated at 250,000 to 400,000 tons annually (Umbada 1989). This was met with widespread disdain: in the streets of Khartoum, people taunted the government for exporting grain to feed the horses in the stables of Saudi Arabia.

The effects of this famine were grave in eastern Sudan. During my first visit to the region in the 1980s, as a volunteer with a relief organization, many Beja groups were dying silently. The effects of famine were worsened by the unfavorable conditions of the Beja: their dependency on herding and small-scale rain-fed agriculture, their political underrepresentation, and the absence of development projects to compensate for the breakdown in their agro-pastoral economy and to provide them with viable alternative survival strategies. This disadvantaged position has continued to place most Beja pastoralists at risk when faced with successive droughts and famines.

Surviving Famines

The history of the Red Sea hills is replete with episodes of drought and famine that differ in their devastation and severity. The British administrative records in both Sinkat and Khartoum and local narratives of famines attest to the Beja historical struggle with the paucity of their economic resources. Most Hadendowa men and women whom I interviewed in 1989 recounted the famine of *sanat sita,* "year six," referring to the terrible year of 1306 in the Islamic calendar (the continental African Sahel famine of 1888–89; see Bayoumi 1979; Hamid 1996). The effect of the 1888–89 famine was aggravated by the long war between the colonial regime and the Mahadia nationalist movement. Thousands of southern Beja, who lived near the Gash and Baraka deltas, and who supported and fought with the Mahadi, were killed in the war or died as a result of the famine. This year was also marked by the invasion of locusts and the destruction of sorghum fields in the Beja region, the failure of crop production, the death of animals, and a rise in the mortality rate due to starvation and a cholera epidemic (Newbold 1935).

A five-year decrease in rainfall that had dried the vegetation cover on the Atabi plains, leaving scarce vegetation for animal survival, was documented in 1910 and 1911 (Dahl 1988). From 1925 to 1928, the northern Beja experienced episodes of drought and famine. The director of public works in the Gash Delta reported in 1927 that the lack of rainfall had rendered the grazing land around the delta inhospitable for many Beja pastoralists. In 1928 many Beja pastoralists and mine workers around Gabait were reported to have received sorghum as a relief provision from the British colonial administration (Graham 1927). These years were particularly difficult for the Bishariyyin, who consequently moved to the rich Hadendowa land around the Atbara River. This led to increased friction between the two groups. The director of public works also noted that while cotton picking was under way around the delta, "additional herds from further north came in and stayed beyond the permitted area. The principal contributing cause was the absence or exhaustion of grazing in the surrounding regions" (Graham 1927). This administrative report brought into focus other reasons for the drought in these years, such as diverting water from the Gash River for irrigating the cotton fields in the Gash Delta, thus blocking the flood of the Gash River from reaching previously well-irrigated northern areas.

During 1925 to 1928, drought was also reported on the Atabi plains (Dahl 1988). The Amarar lost one-third of their sheep, while the northern Beja lost three-fourths of their sheep and goats. The Bishariyyin, the Amarar, and the Beni Amir also suffered tremendously during 1936. During World War II, famine also took its toll among the Beja in Musmar, Halib, Atbara, and the Gash Delta. The spread of mange resulted in the death of most of the animals of these Beja groups.

In the years 1947 to 1949, the authorities in Kassala reported a sweeping famine that reached both Kassala and Qadarif (Morton and Fre 1986). Kassala, Tokar, and Qadarif are large towns in eastern Sudan, and they host vast areas of mechanized agriculture in the region.

The famine was attributed to the low production of grain in Qadarif. The severity of this famine was felt by all Beja in eastern Sudan, as evidenced by high mortality rates for both humans and animals. Local relief agencies and the Egyptian government distributed relief in the form of grain and clothes. The Hadendowa, who were severely affected by this famine, moved to the Tokar and Gash agricultural projects. This resulted in clashes between them and the cultivators in the two projects (Morton and Fre 1986).

During the 1950s, however, the Beja enjoyed better rainfall and crop production. Subsistence agriculture in southern Qadarif was substantial, and the grazing land around the coastal plains, especially around Sawakin, supported many nomads. In Tokar, on the other hand, famine conditions predominated. These conditions were reflected in poor pastureland and the movement of nomads searching for richer grazing land, high sorghum prices vis-à-vis low animal prices, and the distribution of seed and grain as relief (Morton and Fre 1986).

While the early postindependence years passed with no large-scale reported droughts and famines, many Hadendowa women in Sinkat town cited 1967 as a disastrous year for them and their animals. This year is referred to as the *italawia* (derived from *italaw*, lightning), meaning a season of heavy lightning, thunder, and rain, which was followed by two years of drought. Kaltum, a forty-year-old Hadendowa woman, related how animals died of the intense humidity and were carried away by massive floods. She stated:

> During the *italawia* the rain was heavy, and the striking thunder and lightening were scary. The flood took most of our animals, and we were left with nothing to survive on. First, we moved to Sinkat town from Hadarbab, where the government sent us on special trains to the agricultural areas. They took us to the Gash area [around Kassala]. Other people were moved to Tokar and Qadarif. I recalled that we got off the train at Hadalia, where we found trucks waiting for us to take us to the Gash area. In the Gash, you know, there was both government-sponsored agriculture and subsistence agriculture. We were relocated to Wagar [a small town near the Gash area] where we worked very hard harvesting. We worked according to a sharing system called *altusa'* [ninth]. Say you harvest nine sacks, one sack is for you and the rest is for the tenant. After the harvest we had some sacks of grain. We were again moved, with our grain, to our home areas. I recall during that particular year the harvest was a success because there was no *yawaib* [locust].

Kaltum recalled that the early 1970s were relatively better than what she had experienced in previous years. However, in 1975, during Numeri's regime, there was another phase of drought in the hills. During this period,

Kaltum maintained, the rain was scarce and some of their animals died. This is when many families moved to Sinkat town. Kaltum described it in the following way: "Because of the spread of *hisra* [measles], which took the lives of many children in Sinkat, people whose animals lived preferred to stay in their home areas. During this period the government distributed grain. I recall it was yellow grain sent by the Americans. This is why we used to call it *amrikani*. The grain was distributed by local people and not by the Khawadas [Europeans] though."

The Hadendowa, like other Beja in the region, have faced this cyclical dilemma of poverty, famines, sickness, and death armed with their own coping mechanisms and survival strategies. Even during years of bounty, Hadendowa pastoralists have roamed the area searching for pastureland. In the rugged, semiarid terrain of the Red Sea region, the Hadendowa move between the *auqunub*, to make use of winter rain, and the *aulib*, to take advantage of the rainy summer season. As each Hadendowa lineage occupies an independent territory within the larger collective land, members of different lineages have the conditional rights to use the land of other lineages for settlement and grazing during seasons of scarcity. Hassan Mohamed Salih (1976) has defined two systems of land rights among the Hadendowa: *asl* and *amara* rights. While *asl* (original) defines the ancestral right of each lineage in its territorial land, *amara* acknowledges the temporary rights of other lineages.

These *amara* rights are agreed upon among different lineages and are managed through the *qaudab* payment (an animal or money gift given to the leader of the host group for recognition of his group's land rights). According to the *qaudab*, members of the guest lineage can use the land for pasture during certain months but cannot establish permanent residence because prolonged settlement can result in long-lasting conflicts over land ownership. Even in towns where land ownership is organized according to urban regulation codes, the Hadendowa struggle to maintain their land-tenure system. I asked Asha, a Hadendowa woman who migrated to Sinkat town as a result of the famine of the 1980s, about an uncompleted mudroom near her tent. She responded: "My tent is very small and my son who goes to school now asked his friends to come and help him build this mudroom. He wanted a comfortable place to put his books and things. They dug a hole and made the mud over there. But when they started to build the room, individuals from the Imirab group [who claim ownership of the Sinkat area] came and told them to stop building. They said to me, 'We have allowed you to settle and to erect your tent, but not to build a mudroom.' It is because the tent is removable but a mudroom is a sign of permanent residence."

When I asked Asha if she felt a sense of injustice because of this confrontation she paused and then responded: "Not really, because we [her lineage members] would have done the same thing if the Imirab came to settle [permanently] among us. This is why I told you that we don't like to leave our home area for long and to be looked down upon and ordered around by others. In our place we live freely; nobody can prevent us from having water and fresh air."

Yet both in their home areas and when temporarily residing with others, Hadendowa families take pride in their collective land and animal wealth as the backbone of their economic survival and social well-being. In areas where agriculture is not prevalent, animals are the main source of economic survival. Camels, goats, and sheep determine a family's wealth, social status, and endurance during economic crises. Goats and sheep are owned and herded primarily by women and young children. These animals are valued for their milk and meat as well as for their worth in social transactions, especially as bridewealth. The Hadendowa's essential morning and evening meals *(tamhasa* and *audrar)* consist of porridge made of sorghum flour and milk (fresh or sour). Camels, on the other hand, are owned and herded by men. They are valued for their milk and are considered a long-term capital investment. During cultural festivals, the camel race, a favorite male sport, is a site of demonstrating lineage wealth, men's courage, and tribal solidarity. Camels are also a means of transportation during seasonal movements and the link between the Hadendowa in the hills and the market economies of urban centers, where men exchange animal products for grain and other foodstuffs. Above all, camels embody meanings of fertility, health, love, honor, and the bounty of the land as expressed in men's and women's lyrics and songs. In fact, both men's and women's dancing resembles a camel's body movements. Moreover, each lineage engraves its tribal mark on the bodies of its camels as a sign of tribal identification, especially during disputed boundary crossings.

This form of animal wealth, however, has always been at stake during the different cycles of the Beja famines. The devastating famine of the 1980s took its toll on Hadendowa lives and economic resources. Most displaced Hadendowa women whom I interviewed attributed the causes of the famine to *audimim aubrinau* (the gradual disappearance of rain), the death of animals, and soaring sorghum prices, which led most families to migrate to Sinkat town. Most of these women also commented that their choices to stay in their homeland despite clear signs of famine had worsened the situation. Such decisions are attributable to adherence to the ancestral land, reluctance to migrate to town, and the hope for a better rainy season. Thirty-five-year-old Diab, a Hadendowa from the Gamilab lineage, stated: "During the last famine, there was little rain, but we did not leave our homeland immediately. Trees began to die and so did our animals. There was no rainfall during *tihibi* [summer], so we hoped that bounty would prevail in *mutwai*

Girl tending goats (note *saulit wahalit* hairstyle for little girls)

[winter]. But there wasn't enough rain to water the grass in the *auqunub* during winter. When it was all dry, we began to starve, and we had to make a choice either to die or to live for our children. This is when we decided to leave our homeland."

As subsistence agriculture proved to be a risky business, reliance on the market for grain supplementation became one of the viable strategies that families adopted during droughts and famines. The shift in favor of certain trade commodities, such as sorghum, during economic crises added to the severity of famine and the vulnerability of pastoral Hadendowa. The inflated sorghum prices and the deflated value of animals rendered it difficult for most Hadendowa to survive without risking the loss of their remaining livestock. In times of crisis, small animals were either slaughtered or sold cheaply in exchange for *dura* (sorghum, which is now largely distributed by relief organizations). With few remaining animals to exchange for grain, the household economies of most migrant families remained at risk. Based on the findings of RESAP, Leif Manger concluded that with an estimated "annual requirement of about 750 kg of grain per family, and an average herd of 10 goats, the Hadendowa's prospects of viability in this type of situation [were] quite poor. Selling the total herd in January 1991 would bring 10 *rubu* of grain, i.e., a fraction of what a household needs annually" (1996, 129; see also Egeimi 1994).

The continuous deprivation of the Hadendowa in such a marginal economy endangered their migratory way of life and led to new survival mechanisms, most of which also contributed to the process of desertification (Abu Sin 1990). Consecutive cycles of drought and famine made it hard for most Hadendowa to replace their lost camels, whose cost rose substantially, and shifted many household economies to reliance on small animals. Although small animals present a viable survival strategy because of their higher reproduction rate in comparison with camels, their overgrazing also feeds back into the cycle of desertification (Abu Sin 1990). Furthermore, other strategies for survival, such as charcoal production as a widespread activity in the area (despite the Hadendowa taboo against cutting live trees), simultaneously posed a serious threat to the ecology of the region (Manger 1996).

Migration to towns during economic crises has also been one of the vital strategies that most Hadendowa pastoralists adopted to support their disintegrating economies. Accordingly, the urban population in the Red Sea region has increased substantially during the last two decades (Abu Sin 1990). In 1990 the urban population in the Red Sea region rose to 380,000 persons compared with 160,000 in 1973, marking an increase of 138 percent, with an annual growth rate of 8 percent. This rise corresponded with an 18 percent drop in the rural population (Abu Sin 1990). The city of Port Sudan

**Table 1. Animals owned before and after 1984–85 famine
(sample of 50 families)**

Animal	Number of animals before drought	Number of animals after drought
Sheep	962	18
Goats	1,570	116
Camels	104	3
Donkeys	31	0
Cows	7	0
Chickens	0	179
Total	**2,674**	**316**

Data from author's fieldwork, 1989

alone, Abdel-Ati (1996) noted, represents 80 percent of the urban population of the Red Sea region. Most of this migration, however, was confined
to major towns in eastern Sudan and did not spread as far as Khartoum.
The reason for this, most Hadendowa explained, was their commitment to
stay within their territorial boundaries so that they could return to the hills
if their situations improved. Although many migrants ended up choosing
urban life, other families adopted a dual strategy of commuting between
towns and rural areas. The Hadendowa's marginality in these urban centers
was exacerbated by their lack of skills and qualifications deemed necessary
for competing with dominant groups. This is a consequence inseparable
from the emergence of cities in the Sudan as part of the colonial and postcolonial economic projects that favored specific ethnic groups and supported
certain social classes. The poor have always been relegated to the margins
and denied their equal share in education, health services, and even food.

Relevant to this, Abdel-Ati maintains that the development of a city
such as Port Sudan has always been linked to the development of the relatively more prosperous parts of the country, such as Gazira and Khartoum,
more than to the Red Sea region, which further highlights Beja political exclusion (1996, 105). This factor, in addition to the centralization of development planning in the capital, Khartoum, have been blamed for the failure
of projects meant to benefit the vulnerable population of the Red Sea area.
Both colonial and postcolonial efforts to initiate development in the region
have focused on short-term solutions such as humanitarian aid and the
movement of nomads to work as cheap labor in the agricultural projects of
Gash, Tokar, and Qadarif, as we have seen in the case of Kaltum. This "hit-
and-run" attitude toward development has its foundation in predominant
perceptions of nomads as lazy, backward, and favoring "antimodernity."
Abdel Ghafar Ahmed (1980) is right to assert that colonial and postcolonial

View from shanty settlement outside Sinkat town

planners have perceived the Beja, like other pastoralists, as difficult to administer because of their lifestyle and the rugged terrain they inhabit. Consequently, relocation to agricultural projects—which are part of both colonial and postcolonial liberalization policies and agricultural plans to gear mechanized farming toward export production and not to integrate and promote agro-pastoral economies—has often been the facile solution (see Egeimi 1994).

Displaced Hadendowa thus must struggle to maintain their survival, given the meager opportunities available to them in their rural areas and in towns. In Sinkat town most Hadendowa migrants live in unsanitary, crowded settlements outside the town center. While men spend their days in the market working or searching for work, stay-at-home women also try to contribute to household earnings. Most married women rely on their husbands' and sons' work in town or as *muzawria* (dock laborers) in Port Sudan to support their families. Although *muzawria* jobs pay less than the minimum monthly wage (around 30,000 Sudanese pounds [LS], equal to ca. US$12), it is steadier than the irregular jobs provided by the main market in Sinkat (see table 2). Some married women also sell mats, eggs, and

Table 2. Husbands' occupations (sample of 85 families)

Husband's occupation	Frequency	Percentage
Relatively steady jobs at Sinkat market (baker, butcher, cobbler, waiter, tailor, small shop owner, construction worker, goldsmith assistant)	23	27.0
Irregular jobs	17	20.0
Government employee (mostly soldiers, nurses, 1 teacher)	16	18.8
Herding and farming (commuting to rural areas)	13	15.3
Dockworker (Port Sudan)	10	11.8
Driver	2	2.4
Tribal leader (aumda)	1	1.2
Guard (qafir)	3	3.5
Total	**85**	**100.0**

Data from author's fieldwork, 1998

candy at the Port Sudan–Khartoum highway bus terminal. Most Hadendowa are unaccustomed to eating chickens and eggs; however, raising chickens has become one of the strategies by which women try to earn money to fend for their families.

The majority of widows and divorced women who have no sons (or have young sons) or male relatives to support them work as maids in the households of northern Sudanese, Kurds, and the few Beja elite in town. Most of their work includes cleaning and washing clothes, which is strenuous and provides little monetary gain. Tuhmad, one of the widows interviewed in 1998 and a mother of four children, worked two to three days a week washing clothes in the *hishan*. She worked from 11 a.m. to 6 p.m., earning LS 700 for every dozen garments she washed. Depending on demand, Tuhmad said that her income would not exceed LS 20,000 (about US$10) a month. This economic dependency, according to some Hadendowa women, has deprived them of their *durarit*. Women who were previously cared for by their husbands and male kin in a local pastoral economy are facing new economic situations that put them at the mercy of those for whom they work. Additionally, divorce rates have risen after the famine as a result of many husbands leaving for town and abandoning their families. Other husbands have simply not been able to meet their household

Selling mats at bus terminal

responsibilities, a main criterion for being an honorable, responsible man (see Hjort and Dahl 1991).

Many women commented that living in town and being without men had made them more vulnerable and subject to harassment. Haisha, a divorcee, said, "During the relief distribution we used to rush in order to get our food rations. One day one of the local men who was responsible for the food distribution shouted at us and pushed us back. 'Why are you pushing and rushing like this? Don't you have men to do this for you?' I felt as if a knife had pierced through my heart, and I shouted back at him, 'If we had any able men left, we wouldn't be here waiting for your food.' But the food was not even his, it was sent by the Khawadas."

During the early days of famine, families supplemented their income by selling relief provisions such as oil, flour, and milk that were distributed by the various NGOs working in eastern Sudan. The intensity of the 1980s famine went beyond the national level to attract the attention of several humanitarian organizations worldwide. Abdel-Ati reported that there were seventeen NGOs working in eastern Sudan at the onset of the famine, saving 40 percent of the threatened population by supplying relief provisions (1996, 116). The Hadendowa who were not used to the kind of food distributed by these organizations and associated it with ill health and in-fertility sold their relief provisions to buy grain, which proved to be a viable strategy for them at times. Yet this strategy was also responsible for many tribal conflicts. For example, since most NGOs could not reach each lineage in its own area, they depended on *shaikhs* to distribute the provisions. However, some *shaikhs*, referred to as *iqatha shaikhs,* would sell these provisions and fail to distribute the money fairly among their people, which resulted in many charges against them.

Some Hadendowa lineages also appropriated certain cultural regulations, such as the *qaudab*, to draw in external resources such as relief provisions. Since food was distributed according to the existing number of *diwabs* occupying a specific lineage territory, many *shaikhs* began to mobilize other sublineages to reside in their area during relief distribution in order to exploit more foodstuffs. In return the *shaikhs* of the guest lineages paid the *qaudab*, the symbol of respecting land rights, to the *shaikh* of the host lineage by relinquishing some of their relief shares. An Oxfam officer explained a similar incident: "We knew that the number of people [in an area] had increased, but we could not violate the rule that food should be distributed to whoever needs it in an area. Furthermore, the *shaikh* of [the area] convinced us that those were his people, so it would be insulting to contradict his claim."

Besides saving lives, relief provisions also reinforced gendered lineage politics and existing power relations. Some Hadendowa women complained that because they had no husbands or close male relatives to fight for them, their families had been denied access to relief commodities. Madina, age forty-five, whose husband died during the famine, said, "During one winter we almost died because of the cold weather. One organization distributed blankets, but some people who were close relatives of the *shaikh* got their share and we didn't. Sometimes we hear about such distribution, but we don't see it. It was a widespread practice that some *shaikhs* would collect them, sell them, and use the money."

Thus for the Hadendowa, famines meant inescapable realities grounded in local, national, and global politics. The disastrous impact of droughts and famines on families manifested itself in ill health and high infant mortality rates. In 1984 UNICEF reported a 10 to 20 percent infantile death rate in a population of eighteen thousand in the Duraudaib camp in eastern Sudan. In Haiya, another town in eastern Sudan, only 29 percent of the children were reported as unaffected by malnutrition, while 50 percent of them were suffering from vitamin A deficiency (Oxfam Nutritional Surveillance Team 1985).

The social impact of famine and displacement was further reflected in changes to existing familial relations, kinship organization, and cultural

values, especially those pertinent to honor. The rate of destitute women re-
sorting to prostitution in Sinkat was alarming. It was a phenomenon that
most women whom I interviewed frowned upon but could not deny. The
disturbing number of prostitutes in 1984–89 led the authorities in Sinkat to
involve tribal leaders to resolve the situation with the "guardians" of these
prostitutes. This effort proved to be unsuccessful because many families
relied on the incomes of their daughters during the height of famine. To
complicate the situation further, some Muslim extremists among the Beja
youth initiated the "committee of fighting immorality," which confronted
the female leaders of these households and threatened to set fire to their
homes. This confrontation warranted the intervention of the police, who
granted the women safety until the matter was resolved by tribal authorities.

The cycle of destitution and famine is unending in eastern Sudan. In
February 2001 the Sudan News Agency (SUNA) reported a new episode of
drought and starvation that had displaced some ninety-eight thousand
people who deserted their villages to seek refuge in urban centers. As a result, 75 percent of those affected have sold and/or consumed all their livestock. Quoting a report by a group of national and international NGOs, the
agency reported that the hardest hit areas included Haiya, Duraudaib, Sinkat, and Halib. Although some of the displaced people were reported to
be working in agricultural areas, the Humanitarian Aid Commission in the
Red Sea province reported a 100 percent unemployment rate. According
to SUNA eighty-five thousand tons of rice donated by Italy were the only
form of relief received, and this amount was below that required to feed the
needy. The rise to power of the Islamists in the Sudan in 1989, which fueled
the continuing civil war between the north and the south, the imposition of
American and Western economic sanctions, and the shift in humanitarian
politics, have exacerbated the vulnerability and marginality of a large section of the Sudanese population.

Despite this vicious cycle of local and global inequalities, the Hadendowa anchor their concepts of resiliency and honor in an imagery of a
resourceful land vehemently guarded by their ancestors. Through their
struggle to manage the capriciousness of power hierarchies, the Hadendowa engage in continuous negotiations over the ancestral land as a site of
transforming identities.

Land and Descent: The Controversy of Honor

I met Haj Hamid in the village of Aukar in eastern Sudan, which is claimed
to be the original Hadendowa homeland. Although the arid village is almost deserted due to continuous droughts and famines, Aukar is a key site
and a significant historical place for the emergence of the Hadendowa as an

autonomous political group. Haj Hamid, a sixty-five-year-old Hadendowa, began our conversation by relating a grand narrative that describes the Hadendowa's multifaceted ways of organizing their kinship relations and constructing their collective identities. He recounts how the group emerged from the intermarriage of a hybrid Beja-Arab holy man named Barakawin (the fearless) with the daughter of the Beja king, Hadat (the lioness). The two had seven sons and seven daughters, and their descendants founded the existing fourteen Hadendowa lineages. In Aukar the lineages fought victorious battles with invading foreign and national powers that sought to dominate them and expropriate their land. Through a system of fission and fusion, these lineages then broke into *adat*s and *diwab*s. This segmentation process, according to Haj Hamid, is a response to the population increase of one sublineage within a limited area, which leads to pressures over land. Eventually, the sublineages split in order to search for new grazing land. On the social level, conflict over land ownership and over women can also contribute to lineage segmentation. Haj Hamid offered the following illustration of this process:

> Let's assume that Hamid is one of Barakawin's sons who moved out from his father's original homeland. Hamid's family would be called Hamid *indiwab* [family or sublineage]. When Hamid's family multiplies, we would refer to them as Hamidab [those who belong to Hamid or the lineage of Hamid]. Let's then assume that Hamid has a son whose name is Awadnun, who also gets married; his family increases, and he moves out of his father's homeland for one reason or another. Awadnun would then form a section of the Hamidab lineage that we would call Hamidab-Awadnunab [those who relate to the Hamidab through their grandfather Awadnun]. Awadnun would thus have created a new *diwab* of the Hamidab lineage.

At present each lineage occupies a specific geographical area and constitutes an independent political unit. The members of each lineage trace their descent seven generations back to Barakawin through his seven sons and seven daughters.

Haj Hamid's narrative highlighted the courage of the seven sons in surmounting difficulties and hardships and restoring the *durarit* of the collective group. While we were conversing, he pointed to the graveyard where the Hadendowa ancestral grandmother, Hadat, and her husband and seven sons were buried. Commenting on what distinguished Hadat, Haj Hamid said, "She was a religious woman and a virtuous wife. Our people visit her grave carrying food and water to be consumed by the needy." When I asked Haj Hamid about Hadat's seven daughters, he said, "Nobody knows their names or where they were buried, but we all know that they were married to foreigners [non-Beja suitors], and their descendants formed the other seven lineages."

Haj Hamid's grand narrative establishes the hybridity and honorable status of the seven dominant Hadendowa lineages. The interaction with the hybrid Beja-Arab *sharif* (honorable) was celebrated as an intermarriage with a similarly honorable woman, Hadat, the daughter of the Beja king Shakautail. She is thus not only respected for her religiosity, virtue, and fertility but also for symbolizing a hybrid identity resulting from a mutual alliance with a foreign power. The grand narrative, therefore, bespeaks a repertoire of knowledge that describes Hadendowa kinship logic and their construction of a distinct identity whose meanings are negotiated through the notions of honor and the power and danger of foreignness and its impact on regeneration.

The Hadendowa notion of *durarit* revolves around the "purity" of descent and the protection of ancestral land, and each lineage acts independently to guard these two elements of honor. All lineages, however, unite to defend their collective honor from the intrusion of non-Beja groups. Therefore, competition with adjacent nomads over economic resources represents a major threat to Hadendowa autonomy and puts their honor at stake.

After the clearance of vast areas for mechanized farming in the Tokar Delta, Gash, and Qadarif, the Hadendowa were restricted to a limited area of grazing land. The focus on cash-crop production had failed to absorb the majority of vulnerable pastoralists in the area during periods of economic crisis (Egeimi 1994). The Hadendowa situation was worsened by the consequent movements of other Beja from the west and the north into their territories, such as the movement of the Bishariyyin, the Amarar, and the Atman. Pressure on the Hadendowa grazing land was also exacerbated by the migration of the Rashaida from Arabia in 1846 and the movement of the Beni Amir in the 1960s following the war in Eritrea, which led to more conflicts in the region (Mohamed Salih 1976). Since the protection of collective land is vital, the Hadendowa charge certain lineages with the duty of territorial defense against external intrusion. As Andrew Paul notes: "[O]n the east, the Gemilab maintain the frontier against their traditional foes, the Beni Amir, the Besharin on the west are kept at bay by the Shaboidinab, and the Mahmodalihadab, a small section of the Atbara, are responsible for preventing trespass by the Shukria" (1954, 6).

For the Hadendowa maintaining purity of descent is synonymous with protecting land. Lineage members, who descend from a common Hadendowa ancestor, share the same blood, considered a mutual source of honor. It is the duty of lineage members to protect this kinship bond from loss by marriage with outsiders. Hadendowa men and women, however, often explain *durarit* as an emotional influx, or hot blood, emanating from one's heart or guts, a process that in turn triggers a feeling of jealousy or a willingness to protect their land and descent. In this context *durarit* represents a sense of moral commitment that reinforces one's identity and social position within the collectivity. The meanings of *durarit*, however, encompass other domains of social practices and can vary according to social settings: it can mean *hasham* (modesty), *hamaustib* (respect), generosity, or *dawrib* (nice, beautiful) to commend acceptable moral behavior and adherence to cultural codes. The Hadendowa name that some women gave me was Dawrita, which connotes "the one whose moral behavior fits nicely."

The idea that honor emanates from blood, the hot element of the inside, underlies Hadendowa symbolic logic, which uses the human body as a medium for generating knowledge and cultural practices. As a discourse on social relations among lineage and sublineage members, the Hadendowa describe purity of descent as the main criterion pertinent to honor. Haj Hamid's narrative represents a version of many narratives used by the Hadendowa as testimonies of their honorable descent. Those who trace their descent to Barakawin through his seven sons (henceforth "sons of sons' lineages") assume superiority over lineages formed from the intermarriage of Barakawin's and Hadat's daughters (henceforth "sons of daughters' lineages") with foreign men. The foreign men said to have married Hadat's and Barakawin's daughters were from the Shaiqiyya, the Jaalyinn, the Funj, and the Shukriyya, Muslim, Arabic-speaking groups from northern and central Sudan. Foreign suitors also included men of West African and Kurdish origins. Unlike sons of sons' lineages, the descent lines of sons of daughters' lineages are cut off from their foreign fathers; they are incorporated into Hadendowa kinship organization by virtue of matrilocal residence, through male offspring lines. They become dependents of sons of sons' lineages and reside in their territory.

Foreignness as a threat to social order is a central theme in Hadendowa narratives of identity and regeneration. Foreigners, a category that includes colonial Europeans and Turks, the ruling elite of Arabic-speaking northern Sudanese, and other non-Beja groups, are seen as dangerous to social integrity and often depicted in the Hadendowa social imagination as intrusive jinn, which women describe as spiritual entities that manifest themselves in human and other natural forms. Thus members of dominant groups often explain the foreign association of dependent lineages with reference to liaisons with spirits. Hawwa, a forty-two-year-old Hadendowa woman who belonged to one of the dominant lineages, explained that "Barakawin had seven sons only. But when he was fighting other non-Beja groups in the area, he asked God to send him seven jinn to aid him in his fights. God sent Barakawin the seven jinn, who stayed with him, and he later passed them to his seven sons. The jinn married Hadendowa women and formed the sons of daughters' lineages."

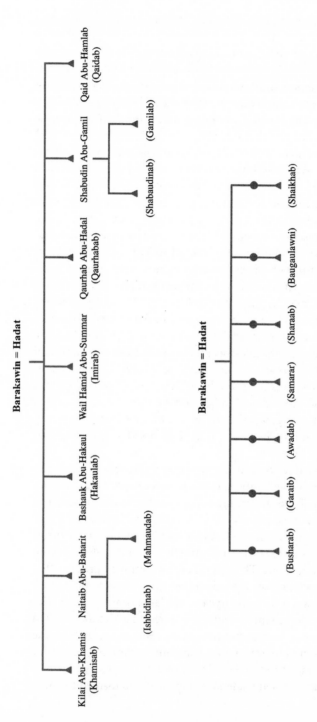

Barakawin = Hadat

Kilai Abu-Khamis (Khamisab)
Naitaib Abu-Baharit
(Ishbidinab) (Mahmaudab)
Bashauk Abu-Hakaul (Hakaulab)
Wail Hamid Abu-Summar (Imirab)
Qaurhab Abu-Hadal (Qaurhabab)
Shabudin Abu-Gamil
(Shabaudinab) (Gamilab)
Qaid Abu-Hamlab (Qaidab)

Barakawin = Hadat

(Busharab) (Garaib) (Awadab) (Samarar) (Sharaab) (Baugaulawni) (Shaikhab)

Busharab, descendants of Shaukriyya (Muslim, Arabic-speaking group from central Sudan)
Garaib, descendants of West African or Funj
Awadab, descendants of Shaiqiyya (Muslim, Arabic-speaking northern Sudanese)
Samarar, descendants of Kurds
Sharaab, descendants of Jaaliyyin (Muslim, Arabic-speaking northern Sudanese)
Baugaulawni (?)
Shaikhab (?)

Sons of sons' lineages (top) and sons of daughters' lineages (bottom)

Here members of the dominant lineages use jinn narratives as a strategy to undermine the status of incorporated groups and to discourage exogamous marriages. In the context of reckoning descent, purity becomes a social construct derived from the natural idiom of blood, a symbol of life and regeneration. Endogamous marriage is seen as the means by which honor and kinship are buttressed.

Narratives that undermine the honor of sons of daughters' lineages not only discourage exogamous marriages but also employ discursive strategies that discredit the status of both a foreign husband and his Hadendowa wife, as manifested in the story of Bura.

Bura (a female name that means "the spinster"), the sister of Gamil, who founded the Gamilab lineage, was married to Hamid, a man from the Shukriyya, an Arabic-speaking group from central Sudan. Hamid, as presented in the narrative, was a *hasbib* (refugee), who fled from his group after killing a man, an atrocious criminal act. Refugees acquire a dependent status through their incorporation into the kinship system, but they have the same rights as other Hadendowa. Thus Gamil protected Hamid, made him herd his animals, and later asked him, despite his refugee status, to marry his sister—an offer that Hamid readily accepted. Since the husband can enter his wife's tent only at night, Hamid was not able to see his wife's face. One day, he decided to sneak into her tent without her knowledge. Seeing her face, he was shocked by her ugliness and fled the camp. By then Bura was pregnant and later gave birth to a boy whom his uncles named Bushara (the sign of bounty). Although Bushara's *durarit* was contested because of his foreign patrilineal descent, he was able to build his *durarit* by accumulating wealth in land and in sons. Bushara and his sons were able to achieve independence from their host lineage by expanding their own territory and establishing a recognizable status among other Hadendowa lineages.

Bura's story is similar to other stories that members of dominant lineages relate about the status of dependent lineages. The story of Madina, the daughter of Bashuk, the son of Barakawin, is another case in point. Madina is said to have been given in marriage to a man from the Funj, a group from central Sudan whose Islamic kingdom flourished in the sixteenth century and subdued many groups, including the Hadendowa. The descendants of this group are denigrated as being the grandsons of a beggar and are called Qarib after the *qaraa* (bowl) that their grandfather used to carry while begging. Haj Taha, who is from the Qarib lineage, explained how members of dominant lineages often regard them as Funj, Falata (Fulani), or Khasa (a pejorative term used to refer to the Beni Amir), but they are none of these; they are pure Arabs. According to some Hadendowa, West Africans, Beni Amir, and some groups from western, central, and southern Sudan are racialized and associated with blackness and slavery. Members of these groups are often said to possess dangerous powers that threaten fertility and regeneration.

These narratives, however, are widely contested, and their meanings are altered according to who is telling the story (see Leach 1954; Bowen 1993). Thus the acquisition or lack of *durarit* is based on internal dynamics and shifts of power. Though honor can be marred as a result of blood mixing, it can also be reinstated through a man's courage and that of his male heirs in defending and extending their territorial boundaries, as in the case of Bushara. An inability to defend land and the purity of descent leads to submission to others, violates the integrity of the group, and reduces men's and women's honor. Abu-Lughod describes a similar correlation between honor and political autonomy among the Awlad Ali Bedouin of Egypt, who view honor as a shield from external domination. A man of honor among the Egyptian Bedouin is one who manifests his independence and unwillingness to submit to others (Abu-Lughod 1986; see also Bourdieu 1965; Campbell 1965).

Lineage debates over honor are not one-sided since dependent groups contest the monolithic descent frame by linking their descent to the Prophet Muhammad, the epitome of honor. While sons of sons' lineages foreground hybridity (being Beja-Arab) as the source of their honor, sons of daughters' lineages identify themselves as "pure" Arabs to contest the narratives of dominant lineages. According to this narrative, Hadat was a pure Arab who came with her father from Hijaz to Sawakin, where she met Barakawin, another Arab holy man. Hadat and Barakawin married, and their descendants founded the existing Hadendowa lineages.

With the expansion of Arab power in eastern Sudan and the conversion of the Beja to Islam during the fourteenth and sixteenth centuries, the Beja began to embrace Arab identity. Although they resisted the intrusion of the Arabs ferociously, Arab descent became a sign of high status and superiority (Mohamed Salih 1976, 17). Honor is thus not an immutable category. Instead, its meanings are embedded in the varying contexts of power relations and social practices. We have seen, for instance, how hybridity is legitimated to foster the social status of dominant lineages and used by them as a strategy to dishonor dependent lineages. As much as the grand narratives are meant to aggrandize the honor of the dominant groups, "dependent" lineages counter these grand narratives by using their own transcripts (cf. Scott 1990). This controversy evokes various questions regarding how historical and social interactions with foreign groups occur. Certain Hadendowa groups may have come to power at crucial moments that entailed establishing novel regulations related to patrilineality, endogamy, and matrilocal residence.

Such indeterminacy about honor and social status was expressed by Haj Hamid when I communicated to him the counternarrative. On hearing the narrative, he laughed briefly and said, "Different people usually say different things, but we are all Hadendowa who came from Barakawin and Hadat. But Hadat was a Beja who gave birth to the bravest Hadendowa sons." In this regard Edmund Leach is right in viewing such tales and mythologies as a language of social controversy (1954, 264) and not as factual statements. The Hadendowa men and women interviewed, however, were very cautious about divulging information about lineage honor and dishonor for fear of provoking tensions among different lineages. Many informants were quick to emphasize the significance of being Hadendowa before delving into the controversies among lineages over land and honor. Fatumab, a senior Hadendowa woman from a dominant group, recited this poem she had composed when I asked her about the differing status of lineages.

Barakawin tihaianaib inda	The sons of Barakawin
Tisharif ilawitib	are descendants of the Prophet.
Sabatdairt haifrain	They are born with wisdom [humor,] and generosity,
Hauba hibat hiabu	and their ancestors have many blessings on them.
Tishwa ikarim ratnai	They asked God to help
Tutaur saadamia	increase their numbers through sons of daughters' lineages.
Tikul ana babiya	My fathers are from the Kulit [a Hadendowa lineage].
Haui mitab anihauk	I can describe them for you.
Hamaut tidari abkaba	Their territory extends from Hamaut to Adurus [vast land].

This debate over honor and identity unfolds in actual settings when dependent groups contest dominant lineages' claims over their ancestral land. Lineage boundaries are marked by natural symbols such as mountains, hills, and seasonal water streams. The Hadendowa migratory lifestyle necessitates certain land regulations for boundary protection. As a result, lineages accept reciprocal land use on a temporary basis and manage this through *qaudab* payment. Dependent lineages, which reside within the territories of the dominant groups, also pay the *qaudab* in recognition of their hosts' land rights.

Despite such regulations, conflicts over land ownership between different Hadendowa lineages arise frequently. This is because lineages, especially

incorporated ones, aspire to enhance their honor by achieving independence from their host lineages. The case of the Amarab and Baulauwab lineages (not their real names) illustrates this point. During my fieldwork the
disputes between the two groups reached a serious level. In fighting against
the Baulauwab and justifying their land rights, the Amarab, who assume the
ownership of Hamawaib territory, insisted that their opponents were their
dependents who should continue to herd their animals, harvest their land,
and pay the *qaudab*. To undermine their opponents' status, the Amarab asserted that the Baulauwab were descendents of a marriage union between
a mentally ill Amarab woman and a foreigner. The root of the conflict may
also be traced to socioeconomic changes as the Baulauwab have grown in
numbers and some of them have been successful in business. My assistant
reported, "One of their sons was a University of Khartoum graduate, and
he is the one who insists that land should belong to whoever cultivates it."

Empowered by their members in towns as well as by the transformation
of their economic and social status, the Baulauwab started to cultivate the
land for themselves despite warnings from their host lineage. They authen-
ticated their land ownership using documents signed by an *aumda* during
the British colonial regime. In response men from the dominant group mo-
bilized and confronted the Baulauwab members, destroyed their fields, and
killed one of their men. The fight also resulted in the wounding of men
from both parties.

After the fight the police and the court personnel in Sinkat town, headed
by the elite class of Arabic-speaking northern Sudanese, intervened. The
officials in town (whose role is to discipline, control, and prevent "the
chaos" of the "Arabs," through the power of the state) are always baffled by
these disputes (see Foucault 1977). Although the Beja sometimes identify
themselves as Arabs, non-Beja urban Sudanese use the word pejoratively to
denote an inferior, nomadic lifestyle. One government functionary said
that he could not understand how such conflicts became so tense and led to
killing over an arid land that is good for nothing.

The Hadendowa often resist government interference in their internal
affairs. Therefore, state courts include group leaders and lineage customary
laws to ensure the effectiveness of their procedures. The involvement of the
nazir, the top authority in the Hadendowa political organization, has been
significant in such situations, as his judgment is respected. In the case of
the fight I described, the police arrested the members of the dominant lineage whose attack resulted in the killing of the Baulauwab man. When I left
Sinkat town, some of the accused men from the dominant lineage were still
in jail, and they refused to confess to the murder. Since the accused were
fighting for an "honorable cause," that is, defending their land, their lineage

members would be dishonored if they incriminated them. A northern Sudanese official at the Sinkat police headquarters told me that he was astonished by the number of people who came to him as mediators attempting to resolve the problem in the interest of their own group: "Every member of a group who lives or works in town feels responsible to come and talk on behalf of his group in order to protect the collective land. This is the only place in the Sudan, I think, where people deal with land ownership as a collective entitlement. In other parts of the country, land is claimed on an individual basis."

The Hadendowa have always maintained a loose alliance with the central authority, which is viewed as both foreign and superior and thus poses a continuous threat to their social values and power over land. In critical times, however, the Hadendowa strategize to mobilize external power to their own advantage. In 1998 a fight between two young Hadendowa men from different lineages led to the killing of one and the serious injury of the other. Although the town was shaken by the event, the murderer was assisted by his lineage members and fled to his rural village to seek refuge. Although the police eventually found his hiding place, his lineage members refused to cooperate or to divulge any information that may have led to his implication in the killing. On the other hand, members of the victim's lineage offered to help the police, who permitted them to join the search for the murderer on the condition that they not take matters into their hands. Although controversy arose over the cause of the fight, it was rumored to have been triggered by the violation of "private boundaries," which usually involve "female honor." This is a sensitive aspect of honor that, like conflict over land, can lead to disputes among men, families, and lineages. Women, like land, are seen as vulnerable and their boundaries can be violated by the intrusion of others. Men's honor is therefore also linked to their ability to guard their "private boundaries" and to ensure the modesty of their women. This aspect of female honor, as related to land, was expressed by Haj Hamed, another Hadendowa, who maintained: "Land is honorable. If someone trespasses on your land, it is as if he openly violated your private space. If you defend your honor, you deserve to be a man, and if you fail, you will never be. Women who have no men to protect them are as vulnerable as unprotected land."

As *asl* and *amara* determine rights and obligations toward collective land, private land, especially where cultivation is practiced, is inherited through the patrilineal line and passed from fathers to sons. According to *auslif*, women are excluded from land inheritance. As *auslif* regulations are predominant among the Hadendowa, shari'ah (Islamic law) is also used when considered fit. When the subject is women's claims over their father's land, for instance, shari'ah is rarely called into question. Women's land ownership is considered taboo and is said to bring *sa'am*, poverty and misfortune. Rarely do fathers include their daughters in their wills even when they allocate their property according to shari'ah (i.e., women should get half the men's share). Among the fifty women I interviewed in 1989, only four said that they inherited land according to their father's will. Of these four, one had lost her land rights because her brothers persuaded her to give up her share on condition that they would relinquish her allotment in produce and grain. Another was denied her share; she maintained: "When we were in our rural area before the famine, we had a sizable piece of arable land and many animals. After my father's death, my brothers divided his property among them and ignored me. I felt mistreated and insisted on having my share according to shari'ah, as my father had intended. But my brothers refused. Some of my relatives tried to talk me into complaining to the government [judge], but I refused because it is *aib* [shameful] for a woman to take her brothers to court. Women who act like this are seen as outcasts; they have no men to protect them."

Women's exclusion from land inheritance has its foundation in established gender roles. Although women customarily do not own land or camels (men's wealth), they do have absolute ownership over the tent, the icon of group regeneration. A woman has the right to prevent her husband from entering her tent, especially in cases of mistreatment. The tent, the locus of reproduction and nourishment, is also the site of *aumkir* between husband and wife, especially during times of economic distress. A Hadendowa popular proverb, "Women should only be consulted in matters of fear, thirst, and hunger" *(Mihinan tina tirau titabat bahain miraukwi tiwawa taraqau)*, speaks to women's centrality in matters concerning their families' survival. Women's honor, however, is tied to their modesty and their ability to regenerate the patrilineage.

Despite these restrictive codes, extramarital affairs occur and can jeopardize the honor of both men and women and lead to serious conflicts that require the intervention of tribal and police authorities. When brought to the attention of the police, women's involvement as the cause of such conflicts is often masked or expressed through latent codes. The following case, which was reported to the Sinkat police and later explained to me by a Hadendowa *shaikh*, reveals a latent discourse through which certain lineages disguise involvement of female honor when encountering external authority.

Sinkat police station, October 17, 1989, a dispatch from the Brasit bus station to the police station in Sinkat stated that thirty-two-year-old A and B from the same lineage fought and caused serious injuries to each other.

Here are excerpts of the dialogue between the investigator and the conflicting parties:

INVESTIGATOR: A, what are the reasons behind the fight?

A: It was because B told me that my brother had insulted him. I told him not to pay attention to my brother because we are relatives. While we were discussing this issue, he struck me with his sword twice and cut off my finger. I struck back at him with a cane.

INVESTIGATOR: B, is this true?

B: I was sitting in the Brasit bus station when A suddenly hit me on my left leg with his cane, and when I tried to draw my sword I unintentionally hit him.

INVESTIGATOR: A, what are the reasons behind the fight?

A: Merely old problems and I told him not to come to my place.

B: A had killed my camel and disposed of its body improperly.

Ostensibly, the fight was generated by A's indecent disposal of B's camel. The investigator took A's answer about the causes of the fight at face value and did not probe further. The case was settled, however, according to legal injunction 127, disturbing the public peace, and a fine was paid. Beyond the manifest reason lay the latent explanation behind the fight, namely, that A had suspected B of having an affair with his wife, which required A to stand up to his rival in order to clear his public image. Thus instead of confronting B, as comparable cases from the Middle East might suggest, A took the matter into his own hands by killing B's camel and leaving its carcass in the open. In this case, A's affront is not a personal one that could be mitigated by divorcing his wife but a public one that A dramatically realized (Goffman 1959, 30) by the public killing of the camel. Stealing a camel or killing it for consumption is regarded as mere theft, but disposing of its body in such an offensive manner is equivalent to exposing the rival's deed to the public eye and accusing him of an honor violation. Thus, unless the rival accepts the accusation and is prepared to defend himself, he himself would be dishonored once and for all (see Pitt-Rivers 1965; Campbell 1965). Here the metaphoric association between women and land resonates with that among women, camels, and sexuality. Female genitalia are referred to as *aukam* (camel). Land, women, and camels are also central elements in most Hadendowa songs about love and belonging. The three are associated with fertility, health, and identity. By bringing one's grievance into the public sphere, through symbolic representation or actual confrontation, a person begins a jurisprudential process whereby the tribal *aumkir* (council) may intervene to resolve the problem.

The abovementioned case was reported to the police because it took place in a shared urban public space (the Brasit bus terminal). In rural areas, as many women explained, the case could have been resolved according to a

Camel race during Haulia (Sinkat town, 1980s)

tribal *tihalifa* (council of oath), which deals with issues of dishonor and divorce. The council includes the closest kin of the spouses and other respected old men known as *shaikhs* or *aumkir* (wise men). In cases of infidelity or suspicion, the husband and the accused man will be present. Young wives are not allowed to address the *shaikhs,* though among certain groups a woman can be present to defend herself. Both the husband and the accused are sworn in, and the accused is convicted if there are witnesses who have seen him frequenting the wife's tent in the absence of her husband. In this case he is obliged to pay the husband a sum of money called *hasham. Hasham* includes both big *hasham,* which is paid when the accused is proven to have frequented the woman's tent, and small *hasham,* which is paid when the wife is proven to have visited his place. If the wife is found innocent, she has the right not to resume a relationship with her husband until her name is cleared, and her husband pays her the *tisanit,* a gift of gratification to win her consent, and the *taqar,* retribution to declare her honor.

Although a man can divorce his wife if she is found guilty, his *durarit* requires him to face an equal, for instance, the man who violated his honor, rather than offending or battering his own wife. The popular Hadendowa proverb *Autak waio tandiau titakat tida rabatak kiki* (the man who batters his wife is not a man) explains a woman's position as honorable subordinate. A man challenges his peers to establish his manliness. Thus by challenging a woman, his honor qualities are questioned. Honor should not be wasted on trivial matters such as fighting minors but should be enhanced to challenge "real enemies" and to protect the collectivity. One woman, Amna, attested to this point when she recited this popular Hadendowa poem:

| Tidurari wahafauku waria hariauk shibaubu | Do not waste your *durarit* on trivial things. |
| Afal sabit hasaitu Wadaui durrit rabandi | Save it for serious matters, such as an attack by enemies. |

This gendered aspect of *durarit* is rooted in the definition of men's and women's social place and in the intertwined concepts of identity and regeneration. Knowledge about these complex meanings enters the daily experiences of individual Hadendowa through narratives, debates, and territorial fights. In situations of high mobility, displacement, and interaction with others, meanings of honor and belonging incorporate both local logic and powerful external realities.

In new urban settings, the Hadendowa filter novel urban practices through their own local lenses to make sense of their marginality and dislocation. Many women whom I interviewed shunned urban lifestyles, lamenting an ancestral heritage that embraced their sense of honor and independence. Other families, however, are settling into urban centers, viewing them as the only refuge for survival. As one Hadendowa woman maintained, she felt less vulnerable in town since three of her children had died of starvation in her village.

Thus the process of constructing Hadendowa identity continues among a new generation of Hadendowa men and women who are appropriating available urban opportunities to survive and enhance their familial connections. Indeed, this endless process of identification is "constituted in relationships" (Kurkiala 1998, 40; see also Henborg and Kurkiala 1998) and rooted in specific points of reference such as places, symbols, and ideas of social becoming. It is thus a fluid process that at times fixes certain concepts and opens others up for negotiation and controversy. We have seen how Hadendowa concepts of honor and identification engage old and new ideas and experiences to enable people to reclaim power over a famished land that is seen as the bedrock of their *durarit*. *Durarit* itself is not fixed in space and time; rather its meanings are produced with reference to alterity and are interwoven with other cultural idioms and gendered practices of fertility, health, and regeneration to allow for future maneuvering (see Marcus 1987; Gupta and Ferguson 1997).

Chapter 2

Historicizing Foreignness

Alterity, Disease, and Social Vulnerability

Say: "I take refuge with the lord of men
the king of men
the God of men
from the evil of the slinking whisperer
who whispers in the breasts of men
of jinn and men."

                                                    Qur'an

Hadendowa perceptions of fertility, danger, and disease encompass a set
of beliefs in the evil eye *(lailit)*, spirits *(jantaib* or jinn), and in mysterious
diseases *(tisaramt)*, whose explanations lie in the gendered "di-vision"
(Bourdieu 1990) of body space and in cultural notions of honor *(durarit)*,
identity, and regeneration that are constantly threatened by increasing
"foreignness" and displacement.[1] These anxieties concerning danger and
disease, I argue, project an image of the modest Hadendowa woman as an
embodiment of honor, affinity, and fertility subject to violation by the un-
regulated morality of the foreign world. The stories and narratives of vulnerability and marginalization that women expressed through the imagery
of woman-as-land project a flexible scaling of morality and honor through
which discursive practices about the dangers of the evil eye, spirits, and

---

1. Most women interviewed used the terms jinn (Arabic) and *jantaib* (Tu-Badawie)
interchangeably to refer to spirits.

tisaramt reference broader concerns about the embodied spatiality under assault. Through gendered models of body space, metaphorical categories and symbolic rituals are projected internally and externally to comment on Hadendowa social order and its "governmentality" (Foucault 1991).

The Hadendowa conceptualization of danger and disease defines particular external threats that are said to undermine the collective code of *durarit:* the integrity of the ancestral land and the pure blood of descent vested in women's procreative power. These perceptions underscore the Hadendowa's ambivalent relations with others, as represented by government authority and institutions as well as foreigners in general, and stem from the notion that their land is exclusively theirs *(hash hashun, balad baladun).* This does not imply that the Hadendowa are isolated or lack interaction with outsiders. On the contrary, their land has for centuries been a passageway for different groups. The Hadendowa, however, always subjected these foreigners to scrutiny and suspicion. Indeed, both Western and Sudanese scholars have represented them as simultaneously aloof and warrior-like (e.g., Paul 1954; Mohamed Salih 1976). Little attention has been paid, however, to how Hadendowa cultural constructions of identity have physically and emotionally tied them, through a code of honor, to their ancestral land. From the Hadendowa perspective, repeated colonial invasions and their social consequences account for their complex framings of external danger. The danger of the outside stems from their fear of losing the very source of their social being.

The Hadendowa physical landscape is a vast, dry area surrounded by mountains that open up to the Red Sea. Significantly, most Hadendowa narratives about external danger feature the sea, which is infested with immoral, deceptive spirits. The fear of the sea and its spirit inhabitants evokes the historical actualities of the foreign invasions of Beja territory, reading foreigners as supernatural transgressors of Beja indigenous space who build colonies for themselves outside Beja jurisdiction, thus undermining their power and authority and rendering them marginal. This imagination of foreignness thus cannot be read apart from the history of urban colonial development in eastern Sudan. Although there are many towns in eastern Sudan whose establishment is associated with colonialism and other historical interactions, I will focus here on Sawakin, Port Sudan, and Sinkat since they are referred to most often in the interviewed women's stories about foreignness.

The ancient port of Sawakin and the city of Port Sudan are the main entrances to eastern Sudan from the Red Sea. Sawakin's strategic location has made it the most famous port on the Red Sea since the Sixth Dynasty of the

Pharaohs (3000 BCE). At the height of its prosperity, Sawakin was a harbor for ships from all over the world, facilitating close links with Ethiopia, Egypt, Arabia, Yemen, India, and China (Hamadi n.d.). It was successively occupied by the Ptolemies, the Romans, the Arabs, and the Turks. By the beginning of the sixteenth century, the army of the first Islamic kingdom, the Funj sultanate, which originated in central Sudan, had invaded Sawakin. During the sultanate's reign, the town grew from a small trading center to a leading port (see Hamadi n.d.). The Beja resisted the Funj fiercely but were ultimately defeated.

Following the demise of the Funj kingdom, Sawakin fell under Turco-Egyptian rule (1821–85), during which it flourished as a cosmopolitan center. Consequently, new houses were built in Sawakin resembling the Turkish style of other Red Sea ports such as Jidda and Massawa. The new buildings, mostly two- to four-story stone houses, were built on the island and inhabited by government officials and merchants, while the Beja lived in timber and mat housing on the periphery. Bounded by such structures, urban centers were meant to create a familiar atmosphere within which the ruling elite could govern properly and manage the affairs of the colonies.

Sawakin thrived as an urban center during Anglo-Egyptian rule (1896 – 1955) as a result of the extension of the Nile Valley railway, which connected the city with the country's interior in 1905. With the construction of the railway and increasing demand for labor, more people from central Sudan crossed Beja land to Sawakin, contributing to its heterogeneity. The city's growth as a hub of "foreignness" was reflected in its largely mixed community. In 1913 Arab families controlled the largest businesses in Sawakin, while Muslim pilgrims, mostly West Africans, returning from Mecca decided to settle in the city (Roden 1970, 7). During times of pilgrimage, Roden reports, the West Africans residing in Sawakin outnumbered the indigenous residents. Moreover, there was an Indian community that occupied its own quarter on the island, as well as substantial Greek and Italian quarters (Roden 1970, 11). The status of Sawakin as a cosmopolitan port, however, changed rapidly after the colonial government decided to establish a new harbor sixty kilometers to the north.

Port Sudan, the new harbor, was designed as a modern port to meet the demands of the twentieth century and to serve the colonial government's interest. In 1906 the city was connected to the railway line, which transported exports and imports and brought more people from central Sudan into contact with the opportunities of the expanding market economy. Like Sawakin, Port Sudan developed as a new "city of contrasts" (Perkins 1993, 137), with an urban center designed mainly for Europeans and the merchant class and unplanned areas to which local people, mainly Beja, were relegated. With the establishment of these colonial centers, Beja claims to their portion of land designated for urban development became even more tenuous. Even when recognized by colonial administrations, the Beja claims were compensated with insignificant sums (Perkins 1993, 39). The postindependence era in the Sudan, however, witnessed the emergence of a much larger national power with which the Beja had to grapple.

Sinkat, the fieldwork site, is another example of an urban colonial center, which was originally established by the Turks and later used as a summer resort by the British. The small town is characterized by wide, sandy streets and cement, brick, and mud houses built in an orderly fashion and mostly owned by northern Sudanese, Sawakinese (a mixed group of Beja, Arabs, and Turks), Kurds, and Ashraf. The Ashraf claim to be descendants of the Prophet Muhammad; they are devoted followers of the Mirghani family, the spiritual leaders of the Khatmiyya (a major mystical brotherhood), the majority of whom live in Port Sudan, Sawakin, and Sinkat (see Voll 1969). They have intermarried with the Hadendowa and speak both Arabic and Tu-Badawie. The Hadendowa, except for a few elite, reside in the unplanned areas on the town's outskirts, which are segregated from the center by major perennial streams. The history of urban development in eastern Sudan reveals an invasion of "foreignness" that is in every regard a negation of Hadendowa moral codes and ideologies of spatial governance and organization. Migrant Hadendowa perceive town dwellers as a crowd whose members do not represent a unified collective entity organized by a specific moral code. They see diseases, alcoholism, theft, dishonesty, and sexual laxity as afflictions prevalent among city dwellers. These views are, however, subject to contestation and negotiability.

Proximity and Distance: The Social Scaling of Honor

The Hadendowa construction of gendered body-space honor resonates with their social scaling of proximity and distance, which incorporates their perceptions of and relations with the different groups that live within and without their boundaries. For instance, the Hadendowa consider Ashraf, Sawakinese, Kurds, and northern Sudanese as urban dwellers whose moral behavior negates their own code of honor. The Hadendowa-Ashraf relationship is one of tension and negotiability. Although the Hadendowa consider the Ashraf to be socially distant because of their non-Beja origin, they also regard them as socially proximate by virtue of their religiosity and prophetic descent. Hadendowa men and women alike rely on the baraka (blessing) of the Khatmiyya saints to cure sicknesses and alleviate other kinds of misfortune. The Hadendowa's religious commitment to the Khatmiyya Sufi order is manifested in their observation of its various religious ceremonies, such as the Haulia, the widely celebrated annual memorial of Alsharifa Maryam, the granddaughter of the founder of the brotherhood.[2]

During the Haulia, the Hadendowa arrive from different parts of the region and gather at the tomb of the saint, situated at the town center. Hadendowa leaders come laden with gifts to be distributed to the needy in the name of Alsharifa as signs of devotion and respect. For the Hadendowa in the region, the Haulia symbolizes a glorified day that is often equated with the two Muslim religious holidays of Aid Alfitr (the post-Ramadan fete) and Aid Aladaha (the sacrifice fete). During the Haulia, men, women, and children don new clothes and wander cheerfully along the roads of the small town to visit relatives and neighbors and to wish them bounty and prosperity. Despite this strongly religious observance, the Hadendowa often negotiate their commitment to the religious order against an "authentic" Hadendowa identity that celebrates meanings of common blood, territoriality, and honor.

The Khatmiyya, through the influence of the Democratic Unionist Party (DUP), have also played a major role in the country's political sphere. During the last democratic period (1986–89), a Hadendowa party bearing the name of their ancestral grandmother (Hadat) emerged to join the election campaign against the DUP in Sinkat district. This created increasing tension between the Hadendowa and the Khatmiyya, who always relied on the support of the Hadendowa to win the election. The emergence of the Hadat party came at the climax of the region's devastating famine and coincided with the attempt of the Hadendowa elite to create a new medium to give voice to their people. Some Hadendowa elite openly accused the Khatmiyya of perpetuating poverty and starvation through their inability to take serious stands on development in the region. The emerging party adopted the name Hadat as a slogan to signal unity, identity, and attachment to land during the election campaign.[3] The tensions between the two groups culminated in the victory of the Hadendowa party in the Sinkat district. When the Unionists who won the election in Port Sudan planned to visit Sinkat to support their allies, Hadendowa men equipped themselves with swords in anticipation of their arrival. The Unionists returned to Port Sudan, however, on hearing the news of the Hadendowa's readiness to

2. The Haulia is banned by the current regime because it is seen as an occasion for promoting alliances for the rival political party, the Democratic Unionist Party (DUP).

3. In 1958 the Beja elite formed a political party (the Beja Congress) in the city of Port Sudan, calling for Beja unity and for equal opportunities and distribution of resources. The party is now part of the armed exiled opposition coalition. The Hadat party emerged under the umbrella of the Beja Congress; its local influence dissipated, however, after the end of the democratic period and the rise of the Islamists to power.

fight. The Ashraf, strong supporters of the Khatmiyya in Sinkat, expressed their indignation at this event in religious songs. One of these widespread songs praised the leader of the religious order and denounced Hadendowa claims to ownership of their ancestral land. Instead the song stressed that God had spread the land for his Prophet Muhammad, and since the Khatmiyya are descendants of the Prophet, they have an equal claim to the Hadendowa land and its resources.

Idmianit Sidib Imauqadna ibishwaiyn aun bikhatim nibau	They infringe on his holiness by stoning our *sharif* [descendant of the Prophet]; they aspire [by such means] to achieve a status similar to his, which is unattainable.
Idmianit tidyai hinit wa habib aunur inabi barartau	They infringe [upon his holiness] by claiming that the land is theirs, unaware that God has essentially spread this land for the Prophet and his grandsons [the Mirghani family]

The events surrounding the election also illustrate the Hadendowa's loose alliance with groups perceived as external and the strategies they adopt to accommodate external powers in times of economic stress. During the famine of the 1980s, debate over collective identity was heightened and accusations of betrayal extended to include the northern Sudanese elite, who were held responsible for withholding immediate aid. The Hadendowa, whose attitudes toward Europeans are ambivalent because of a history of colonization and differing religiosity, were baffled by the great numbers of European relief agencies that descended on their land to help mitigate the severity of the crisis. The famine of the 1980s was sometimes referred to as the Khawada to indicate the involvement of many European NGOs in the aid mission. Although cautious about European involvement, many Hadendowa felt gratitude toward the Khawada when compared to the Khatmiyya or the ruling democratic government at that time. The following dialogue between interviewees Tibasharik and Tibatadil speaks to this concern and illustrates this heightened sense of inclusion and exclusion.

TIBATADIL: During the famine our religious leaders and the Khatmiyya urged us to hang the *sunkab* inside our tents to protect us from the misfortune of famine and to bring rain. They prevented us from eating the food of the Khawada saying that the Khawada would bewitch us and count our children . . . But this is not true because the Khawada was the only one whom we found among us during that miserable time. He

[*looking at Tibasharik*] is a man; when you go back to Khartoum tell
them [the government] that we will elect the Khawada next time [*said
sarcastically*].

TIBASHARIK: No, no, we cannot elect the Khawada. How can you elect a
non-Muslim, Tibatadil?

TIBATADIL: Islam is something in the heart and in the acts, so the Khawada
is a Muslim because he saved our lives. And if this is really what you think
[*mockingly*], why did you give your vote to Hadat and not to the Khatmiyya
if you really love Alsharifa [Maryam]?

TIBASHARIK: [*puzzled*] I gave my vote to my kinfolk. The love of Alsharifa is
something in my heart.

[*They seemed relieved and started to sing this Hadendowa song, which
incorporates the role of the Khawada in the relief effort.*]

Hirarair wahiaf tiqirbati lawiqa	He walks around devotedly [taking good care of people]. To help others he ended up in a foreign country.
inadiri kirayida, Hirarira Hauk talama bashauta	Yet [he enjoys the good company] of the people who gather around him [to receive food aid]. He walks around devotedly [taking good care of people]. [He is fair] and does not favor one tribe at the expense of another.

This song is essentially a wedding song that celebrates and idealizes the
Hadendowa groom, who embodies values of honor: hospitality, generosity,
courage, humor, and confidence. During the famine some of the verses of
this song were altered to incorporate the Khawada. Yet this sense of appre-
ciation is also mixed with a sense of danger associated with relief food,
which is suspected of causing infertility and children's sickness. The shift-
ing attitude toward the inclusion or exclusion of others is thus temporal.
When I went back to interview Tibatadil and Tibasharik during my last visit
to Sinkat, their criticism of the Khawada was even harsher. There were
fewer agencies than previously that catered to the needs of the poor, including the Sudanese Red Crescent and the Islamic Relief Agency. Tibasharik
commented on "bad governance" by saying, "All governments are the same
including that of the Khawada. They all come and go, but we have our land
and people." When it comes to issues of honor and belonging, however,
Ashraf, Sawakinese, northern Sudanese, and even Khawadat are regarded as
distant from an "authentic" Hadendowa identity.

The Hadendowa perceptions of the northern Sudanese signify a salient domain of boundary construction within which they identify themselves as Badawait (Bedouin), or Beja, and label other non-Beja groups as Sudanese. Within the latter category, they recognize Arabic-speaking northern Sudanese as *balawait*, in contrast to Badawait. *Balawait*, according to Dirar (1991, 1992, 56; see also Paul 1954, 64), is derived from the word *bellou*, which was the name of the first group that migrated from Arabia and settled among the Beja before the coming of Islam.

The Bellou, also known as Himyarites or Hadareb, which refers to Hadramout (the Bellou's original homeland in Yemen), asserted superiority over the Beja and enslaved some of them. They intermarried with the Beja, however, to consolidate their political power in the area. The Bellou, or Hadareb, a ruling class, were early converts to Islam, and they introduced other Beja groups to the new religion during the fourteenth century (Paul 1954, 66).

The power of the Bellou, or Hadareb, declined after the exhaustion of the gold and emerald mines and the abandonment of the port of Aidhab on the Red Sea in the mid-fourteenth century (Paul 1954, 76). The Bishariyyin, who emerged as the first tribal entity among the Beja, drove the Bellou south to the hills of Sinkat and Erkawit around the sixteenth century. The forces of the Funj kingdom later defeated the Bellou. When the Turks annexed Sawakin to the Hejaz region in 1520, the Bellou were less powerful in the management of the port (Paul 1954, 77). Hadendowa warriors, then a small clan, had driven the Bellou south into the area beyond the Baraka perennial stream by the first quarter of the seventeenth century.

For the Hadendowa, the Bellou, or *balawait*, connotes both the intruder and the superior. Arabic-speaking northern Sudanese are lumped into this historical category because they have held central power since the country's independence. Succeeding the colonial regime, the northern Sudanese elite, bureaucrats, and traders *(jallaba)* have shaped the political economy and the cultural geography of urban centers. They were the first to migrate to rural areas, and they comprise the majority of town dwellers. Rural areas have become sites for the diffusion of the central power of Khartoum, represented by various government institutions that propagate modernity in accordance with a northern Sudanese vision.

The term *balawait*, used by the Hadendowa to refer to the northern Sudanese, is loaded with contrasting cultural stereotypes. Hadendowa women often comment negatively on how northern Sudanese men and women eat their meals together, mix at work and other public places, send their girls to school, and allow their brides to dance in the presence of strange men, behaviors that the Hadendowa see as *aib* (shameful). Married *balawait* women also reveal their sexuality in public by wearing ostentatious jewelry and strong perfumes. These stereotypes, however, are negotiated differently by the old and the new generation of Hadendowa men and women: more members of the younger generation are beginning to see urbanization as a means of gaining power and economic resources. Although the *balawait* are socially distant due to their differing behavior, Hadendowa women also regard them as socially proximate by virtue of their education and adherence to Islam.

By contrast, the term *kishab* associates the neighboring Beni Amir and West Africans with "blackness," "slavery," and "foreign origin."[4] The Hadendowa also refer to the Beni Amir as *khasa*, an Arabic term that also denotes "slavery."[5] The Beni Amir, who are Muslims and speak Tigray, are the Hadendowa's oldest foes and major competitors for land and pasture in the region. This reinforces the Hadendowa's perception of the Beni Amir as foreigners who invaded their land from Eritrea and Ethiopia. Because of the Beni Amir's "foreignness," the Hadendowa believe that their livestock are the source of the mysterious disease *tisaramt*, which endangers women's fertility and children's growth.

Like many urban centers in the country, Sinkat includes many West Africans who have migrated from Chad and Nigeria. The Hadendowa, like many Sudanese, refer to those West Africans as Takarir or Falata.[6] The Hadendowa believe that Takarir men possess the power of both malevolent and benevolent jinn because of their "blackness" and their knowledge of the Qur'an. Although the Takarir intermarried with some Hadendowa families, the descendants of these marriages are considered to be "impure." Hadendowa women who have been given in marriage to West African men are labeled *halaib* (mentally ill), and it is believed that they were wed to the Takarir in order to be cured. Such statements discrediting foreign suitors and their Hadendowa women are common and are meant to undermine the honor of intermixed unions and to assert the significance of protecting the "purity" of descent through endogamous marriage. Saba, a young Hadendowa woman in her late twenties, told me her tormented love story involving a man from another Hadendowa lineage, whose members assume "pure" descent from Barakawin, the Hadendowa forefather. Because her great grandfather is believed to be from the Takarir, her lover's family

4. For a history of slavery in the Sudan, see, for instance, Sikainga 1996.

5. The Beni Amir are comprised of different groups that are divided into subgroups of nobles and subordinates. They speak Tigray, a Semitic language, which differs from the Cushitic Tu-Badawie language.

6. Takarir refers to the kingdom of Tekrur, which was established in Senegal in the eleventh century CE. One of Sinkat's shanty settlements is named after a well constructed by a Nigerian migrant *(bir tikrirait).*

opposed their marriage union. Saba told me that her lover's failure to convince his family resulted in the breakup of their relationship.

Many interviewed women used the term "Halab" (Gypsy; see Boddy 1989, 103) to contrast the *adarawb* (red) skin color of the Gypsies with their own *simrit* (brown) skin color. As is the case in northern Sudan, Hadendowa use skin color as a sign of identifying with a specific group. Although the brown skin color might be categorized as "black" elsewhere, women used the term *simrit* to give the color brown a more positive connotation than the color black, which they associate with *kishab*. Red skin color is also linked to Europeans and people of Arab descent. In the case of the Halab, for instance, members of this group are considered landless people who wander around aimlessly. Both the Hadendowa and the northern Sudanese categorize the Halab as people whose behavior negates their own codes of honor, because they live in open spaces and their men and women mix together. Usually their men are blacksmiths, and their women beg for food or exchange cooking utensils for food and clothes.

Within this cultural geography of honor and social difference, Hadendowa women embody values of honor that stress sexual modesty and proper motherhood. A Hadendowa woman veils her body and face in public and in the presence of men, and she casts her eyes down when walking in the street or talking to men. She also conceals her sexuality in public by not provoking men with her jewelry or strong perfumes. Such codes of propriety emerged as central themes in my conversations with women. My own position as a "*balawait*/northern Sudanese" researcher was scrutinized through these propriety measures. Although I braided my hair and wore a fauta, women questioned my position as a single woman traveling and studying abroad. Most women, however, found means to define me as socially proximate by commenting on the way I kept my eyes downcast or covered my face when walking in the street. This impression became widespread, and wherever I went, women mentioned how so-and-so had seen me walking "like them" in the street. They would then joke: "You must be a Hadendowa who was kidnapped by a *balawait qabilat* (tribe) a long time ago." Women also compared my behavior with that of other *balawait* researchers and educators who had visited them. One woman commented that some *balawait* women would visit them wearing pants and refused to eat their food or sit like them on the ground. She continued: "Some *balawait* women look at us as ignorant, dirty Arabs and think that our food would make them sick." My acceptability, thus, entailed my conformity to behavior that women saw as appropriate (*dawrib*, nice), which in turn led them to respect me. This reciprocal process of acceptability and respect, however, made women feel comfortable discussing some positive values they ascribed to *balawait*-ness. *Balawait* women are also seen as "knowledgeable," "clean,"

and "organized"—attributes that Hadendowa women connect with education, resourcefulness, and sophistication and contrast with their state of
poverty and hardship. Thus the measure of morality is negotiable and
brings into focus the contingent character of what is seen as dangerously
foreign. Although women identified many ethnic groups as morally distant,
certain categories, such as *balawait*, Beni Amir, Takarir, and Halab, emerged
as more critical in women's representation of foreignness, especially during
times of economic crises and distress.

Dangerous Encounters

The Hadendowa speak about different kinds of evil that can be caused by
both people and spirits. The description of this evil, I argue, corresponds to
their social scaling of proximity and distance. People of the same lineage
and sublineage are close to each other by blood, matrilocal residence, and a
common code of honor. Members of other groups become relatively distant if they do not meet the criteria of descent and residence. The gulf between proximity and distance widens whenever we move away from the
Hadendowa physical and social landscape. Such social zoning defines Hadendowa internal and external social relations and underlies their conceptualization of foreignness. Although the criteria for social proximity and
distance are not always consistent in Hadendowa descriptions of foreignness, fear of the evil eye, spirits, and mysterious diseases and their threat to
fertility and social well-being looms large.

The Evil Eye

Ethnographic studies on health and fertility in sub-Saharan Africa and the
Middle East have drawn attention to the evil eye and its dangerous effect on
physical and social well-being (e.g., Reminick 1976; Spooner 1976; Harfouche 1980; Boddy 1989; Delaney 1991; Morsy 1990; Inhorn 1994). Like
witchcraft beliefs in many societies (see Nadel 1952; Evans-Pritchard 1956;
Maloney 1976), the evil eye *(lailit)* among the Hadendowa expresses tensions among close relatives. Outsiders can also cast the evil eye on a Hadendowa person. Brian Spooner (1976) has criticized evil-eye scholarship for
providing numerous cross-cultural examples that fail to theorize the phenomenon and situate its social meanings and practices. A new trend in
studies of the evil eye calls for anchoring its meanings and practices in anal-
yses of colonialism, modernity, identity, and the representation of difference (Ibrahim 1994). In his study of the Rubatab culture of northern Sudan,
Abdullahi Ibrahim shows how the evil eye *(sahir)* is an "epistemological category" that reenacts Rubatab culture and the Rubatab representation of
otherness. If projected inward, *sahir* metaphors comment on Rubatab

moral superiority and the antisocial behavior deemed threatening to their social order. And when projected outward, *sahir* describes an external ethnic landscape "of Muslims and non-Muslims, Arabs and non-Arabs, gibberish and language, and the landed and the landless" (1994, 61). Corresponding to this, evil eye accusations among the Hadendowa are not confined to the network of close relatives. Rather, such attacks may originate in a foreign landscape replete with immorality, evil spirits, and mysterious diseases, which penetrate victims' bodies and threaten their fertility and well-being. This conforms to the interviewed women's understanding that insiders who possess the dangerous power of the evil eye are marginal persons and thus relegated to the domain of otherness. Hadendowa accusations of the evil eye, therefore, are part of an intertwined theory of sickness and health within which the evil eye, evil spirits, and mysterious diseases are seen as eminently dangerous to procreation.

The Hadendowa use the eye metaphor to emphasize evil emanating from envious eye-to-eye contact. The evil eye, according to one Hadendowa woman, is a powerful gaze accompanied by the utterance of envious praise intended to destroy someone's material wealth, especially wealth in health and children. Women describe such intentions as evil when envious people refrain from acknowledging that the disparity between them and those they envy is created by God. Thus praise sealed by saying *ma sha Allah* (by God's grace) communicates good intentions. Failing to utter this phrase can result in transmitting the dangerous gaze and praise to the bodies of the envied, rendering them useless and unable to perform their productive and reproductive roles. Thus the evil eye is always associated with psychological disorders, paralysis, and sudden adversities, especially those related to infertility and child sickness. Women attempt to cure the evil eye with amulets and *mihaya* (blessed water), which they acquire from *fuqara* (religious practitioners). *Mihaya* contains Qur'anic verses written on a wooden board or paper and soaked in water for patients to drink or use to massage their bodies, while amulets usually contain a set of Qur'anic verses that bewitched people, especially women and children, wear or keep in their proximity. Yet treatment for the evil eye may vary according to the severity and combination of ailments a person suffers. Women described curing the evil eye as extremely difficult, since it violates the integrity of the human body and creates an orifice that attracts other ailments associated with spirits and mysterious diseases.

The Spirit World

The Hadendowa theory of danger and disease articulates another source of evil caused by foreign spirits (*jantaib* or jinn) that targets fertility and regeneration. *Jantaib* is a broad category of spirits whose meanings extend beyond orthodox Islamic understanding to reflect the Hadendowa's social order and their interaction with others. Like many other Sudanese and African groups (see, e.g., Alnagar 1975; Boddy 1989; Constantinides 1979, 1991; Kenyon 1995; Kramer 1993; Stoller 1995), the Hadendowa believe in an invisible world of spirits that exists outside their social boundaries. These spirits inhabit the sea, the mountains that surround the villages, seasonal and permanent trees, and empty alleys and yards outside their domestic spaces. As is the case with the Hadendowa social order, the spirit world consists of several "tribes," each of which is organized by specific social values, which, instead of being guarded by honor, are grounded in immorality and deception. Like humans, spirits have physical traits, senses, and emotions. Unlike humans, however, they can transform themselves into different forms that humans cannot mimic (see Boddy 1989).

The spirit world also corresponds to women's conceptualization of social proximity and distance. It is socially differentiated, with white Muslim spirits *(jantaib ailab)* at the higher rank, and red spirits *(jantaib adarawb)* at the bottom. Women describe white Muslim spirits as believers in God and his Prophet, Muhammad. Therefore, Muslim jinn are not harmful and are employed by religious people to undo evil and harm. A Hadendowa woman possessed by Muslim jinn told me that her jinn never disturb her by manifesting themselves suddenly. They begin descending upon her using the greeting of Islam, *al-salamu alaikum* (peace upon you). When she replies *wa alaikumu al-salam* (peace upon you too), they begin conversing with her and explain the reasons for their visit. They may request that she put henna on her feet or recite the Qur'an for them, or they may complain to her about her neighbors who are invading their privacy by throwing hot water into an alley or cutting a tree without their permission. She then promises to obey their orders or to convey their messages.

Red spirits, on the other hand, reflect the colonial experience and include Christian jinn (representing Europeans, Khawajat) and Muslim (yet foreign, Turkish and Moroccan) jinn.[7] Within the category of red spirits, Hadendowa women stress the danger of black spirits *(jantaib hadal)*, which cause "blockage" *(arid)*, invite other forms of red jinn, and ultimately lead to infertility. These red spirit figures are known among Hadendowa women as *ijar*, synonymous with the *zar* type of spirits in northern Sudanese culture. Black jinn differ from women's characterization of the devil *(iblis* or *shaitan)* as a tall, pale character with bloody teeth and a fiery tongue and

---

7. Women describe Turks, Kurds, and Moroccans as people of red skin color. They refer to the spirits' characters with different terms: Khawajat are sometimes referred to as *kustani,* Turkish spirits are called *bashawat* or *atrak,* while Moroccans are referred to as *maghrabi* spirits.

throat who lives in ashes and dirty places. The devil is primarily responsible for triggering antisocial behavior, such as drinking and conflict among kin, for the objective of the devil, from the day of his creation, is to prevent Muslims from adhering to their faith.

It is significant to note that some women also perceive red spirits *(ijar)*, and especially black spirits, as rooted in Islamic history. Interviewee Zainab said that an *ijar* was first known during the time of the Prophet Muhammad. One day the Prophet and some of his companions came across a red-eyed black figure who was walking on his head. The companions asked the Prophet about it, and he replied that it was a male jinn named Ijar, who would manifest himself to people in different forms in the future to confuse them and stand in the way of their prosperity. People then would call this jinn *arid*. Women often describe a black jinn as a male Beni Amir, whom they refer to as Wad Diqni or *jibali* (from the mountains). He always plays the *rababa* (a lute-like musical instrument) while herding his animals in the mountains. According to Hadendowa social scaling of proximity and distance, spirits in the colonial categories of European, Turkish, and Moroccan seem to descend less frequently on women than does the Beni Amir black spirit. While the former categories pertain to a colonial past, the Beni Amir, the Hadendowa's inveterate foes, represent a conflictual present and a form of foreignness within the reach of Hadendowa social imagination.[8]

Red spirits exhaust their hosts with their sudden visits and demands and cause great harm to women's and men's fertility at any point of their life cycle, rendering them socially useless. In northern Sudan, red spirits, although threatening to fertility and bodily integrity, are seen as pleasure-seeking beings who cause milder forms of sickness that might not lead to death (see, e.g., Boddy 1989). For the Hadendowa, however, the concepts of fertility and procreation are so central that red spirits, like other forms of evil, are seen as eminently dangerous and possibly leading to both physical and social death. Encounters with *ijar* require ceremonial feasting and drumming during which the spirit descends on its host and makes its arduous demands. Hadendowa descriptions of red jinn and their manifestation during spirit-possession ceremonies and trances are in many ways similar to the well-documented *zar* practices in other parts of the country. The ceremonies I attended, though, were less elaborate, due to the economic circumstances of many migrants. Some women may forgo the expensive ceremonies by using *ijar* medicine provided by spirit specialists *(shaikhat)*.

Scholars of spirit possession, especially in the Sudan, situate the practice within the analysis of power inequalities as they inform gender

---

8. See also Kenyon 1995 on the predominance of Habash (Ethiopian) spirits in Sennar after the increased migration of Ethiopian refugees to the area.

arrangements and fertility practices. Janice Boddy's (1989) seminal work among the Hofriyati women of northern Sudan is a case in point. In Boddy's analysis of *zar*, spirits are allegories of powerful others whose encounters during trances orient women's consciousness toward new realities external to their gender-bound social world. Through trance experiences, Hofriyati women are able to claim "foreign feminine perspectives" considered morally alien in reality. By so doing, Hofriyati women achieve their "true adulthood" and complete their individuality and selves, which are circumscribed by the "traumatic, disposition-cultivating experiences" of circumcision and marriage (1989, 309). Although Boddy's reading of trance suggests a hierarchy of "better-off external feminine realities" and "traumatized ones," her analysis brings into focus the centrality of women's voices to resisting "hegemonic truth." Hadendowa women's interpretation of *ijar*, however, orients them toward their own powerful cultural realities, which are constantly threatened by poverty, marginality, and dislocation. This interpretation adds to Boddy's contribution an equally significant aspect of power: its danger and women's awareness of its continuous threat to their identity and social well-being. This dimension is apparent in women's employment of the *halafa* healing logic during *ijar* ceremonial rituals and cures. *Halafa* (derivative of the Arabic word *khalafa*) describes an oppositional logic whereby danger caused by the spirits during the act of boundary crossing can be reversed by using objects, substances, and commodities from the spirit domain. The Hadendowa, for instance, fear the danger of jinn living in the sea; therefore, eating seafood is taboo. Juxtaposed to this, however, seashells and fish bones are used as protection from danger and are worn as amulets against the evil eye, evil jinn, and the disease *tisaramt*. This taboo is related to the danger of consuming foreign products believed to affect bodily well-being. The inner body is where health and energy are generated and stored in contrast to the outer body, which, although penetrable, serves as a shield to protect the inner organs. This conforms to the Hadendowa's notion of power within and without. What is inside is deemed more valuable and thus more vulnerable to external danger.

The *halafa* reasoning presented here resembles, to some extent, what Paul Stoller (1995, citing Taussig 1993) has noted about the associations among sympathetic magic, mimesis, and alterity in Hauka rituals. Through "imitative representation" (see also Kramer 1993, 249), the mimesis acquires the powerful properties of the prototype—the other—and thus the sorcerer achieves mastery over it. Although *halafa* logic does not entail actual copying or carving of European figurines, as in some West African examples, its oppositional power renders foreignness manageable through its mimesis, signs, and commodities, which are used to heal the very danger that foreignness causes to societal well-being. External power is made proximate and harnessed to instantiate the mastery of the power within. In the context of *ijar,* sick persons, especially infertile women, like the spirits that caused their illnesses, are rendered marginal by virtue of their contact with external danger. To normalize their bodily state, sick persons are brought into the healing scene as incarnated others in an attempt to exorcise the spirit and neutralize its danger by using its own products and signs such as perfumes, incenses, and cigarettes. These products are either inhaled or consumed through the bodily orifice through which the spirit is believed to have entered the person. In this sense women negotiate their gender predicament by lifting the blame from their physical bodies to the powerful level of the "body politic" by identifying the danger without, a danger that their men also mediate and are expected to protect against.

Sea Spirits

Sea spirits also emerge as important epistemological categories in women's narratives about danger and disease. Although different from *ijar* spirits in their manifestation, encounters with sea spirits can also cause paralysis and fertility mishaps and lead to other forms of illnesses. Women describe sea spirits as mostly females whose deception and immorality negate Hadendowa women's code of modesty and proper motherhood. Sea spirits, like other spirits, have the ability to transform into many characters and can traverse the sea and the land. The prominence of the Red Sea as a pervious orifice in the Beja landscape and its depiction as a spirit domicile parallel Egyptian Nubians' perception of the Nile as a water boundary infested with malevolent spirits (Grauer and Kennedy 1978). These monstrous beings of the Nile are associated with blackness, belligerence, and cannibalism (see al-Guindi 1978). Although the scholars who note these beliefs do not elaborate on how they are connected with the Nubians' conceptualization of fertility, gender, and regeneration, their examples of Nile monsters targeting palm trees, newlyweds, pretty women, and small children are suggestive. Their studies draw attention to the embeddedness of such beliefs in the region's historical encounters with slavery, conflict, and colonial domination—a theme that resonates with the Hadendowa imagination of the dangerous sea and its elusive jinn inhabitants.

The popular narratives of the two female jinn, Tahashaw and Tishawdibyan, who traverse the land and the sea, illuminate this representation. The two narratives can be viewed as vivid representations of how the Hadendowa social imagination reconstructs foreignness. Hadendowa women describe Tahashaw as a beautiful woman who manifests herself to them wearing a colorful body wrap, expensive jewelry, and strong perfumes. Women associate some spirit characters with cleanliness and sweet smells.

Thus bad smells are said to provoke jinn and therefore endanger bodily well-being. Strong perfumes, such as *khumra,* worn by married northern Sudanese women, are also said to cause children's illnesses. Women report these stories as shared knowledge, claiming their authenticity and authorship (cf. White 2000; see also Gal 1991; Hill and Irvine 1992). The story of Dawrit's frightening encounter with Tahashaw is an example of how women perceive and describe their experiences with some spirits.

> Once I was returning to my rural area after a visit to Sinkat town. I was accompanied by some of my friends and their husbands. On our way, not far from the town's outskirts, a beautiful woman who was wearing nice clothes and perfumes appeared to us. I said, *"Bismillah,"* [in the name of God] and shouted, "This is Tahashaw." When I repeated the name of God, she disappeared while mumbling some words in Arabic, *"Ashtatan, ashtatan"* [wither away, wither away]. Then we saw a tall woman standing on the top of the mountain; she became thinner and thinner; it was Tahashaw.
>
> We continued our journey, and when it was late, the men decided that we would spend the night in that area. . . . When I lay down, my body went numb and I saw myself in a beautiful house with nice beds, clean sheets, tables, chairs, and everything. I wanted to say the name of God but could not move. However, I was able to repeat the name of God in my heart. When I repeated the name of God in my heart, I saw myself sleeping in a *kharaba* [ruin; she used the Arabic term]. When I told my girlfriends, they got very scared.

Tahashaw can transform herself into many figures. She resembles a northern Sudanese woman with her provocative perfume and rattling jewelry. She can become a Halab woman who knocks on people's doors to beg them for food, sell them cooking utensils, or ask them for directions. Sometimes she appears to people wearing her body wrap, covering her face like a Beja woman, and then suddenly disappears or takes the form of a female dwarf. Tahashaw meets men and women alike, seduces them with her extravagant materiality, which turns at the end into ruins. She also meets men arriving in train stations and begs them to rest at her luxurious home, which turns into a dumpsite when they wake up. People bewitched by Tahashaw can go crazy or become paralyzed or infertile when they confront such shocking realities. Healing these conditions may involve treatments such as attempts to exorcise the evil eye and spirits or herbal medicine suggested by various medical practitioners. Only those who manage to protect themselves by calling the name of God can survive the spirit encounter safely. My assistant, a young Hadendowa woman, asked Dawrit, "Why do few of us encounter Tahashaw now?" Dawrit replied sarcastically, "Because people themselves become *hashaw* [connoting "jinn"]. Look how our region is pervaded by others."

Tahashaw' narratives may be viewed as a discourse on the powerlessness of the Hadendowa as they encounter foreign presences and a transforming world. Tahashaw could be a metaphor for the process of *balawait*-ization (urbanization in accordance with a northern Sudanese model) that the Hadendowa themselves are undergoing. It is also significant that women's discourses about jinn as "others" depict some of these jinn figures as females who are seductive, alluring, and threatening. Except for male red jinn, women represent the spirits who live in the sea or within and without their social domain as females. This suggests that Hadendowa women see foreign moral behavior as threatening to their femininity, propriety, and fertility, all of which are essential to achieving honor and social security.

The narratives of jinn also underscore a dangerous liaison between Hadendowa men and foreign women, as manifest in the narrative of Tishawdibyan, the female jinn who lives in the sea and, like Tahashaw, seduces men with her alluring beauty. Fatna, whom I interviewed in 1998, gave the following account of Tishawdibyan's story:

> Tishawdibyan is a beautiful female jinn who lives in the sea. Sometimes she comes out of the sea to play on the land. One day a Hadendowa man saw her and immediately fell in love with her. He decided to set a trap to catch her. When Tishawdibyan came near the snare, the man told her about his intention. Since jinn do the opposite of what you tell them, the female jinn did not believe him and began to jump over the snare while repeating the phrase: "If you catch me, do not let go of me." Tired of jumping, she fell into the trap, and the man caught her. The two later got married. Years passed, and the female jinn gave birth to two sons. However, she was bored with living on land and decided to return to the sea. She told her husband that she missed playing in the sea and asked his permission to visit her family and friends and then come back. As her husband did not believe that she would come back, he accepted on the condition that she be tied to a rope while in the sea. The female jinn was able to visit her family and came back to her husband and sons.
>
> Weeks passed and she insisted on going again, but this time she convinced her husband not to tie her because her sons were the bond that would inspire her to return and continue their upbringing. The husband believed her, and she went into the sea. The husband waited on the shore and watched her swim further and further until she almost disappeared. Because he did not know how to swim, the husband could not go with her. He shouted to her, "Are you coming back?" The woman laughed and said, "Didn't I tell you not to let go of what you have [*abkab tikati ba fadiga*]?" Tishawdibyan disappeared and never came back to her husband.

Tishawdibyan's narrative reflects the Hadendowa's abhorrence of the sea, the dangerous orifice in their landscape through which they have encountered different forms of foreignness. Accordingly, women perceive the long, invasion-ridden history of the ancient port of Sawakin as an intrusion by jinn. They consider Sawakin a hub of foreignness established by the descendants of an Ethiopian female slave and a male jinn. The offspring of this liaison mixed with the original Beja inhabitants and later formed Sawakin's modern population, which the Hadendowa refer to as Sawakinese.[9] Such jinn stories are very common among the Hadendowa. Some of my friends who are descendants of Hadendowa women and West Africans (Takarir) maintain that their foreign grandfathers had female jinn, who still live in the sea. Therefore, members of their families are advised not to swim in the sea for fear that these female jinn might kidnap them. A man from one of these families related that he was once sailing in the sea, in Port Sudan, with his friends when a female jinn grabbed his hand and attempted to drown him. Although he resisted her, she was able to snatch his engagement ring, and since then the man had not been able to consummate his wedding, as his fertility had been compromised.

Like other deceptive and immoral female jinn, Tishawdibyan negates the Hadendowa code of modesty and proper motherhood by deceiving her husband and abandoning her children. Just as Hadendowa women can threaten the patrimony through premarital sexuality and exogamous marriage, Hadendowa men can also endanger their progeny by marrying foreign women. Thus women use Tishawdibyan's phrase *abkab tikati ba fadiga* (don't let go of what you have) as a saying to remind both men and women to maintain kinship ties.

The metaphorical associations among land, women, and female jinn present Hadendowa women as the ideal yet threatened embodiment of honor. Because sexuality and fertility are closely tied to notions of female honor, their regenerative potential can readily be wasted by external influence. The danger facing this potentiality stems from the significance of milk and blood as natural symbols of kinship and regeneration that can be violated by boundary transgression, especially when these fluids are shed from bodily orifices (see Douglas 1966; Boddy 1989; Inhorn 1994). Thus sexual intercourse is dangerous, because the semen of the man (synonymous with milk) leaves his body to mix with a woman's blood.[10] And menstruation becomes dangerous because blood, the vital source of life, is shed outside a woman's body in a nonreproductive act (see Gottlieb 1988).

---

9. Many people I talked to maintained that the name Sawakin is derived from the Arabic word *sawajin* (singular *sijin*, prison) referring to the place where King Solomon imprisoned the jinn. Others maintain that it is an appropriation of the Arabic phrase *swaha aljinn* (the jinn made it).

10. Some Hadendowa women believe that mixing a woman's clean blood, after she stops menstruating, with a man's semen creates a child.

Pregnancy, childbirth, and breast-feeding are also vulnerable reproductive stages, central to notions of responsible motherhood. According to fifty-five-year-old Nafisa, whom I interviewed in 1998, it is through a woman's breast milk that "men drink the values of *durarit.*" In this way she emphasized the significance of breast-feeding to raising healthy children, especially sons, who would grow up to embody meanings of collective honor. Nafisa also stressed that a Hadendowa woman, like her ancestral foremother, Hadat, wife of Barakawin, should give her undivided attention to her children's well-being. A careless mother fails to attend to her children and leaves them at the mercy of evil spirits, which may affect their minds and render them disabled. Nafisa maintains that the Hadendowa refer to such children as *bahai natu* (motherless children) even if their mothers are alive. During my interview with Nafisa, a handicapped child came to play with her grandchildren. Nafisa attributed the child's partial paralysis to the negligence of his mother, who had left him alone with his little sister when he was one year old. Leaving little children unattended makes them vulnerable to attacks from evil jinn. Unlike the immoral, sexually licentious female jinn, Hadendowa women are bound by a propriety code that portrays them as responsible, honorable mothers. This representation of reproductive vulnerability is also invoked with reference to notions of mysterious diseases and their threat to women's and children's health.

Tisaramt: *Endangering Fertility and Children's Health*

In relation to fertility and societal well-being, women describe another form of danger caused by the mysterious disease *tisaramt* or *tifgid* brought into their domestic space by foreign animals and products. From within, *tisaramt* results from a Hadendowa ceremony known as *taikam silail* (camel prayer or blessing) during which men attempt to protect the fertility of breeding camels from internal and external danger. These breeding camels are different from *shade* camels, which the Hadendowa use for travel, commercial exchanges, and other common purposes. The majority of the women interviewed, however, agreed that both breeding and *shade* camels could cause *tisaramt* if these camels transgress lineage boundaries.

Hadendowa men attempt to protect the fertility of breeding camels by smearing them with a mixture of red stone *(adal awat)* powder and camel milk. The red stone powder is found in mountain caves, and the Hadendowa take certain precautions when obtaining it. Only old men and women free from the danger of sexuality (and menstruation in the case of women) can procure *adal awat*. Since jinn also live in the mountains, *adal awat* suggests an association with spirits and their danger to fertility. Mixing red powder with milk reflects women's perceptions that milk and blood are vital forces of reproduction and therefore can be jeopardized. Protecting

Camel stamped with red hand mark for protection

camel milk by using a red substance from the foreign domain of jinn is believed to counteract the evil it may cause to both human and camel reproduction.

According to *halafa,* the camel fertility of one sublineage (representing interior fertility) is at stake if it crosses the boundaries of another lineage. The positive value of breeding camels is thus reversed during transgression; therefore, these camels or any person or object that comes into contact with them can cause miscarriage, infertility, and child death.

From without, the Hadendowa believe that *tisaramt* can be caused by the Beni Amir's animals and other foreign livestock and products. Recently, and with Hadendowa migration to towns and their introduction to relief food distributed by local and international organizations, fear of *tisaramt* has been extended to include foodstuffs such as powdered milk, bottled oil, and canned foods. Many women associate their infertility, especially after their migration to urban centers, with eating relief food (see Rene 1996; White 2000). Eating such food and contacting foreign products during pregnancy is thought to lead to miscarriage, child death, or the birth of children with body ulcers and other deformities that may lead to their death. The women's understanding of the effect of foreign products on their health suggests the Foucauldian idea of the covert work of power and its ability to circulate through other means to mold and take control of the body.

The Hadendowa believe that pregnant women can also transmit *ti-saramt* to their fetuses by eating foreign cow and goat meat. The disease is also transmittable through breast milk. It is significant to note that women also associate meat with blood, which can nourish a pregnant woman and her fetus. The symbolism of milk and blood as vital life forces that are susceptible to external danger is at the heart of women's fear of *tisaramt*, as reflected in the following account.

Timani, another interviewee, told the story of a foreign nomadic group that settled in her family's rural area at the time of her grandfather's death. Her family bought a cow from the nomads to feed people who came to give their condolences. Her mother, who was then pregnant, ate some of the cow's meat. She miscarried her baby a few days later. The cow was suspected to belong to the *khasa* (Beni Amir) and to have infected the mother with *ti-saramt*. To cure the mother, the husband went to the place where they had slaughtered the cow and brought back some of the cow's stomach remains, which were cleaned, dried, cooked, and given to the mother to take with *samin* (butter). Timani maintained that her mother became pregnant again, and because her father had not forgotten his wife's *tisaramt* affliction, he went to town and bought a cow stomach, which the mother again ate as a precaution. This protection measure continued until she gave birth to a healthy son.

Tisaramt is contagious and can be passed to children by both parents. Relatives can also get the disease through contact with objects that were close to the body of an infected person. Thus it is advisable not to wear the clothes of infected persons or to use their other belongings. Women also told me that they refrain from braiding infected women's hair, for fear of contamination. When I went to interview thirty-three-year-old Tayyis, I was forewarned not to eat her food or use her cups. Tayyis was married when very young but had no children. Her mother and her mother's sisters were suspected of having *tisaramt* because many of their children had been sick or had died. Her mother's oldest sister, for instance, was diagnosed by religious practitioners as having *tisaramt* after her three miscarriages. Later she had two sons, one of whom was deaf. Tayyis said that when the older son married, his mother protected his wife by giving her *dairwawut* (seven herbs mixed with *adal awat* powder) to take with butter and milk at the onset of her pregnancy. She had to use this remedy until the fifth month of pregnancy and then continued after the seventh month until she gave birth. Tayyis went on to say that because the older son's wife was protected in this manner, her children survived, unlike the children of the wife of the younger deaf son; those children died after birth because their mother had ignored the advice of her mother-in-law to protect herself from *tisaramt*.

Women treat *tisaramt*, like the evil caused by spirits, by employing *halafa* (reverse logic). Hadendowa animal products, such as milk and butter, symbolize the power of kinship and regeneration in contrast to foreign foodstuffs. According to *halafa*, mixing the milk and butter of domestic animals with herbs or red stone powder procured from the spirit domains counteracts and neutralizes external danger.

Like the spirits that inhabit the sea, the water streams, and the mountains, various spirits inhabit trees. Firdaus, another interviewee, said that under each tree branch there are forty types of jinn. According to *halafa*, the Hadendowa use the powers of plants to cure *tisaramt* and other forms of evil (see Jacobsen 1998). Because of the ominous power of healing plants, people who procure them must be knowledgeable about the spirit world, for instance, religious or possessed people. Such knowledgeable persons can negotiate with jinn and convince them to cut their leaves. In this healing domain where power and knowledge imply each other, common people can fall sick or become mentally ill if they use or cut these herbs. Even for knowledgeable people, cutting healing plants requires certain precautions such as leaving seven grains of sorghum, water, or money beneath them or standing opposite their shadows in order not to annoy their spirit inhabitants. Some trees, however, are more harmful than others. Permanent trees, for instance, are less harmful than bushes and other seasonal plants. This resonates with the Hadendowa kinship logic that permanent residence among them is essential for closeness, while temporary residence and frequent movements denote distance and uprootedness.

Both red jinn and the disease of *tisaramt* can be inherited, through the female line in the case of red jinn, and through both male and female lines in the case of *tisaramt*. While red spirits are usually associated with fertility traumas, *tisaramt* is frequently associated with venereal diseases such as syphilis, which are blamed on the indulgence of Hadendowa men in urban lifestyles involving immoral behaviors. Men are more mobile than women and can bring *tisaramt* to their wives through the interaction of their semen with the women's blood, which nourishes the child in the womb and transforms into breast milk, which nourishes the child after birth.[11] Therefore, *tisaramt* can be transmitted from men to women through sexual intercourse and through contact of both men and women with foreign products and objects that ultimately stunt children's growth and endanger collective fertility. The doctor at Sinkat Hospital confirmed the connection that some

---

11. On the symbolism of milk and blood in Africa and the Middle East, see, for example, Altorki 1980; Jacobson-Widding 1991; and Delaney 1991.

women made between *tisaramt* and syphilis. But the staff at Sinkat Hospital bemoaned their financial inability to carry out health campaigns that would communicate information about sexually transmitted diseases (including AIDS) to encourage reporting of such symptoms.

Hadendowa women's perceptions of danger and disease reflect the world beyond their boundaries, a world that becomes visible through the infiltration of others into their homeland. Such perceptions plot a cultural geography of honor and social difference within which women see foreignness and boundary transgression as highly charged and dangerous for physical and social well-being. In this context the female body, as a fertile womb and as a site of political struggle (Greenhalgh 1994), can be seen as mirroring the Hadendowa concern with keeping their societal boundaries intact (see Douglas 1966). This theme of embodied spatiality describes a "contested moral geography" (Auslander 1993) within which both men and women occupy precarious positions.

Hadendowa women's gendered representations of the body invoke broader social, political, and spatial relations that are central to feminist theorization of gender identities, procreation, and women's social place. By using their own propriety codes, women view power not only in oppositional terms but also as a multifaceted structural force within which different social categories are implicated. This "feminine" perspective situates women's narratives and the symbolic logic of danger and disease within a connected local-global context that shapes and reinforces cultural meanings and practices. Within this larger context, the Hadendowa find themselves occupying a marginalized location and contending with "foreign forces" they perceive as posing serious threats to fertility and regeneration. Narratives of danger and disease, then, offer a glimpse into the multiple ways by which women give consent to and subtly resist power asymmetries (see Abu-Lughod 1986; di Leonardo 1991). Such relations of power and inequality are negotiated through the *halafa* ritual power and its mimetic ability to convert foreignness into a positive force to restore the power within. *Halafa* ritual media, as both signifying practices and techniques of power (Foucault 1980; Comaroff and Comaroff 1993), are settings for social transformation, empowerment, and the construction of collective identities.

Chapter 3

Performing *Durarit*

Constructing Gender
through the Life Course

Durarit ranshit aunaw kaya uqamia
Mamad alqauwab awdai amail babauk

[(The groom) working courageously to build his *durarit*
generous, he never blames his destitution.]

From a popular wedding song

Muhammad, a Hadendowa driver who was taking us, a group of NGO
workers, both Hadendowa and northern Sudanese, to attend a wedding in
the *khala,* was proud to point out the boundaries of his ancestral land.
Ali, a Halafawi (Nubian) from northern Sudan who is known for his relent-
less teasing of, and disagreements with, Muhammad said, "What ancestral
land? Do you call these dry hills your ancestral land? What does this empty
land do for you, hungry people? You should relocate." Muhammad's voice
sharpened as if he were ready to strike back. "Relocate! You don't tell a Ha-
dendowi to relocate; it is your people who are *murahalin* ["being moved
around," referring to the forced relocation of the Nubians from Wadi Halfa
after the construction of the Aswan Dam and the massive flooding of the
Nile in the 1960s]." Muhammad continued, "We might be monetarily poor,
but we are rich because we have roots in this land; we have people who, as
poor as they are, come together to sing and dance at weddings to break the
silence of these hills. You know why these people are rich? Because they can

offer their last meal to their guests, and they come to your aid when you are in need. When you smell the fresh air of these mountains, you know where you belong, and when you are dying here know that you will have a grave."

The land stretched ahead of us, marked with clusters of tents and scenes of women wrapped in their colorful *fautas* creating a distinctive contrast against the grayness of the landscape. As we have seen, the cultural richness that defines the contours of this land is experienced through the gendered "di-vision" of men's and women's social place within a constructed moral geography that enhances the meanings of *durarit* and the regeneration of the patrilineal lineage. The notion of *durarit*, as symbolic and economic capital (Bourdieu 1990), constructs meanings of identity between lineage and sublineage members based on a common territory and blood descent. *Durarit* is thus inherited and can be fostered through wealth in land and children, especially sons. It can, however, be tarnished through moral and social behavior deemed threatening to the social order. Although men and women alike can be born with *durarit*, the means of enhancing male and female honor are inherently gendered and marked through the territorial division of the social space.

Hadendowa gender logic organizes the social space of men and women within which they achieve their gender identities and experience their social roles. These "di-visions" are at the heart of Hadendowa matrimonial and patrimonial practices, which stress the significance of fertility, regeneration, and wellness. Within these spatial divisions, two complementary domains of social practices can be identified. The first can be described as a covert space for women associated with sexuality and vulnerable reproductive events that begins with marriage and the creation of a *bidaiqaw* (tent) and unfolds with pregnancy and birth. The second is an overt social domain for men, distant from the powers of sexuality and fertility, within which they enhance their *durarit* by protecting the land and descent. The Hadendowa's contrasting notions of femininity and masculinity extend beyond these spatially embodied gender asymmetries, however, to discern an integral domain of foreignness that informs the organization of gender and social life.

Gendered *Durarit*

Marriage and the creation of a tent begin the cycle of procreation. It is the cornerstone of both regeneration and cultivation of honor pertinent to the development of individual gender identities. Within marriage both girls and boys transcend the state of childhood and move into adulthood. Children are wed at a young age. Girls are usually wed shortly before or after their menarche and boys after puberty. This pattern is observed mostly among rural Hadendowa and those who have migrated recently to towns. Age at marriage is slightly higher among families who have lived longer in towns due to many factors associated with urban lifestyles. Khadija, a senior Hadendowa woman, related this phenomenon to the difficult economic situation in town, where families may find it hard to pay the bridewealth *(ausaf)*. She said, "We used to wed girls and boys at age ten and twelve; now we marry girls at age eighteen and boys at age twenty. This affects couples' ability to have many children in the future." She then asked me at what age people marry in Khartoum and America. When I told her that people generally marry at approximately twenty-five years of age or even at thirty, she put her hands over her head, expressing astonishment, and responded, "You definitely do not have time to have children there. This is not good; children are treasure, and they are the sweetness of life. How can you live without them?"

As the construction of the tent marks the consummation of marriage and the beginning of a new social life in the *diwab,* it is also tuned to the construction of male and female identities during the experiential life cycle, which is rooted in the rites of association with, and separation from, the tent.

When very young, male and female children belong in their mothers' spatial domain and are treated equally. Hairstyles symbolically mark their growth and achievement of gender identities. The use of hair in rites of transition suggests a correspondence between the head, the source of reason according to Hadendowa women, and consciousness about gender identities and roles. Mothers believe that children start to develop a partial ability to feel and discern between the ages of three and seven months. This transition is marked by shaving children's hair, which women refer to as "belly hair," and allowing it to grow naturally until children begin to walk and talk, when they are more able to reason. At this age, however, children are still defined as *dabalaub* (little ones), whose gender identities are not fully achieved. Not until age five is gender differentiation symbolically marked. At this stage children wear their hair in the *saulit wahalit* style, usually after circumcision, characterized by shaving all their hair and leaving a short front clump for boys and both front and back hair clusters for girls. This represents a stage by the end of which boys' hair is left to grow thicker and upward, while girls wear their hair downward, implying the differing meanings of openness and covertness associated with masculinity and femininity.

Male and female circumcision is another significant gender identity rite performed on children at age five or shortly before puberty. The operation is thought to enhance health, purity, and sexuality. The Hadendowa believe

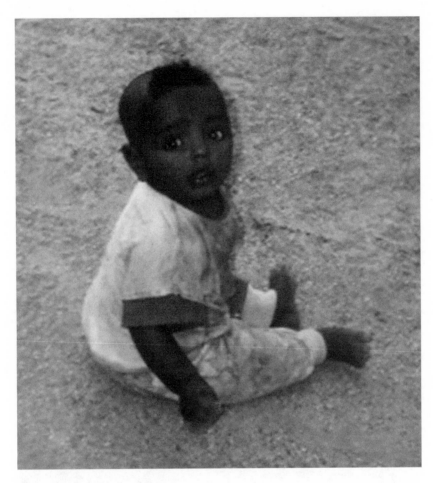

Saulit wahalit hairstyle for little boys

that circumcision, when practiced at an early age, enhances children's health and shields them from diseases caused by evil spirits. Such diseases are associated with feces and other harmful residue that affects bodily well-being. Opening the "closed" male organ in circumcision is said to eliminate the pollution and danger of the spirits. Female Pharaonic circumcision, on the other hand, reduces the vaginal opening, which Hadendowa women consider to be wide in uncircumcised girls, and serves the purpose of curtailing possible penetration by malevolent spirits that cause menstruation, hemorrhage, and infertility. It also guards a girl's virginity, the symbol of intact fertility, from being wasted by a premarital sexual experience. Both the pain and the festivities that accompany the operation inscribe on

Tatau hairstyle for pubescent girls

children's bodies and dispositions different meanings of propriety derived from bodily integrity, purity, and reproductivity (Bourdieu 1990; Boddy 1989; Gruenbaum 2001).

Children become fully aware of their differing gender identities and roles at puberty. Girls begin to achieve their feminine identity even before puberty by engaging with their mothers in household tasks such as taking care of younger siblings and bringing water. With menarche they are considered young adults, as manifested in their descending *tatau* hairstyle. They now cover their hair and bodies with *kiyaus* (half *fauta*). In Sinkat town the *tarha* (scarf) and lengthy dresses are accepted among some Hadendowa. Since female fertility becomes active with menarche, covering the body and the face is necessary for protecting the potent female body from the dangers and diseases of boundary transgression. Covering is also a sign of modesty in the presence of senior male relatives, which in turn suggests an association between covering and protecting the female body from the external danger mediated by men.

Women consider the postpubescent female body to be porous and bound by the reproductive rhythms of menstruation, pregnancy, giving birth, and breast-feeding, all of which render women vulnerable and susceptible to *aushar* (evil) and diseases that can jeopardize their fertility and their children's health. Women, by virtue of this reproductive capacity, occupy the center of the domestic space. The tent takes its social identity from that of the woman and is related to procreation and sexual intimacy. The association of these vital forces with sexuality and procreation produces ambivalent representations of women's bodies as sources of both negative and positive powers. Both sexuality and reproduction can be sources of honor if they generate patrilineality and of *aib* (dishonor) if women engage in premarital sexual activity or are given in marriage to strangers. Thus it is not surprising that most Hadendowa narratives about land ownership are gendered representations portraying struggles with external powers as conflict over women. Land is seen as a woman who can be violated and taken away from her lineage members. Like the ancestral land that can be violated by others, women's bodies are also permeable and can threaten the social order. Just as the construction of collective identity is situated within the complex linkages of land and honor, Hadendowa women embody the cultural meanings of affinity, motherhood, and regeneration.

Postpubescent girls achieve their *durarit* by observing *auslif* practices, especially those regarding when and whom to marry. A girl's modesty is evident in her actions, her dress, and her body movements. She sits with her legs closed, keeps her voice serene, and keeps her eyes downcast when walking in the street or talking to male relatives. *Durarit,* as Hadendowa women explain, is a broad category that includes both men's and women's willingness to protect the patrimony and blood descent. Thus, women who adhere to modesty are also considered women of *durarit*. ʿAlawia, age thirty-five, once discussed her daughter's marriage in my presence. Her daughter, who had finished intermediate school, was teasing her mother by telling her that she would rather marry an educated distant relative instead of her father's brother's son, who had religious schooling only. ʿAlawia was very irritated by her daughter's sarcasm and responded, "Well, if you refuse your father's brother's son, then you have no honor, *durarit kit bari.*"

A woman's feminine identity and *durarit* mature when she succeeds in marriage and childbearing and child rearing. Her childless marital status is distinguished by her *shadat* hairstyle. As soon as she gives birth to a live child, she alters her braids to a *saulit* style (see figure on p. 35).[1] Many Hadendowa women maintain that the *saulit* (the golden or silver ring) usually marks the birth of the first son. Mothers of girls, however, also wear the ring, hoping to have future sons and grandsons. This is plausible because gold and silver are considered precious ornaments that are also associated with men's space and with protection from spirits. Women also assert that the circular shape of the *saulit* is protective, which suggests closeness as manifest in these two examples of altering children's hair as *halafa*. If a child survives after his mother's successive reproductive mishaps, his hairstyle can be reversed for protection. In such situations, young female children (age five to six) can wear their front hair in a *saulit* style but shaved in the back. Boys wear their hair in a *kulup* style, which is characterized by shaving the middle part of the head in a circle while leaving the front and top circles of hair.

Although reproduction enhances women's and men's *durarit*, childlessness and "son-infertility" do not deny women their ability to become modest, loyal Hadendowa women. Since infertility is often blamed on external agents, such as the evil eye and evil spirits, women interpret the honor of having many sons with reference to *hamaustib* (respect) and *masaib* (blessing). This is also because *durarit* encompasses other domains of practice such as generosity and support for kin. Hibat, a childless Hadendowa woman, lucidly explained: "An old, childless woman with no husband or close relatives to support her has to be more careful about guarding her tongue, her hands, and her feet. These body parts become like her close relatives through whom she will be respected and recognized. I mean she has to guard her tongue from hurting others, she has to be generous and stretch her

---

1. In the *shadat* hairstyle, the hair is divided in the middle and braided downward. The *saulit* braids resemble the *shadat* style, but they differ in that a small cluster of hair is braided in the middle and crossed at the forehead. *Saulit* refers to a silver or golden ring that women fasten at the center of the crossed braids.

hands for the needy, and she has to fulfill her social obligations by visiting others. Then she does not need close relatives or a son to take care of her because other people will be there for her."

Within this gendered spatiality, men take the leading role of defending the patrimony. A well-rounded man achieves his social identity outside the female compound when he reaches puberty and disassociates himself from the tent. Men enhance their *durarit* in the wilderness and the domain of foreignness, from which they have to protect women and children. In rural areas pubescent boys construct their own *shafat* (small rectangular wooden houses) within the boundaries of the domestic space but further from the women's tents. At this stage the boy receives animal gifts from his parents and relatives to start his own herd and prove his independence. His father also gives him a small sword, the symbol of protecting the land, and his male relatives teach him the art of dueling. He wears a man's costume and his hair is fully grown. He is now ready to cultivate the qualities associated with male honor. In town male children also separate from their mother's tents or rooms at puberty and move to small *rakobas* (wooden verandah-like dwellings) or mudrooms, located on the side opposite the female quarter. Since herding is no longer the only viable economic strategy in town, boys at this age are either in school or involved with their fathers or male relatives in petty jobs in the town center.

Within marriage husbands also have to leave the women's compound early in the morning to herd their animals in the open terrain outside the domestic space (in rural areas) or to perform their jobs in the marketplace (in towns); they unite with their wives and children after sunset. For men to dwell with their wives and children during the daytime, when they can be seen and judged, is a shameful act that reduces their *durarit*. Men who stay with their wives during the day are exposed to mockery, and their ability to judge is often questioned even by their female relatives. Pierre Bourdieu (1965) observed among the Kabyle that the respectable man must allow himself to be seen, to show and place himself continuously under the gaze of others in order to be able to face them.

Similarly, a Hadendowa man conceals his private affairs among his peers. Conflicts and fights can arise if the name of a man's wife, his mother, or his sisters is mentioned in public. A man whose mother's name is mentioned in public is justified in fighting the offender in order to restore his *durarit*. Urban Hadendowa men whom I talked with about this taboo recounted various anecdotes as explanations. Omar, an educated Hadendowa man, explained how such taboos create problems for them when they work in towns. After six years of working in a factory in Port Sudan, Omar quit his job because he was asked, as part of a new procedure, to fill in a form that included information about workers' mothers. He maintains, "*Balawait* (northern

Sudanese) do not understand our customs and may ridicule us for them." He went on, "A relative of mine almost killed a *balawait* who jokingly asked him about his mother's name." A woman too should refer to her husband by his firstborn's name and not by his first name (e.g., Abu [father of] Fatna or Abu Omar). Issues of sexuality and marital affairs have to be concealed by both men and women because they signify power and vulnerability. This does not indicate a discontinuation of relationships between mothers and sons, however, for men continue to consult their mothers on serious matters.

This gendered *durarit* rests on the notion that men's bodies, unlike those of women, are less susceptible to external danger. It is by virtue of this relative integrity that men can endure the task of defending the patrimony. In this sense men enhance their *durarit* by being at the margin, in other words, at the source of external power (Douglas 1966). This runs counter to the case of many East African pastoral groups in which men gain their power and social status by being at the center of the domestic space, while women's subordinate status is mirrored in their peripheral location (see Jacobson-Widding 1991). Just as Hadendowa women are simultaneously powerful and vulnerable by virtue of their centrality in the process of regeneration, men are powerful and dangerous by virtue of their marginal engagement in both domestic and foreign social spheres. Their mobility and contact with foreignness is considered dangerous and can contaminate their wives' fertility and their children's health (see Helms 1988 on the association of distance with power and danger). Such gendered division, therefore, represents more than an enclosed symbolic system (Jacobson-Widding 1991) for it locates a host of internal and external fields of power and danger that are mapped onto the social landscape and the body's states of sickness and well-being to signify broader concepts of identity, kinship, and regeneration.

The End of Agency: Marriage, Honor, and Resistance

The theme of "vulnerable fertility" informs women's narratives and explanations of matrimonial practices. We have seen that marriage with outsiders is considered a threat to the purity of the patriline and the honor of dependent lineages. Lineages that claim purity of descent employ narrative discourses that endorse endogamous marriage as the viable strategy to maintain the patrimony. Although marriage among the Hadendowa is endogamous, following the father's brother's daughter's (FBD) marriage convention, matrilocality prevails as an organizing principle. In such a predominantly nomadic economy, land is less significant as private property, and thus it is used and claimed collectively by extended family members who trace their descent (through the male line) to a common forefather.

Mohamed Salih (1976) relates this emphasis on matrilocality to the Hadendowa's matrilineal past, downplaying the centrality of fertility and motherhood to their conceptualization of identity and regeneration. It is through the great number of women's tents, reflecting the number of married children, over a vast territory, that the group asserts its honorable status.

Marriage to one's FBD is preferred to other types of endogamous marriages and is closely tied to notions of regeneration. Although FBD marriage is preferred, in practice marriage to sublineage members is widely accepted. According to the eighty-five women interviewed in 1998, FBD marriage represented 32.9 percent (n = 28), while marriage to relatives from the same sublineage represented 42.4 percent (n = 36). In between came father's sister's daughter's marriage (11.8 percent, n = 10), mother's brother's daughter's marriage (7.1 percent, n = 6), and mother's sister's daughter's marriage (5.9 percent, n = 5). Marriages among the families interviewed were arranged by elder male and female relatives, whose decisions often undermine children's choices. This is not to rule out cases of resistance to parental decisions, but people's choices about love and marriage are also attuned to cultural constructions (Bourdieu 1990; Asad 1993).

Haisha, a married senior Hadendowa woman, explained that although men officiate marriage negotiations, mothers play a key role in these decisions as well, especially if they have strong objections about the groom or his families. Daughters also capitalize on their mothers' power to delay marriage or to impose their own preferences. Love affairs beyond familial arrangements, however, are perceived as violation of *auslif* practices and honor codes. Although songs for female lovers abound, the names of the beloved should always be concealed, especially if the beloved herself is a close cousin. Marrying a classificatory *duriaur* (paternal cousin) or *duriatuaur* (maternal cousin) concerns protecting familial and collective honor. Abdel, a young Hadendowa who works in town, suggested a close linguistic link between *durarit, duriaur,* and *duriatuaur* because they imply the duty of men and women to marry their close cousins in order to protect their own honor. This resonates with this story related by Bahawir, a woman from the Gamilab lineage.

> Our grandmother told us about an extremely beautiful woman who fell in love with a man from the Bishariyyn tribe. Their love story became well known, but her father's brother's sons were many and they were competing to marry her. She insisted on the man she loved, however, and refused to marry the men who proposed to her. Thus her family scorned her. Her father and uncles went mad because she had shamed the family. They tried to convince her, but she refused until her death at age forty. At her grave one of her father's brother's sons said, "We will be ashamed forever if we let our uncle's daughter die a spinster while we are alive," and he married her at the grave.

Such stories of defiance also thrive in practice when a woman takes oppositional actions against her family's decision regardless of the cost of resistance. During the first phase of my fieldwork in the late eighties, the displaced Hadendowa in Sinkat were facing many challenges concerning their economic and cultural survival. Prostitution was at its peak in town as a result of the devastating poverty and destitution. Some women were imprisoned for their alleged involvement in organizing prostitution. I interviewed some of these women in Sinkat's prison, and the story of Fatauma captures this theme of marriage and resistance.

Fatauma, like the woman in Bahawir's story, had fallen in love with a man from another group. She too was engaged to one of her paternal cousins. But her relationship with her lover was serious, and they decided to get married.

When the lover proposed, her family refused vigorously for they saw it as an insult to the *durarit* of her maternal and paternal cousins. When she refused to marry anyone but the man she loved, her family threatened to kill both of them. At this point Fatauma was fed up with her family's threats, and she fled to Port Sudan. She said, "The only woman I knew [there] was a relative who had fled our rural area long before me and worked as a prostitute in Port Sudan. I stayed with her because I could not marry the man I loved." After a while Fatauma herself engaged in prostitution. During this time she refused to marry until she met a man from her *diwab* in Port Sudan. The man convinced her family, and they married. During the period she was living in Port Sudan with her husband and child, no one from her family, especially her father, uncles, and brothers, came to ask about her. "Only my mother, who came infrequently to try and convince me to come back home," she said. When her marriage ended in divorce, she came to Sinkat and became involved in prostitution again.

The two stories of Bahawir and Fatauma present the limit of agency that women possess, especially when they attempt to undermine established power structures, which both men and women are socialized to sustain. Men and women, however, can choose nonconformity to subvert the cultural framing of their love and marriage choices but not without being scorned and marginalized as useless *(anfa'ab kikin)*, unmanly *(rabatak kikin)*, with no *durarit (durarit ka bari* or *kit bari)*, or mentally ill *(halaib, halit)*. As in the story of Bahawir, a woman who refuses to marry is denounced as a *bura* (spinster), her behavior is suspected, and her families' names will be tainted for posterity. According to Bahawir, it was the duty of the male cousin to erase the shame of his female cousin's resistance, even after her death, by claiming her as an endogamous married woman.

Marriage with agnates is often portrayed in terms of sisterhood-brotherhood or blood-milk relations. Most women interviewed, however, mentioned that they prefer to marry their relatives because marrying out means leaving one's source of kin support and thus being subject to mistreatment by people whose interest lies elsewhere (see Abu-Lughod 1986). A man of honor should take care of his wife and children and not subject them to abuse or mistreatment. Kishat (age sixty) commented on her neighbor's husband by saying, "He does not care about his family. He spends his money and time on other women [prostitutes]. He drinks. He is weak because he succumbs to his desires. Our men, before we came to town, were not used to drinking; it makes them unable to stand up to others." For Kishat the ideal Hadendowa man is generous, brave, independent, and trustworthy. *Kulausai* (suspicious) husbands are weak because their overwhelming mistrust can lead to the disruption of marital relations and to tribal conflicts, a calamity that kin attempt to avert.

Although divorced women are looked down upon and are often blamed for breaking up their marriages, men, who have the legal right to divorce, share greater responsibility of failing to sustain their marital relations. Divorce is widely discouraged, and elders often intervene to delay its occurrence. According to Tunur (age fifty), "If a man attempts to declare divorce by saying *titakat taukna fidqat* [your daughter is divorced] in the presence of his family or his wife's family, one of his relatives would quickly attempt to prevent him from finishing the sentence in order to allow the elders to intervene and resolve the problem."

Families also discourage their daughters who ask to be divorced from their husbands. Halima (age forty-five), who has been discontented with her husband for some time, said, "When I went to my family asking to be divorced, they welcomed me with less warmth. Although they were generous with me as usual and we chatted a lot and had good times, they always talked me into going back to my house. They told me that women are identified with their husbands and children. They made me do all the hard tasks that my little sisters used to do. I had to herd, bring water and firewood, and cook the porridge. Over time I understood my parents' wisdom and went back to my house."

Families provide support for their daughters, however, when they are divorced or mistreated. If the daughter lived with her husband far from her mother's compound for any practical reasons, upon divorce she dismantles her tent and erects it near that of her mother. If her children are young, they will remain in her mother's compound, although, following Islamic convention, a husband can claim that his children be raised in his mother's compound. But according to Miriam (age fifty), this is usually *bariauk shana,* "your work comes back to you"; especially if the husband is a cousin, children are considered to be the responsibility of both families.

Women also assert their *durarit* by seeking the support of their male kin during marital disputes. Indeed, a woman who has a strong family background, as reckoned in animal wealth and the social status of her male kin, is in a better position when seeking divorce or objecting to her husband's mistreatment than women who have no strong male kin support. Diab (age forty) related her first marriage experience when she was living in a rural area before her migration to town after the drought: "I was first married to my father's brother's son. We often disagreed with each other. He does not like to work; he is spoiled and dependent on his father. He spent all his time with his parents so he could not fulfill his duties toward me. When I complained to my father, who was the *shaikh* of the *diwab,* he convinced him to divorce me. He agreed to divorce me on condition that he could take back the animal [sheep, goats] gift his family had given me on my wedding [dowry]. We gave him what he wanted, and now I am married to my mother's brother's son."

Fatima (age forty-five), on the other hand, had a different experience. She was married to a man from another *diwab* who formerly had trade relations with her father. Although Fatima had asked for a divorce, her husband refused, deserted her, and married another woman. She said, "He is a difficult person, a *kulausai* person who never stopped nagging me about my behavior. He always imagined that I had relations with other men or that other men were interested in me. We fought frequently, and we ended up with big problems. When I claimed divorce, he refused and deserted me and swore that he would leave me *halaqat* [deserted] until his death."

Fatima complained to her uncles, but they refused to intervene since they had previously objected to her marriage to a non-*diwab* member. Her brothers also failed to convince her husband to divorce her. She remained *halaqat,* and her husband was married to two women from his *diwab.* Obviously Fatima's situation was worsened by the various circumstances that surrounded her marriage: her marriage to an outsider, her father's death, the familial conflict that her marriage had created, and most importantly the fact that men have the absolute power to divorce or desert their wives. These factors combined left Fatima little maneuvering power to change her situation, which she perceived as punishment and abuse from her husband and failure on the part of her male kin to stand up for her. She maintained that she would remain *halaqat* until her husband changed his mind or her family succeeded in convincing him to divorce her.

Fatima's case also confirms women's preference for marriage to close agnates who, except in the worst scenarios, are expected to exert their *durarit* by treating them as sisters and close relatives. Performing *durarit* is mutual, however. Balait (age fifty) often complained about her brother's daughter, Asha, that she had little *durarit* because of her inability to fulfill her duties toward her husband: "If he weren't her uncle's son, he would have divorced her. Yesterday he complained to me [his aunt] that if Asha remains defiant he will take another wife."

Asha's story is instructive for it sheds light on the dynamics of kinship relations as performed within marriage and the circumscription of power and negotiation that both men and women encounter in dealing with pre-scribed cultural codes. Asha was known among her relatives as daring, out-spoken, and humorous. She was also a talented singer, poet, and narrator. Although she was in her early thirties, she found no "shame" in talking about matters related to love and sexuality in our presence, which often made her female relatives giggle and cover their faces in modesty. Some of her female relatives were quick to warn us not to take her talk seriously be-cause she was "mentally disturbed." Others apologized to us for her bold-ness and inappropriate behavior. This degree of discomfort was exacer-bated by our presence since we were regarded as socially distant. When alone in our company, Asha laughed at what her relatives had told us, and she would often insist, "I am not crazy, I just do not say what they always want me to say."

Asha, who lived near her two sisters and her paternal aunt Balait, lost her three young children to famine in the 1980s, after which she decided to move with her family to Sinkat. Her husband worked irregularly as an auc-tioneer dealing in animals and other foodstuff. Since her children's death, Asha decided not to have more children, and she abstained from sexual re-lations. Most women believe that birth control methods are *haram* (reli-giously unsanctioned) and dangerous to health; they often use abstinence to delay pregnancies, resist their husbands, or stop childbearing. It was this decision by Asha to abstain that angered her aunt Balait, who referred to it as defiance that might lead her husband to divorce or polygyny. But Asha saw no point in giving birth to children who would eventually die. "Why should I give birth to children who would die in front of my eyes when I am not able to save their lives? I refused to have sex; why should I? For pleasure! Or to give birth to dead children!" she furiously remarked.

Apparently all of Asha's close female relatives knew about her marital problems. Some pitied her for the loss of her children; others scolded her for her misbehavior toward her husband, who was seen as an ideal man be-cause of his generosity, supportiveness, and moral demeanor. Asha herself would often mention that if she were married to a distant relative he would have given up on her.

One day we found Balait extremely furious because Asha had fought with her husband the night before, and she was confined to her tent, refus-ing to talk to anyone. Balait requested that we talk to her because we were "educated and Asha loved and trusted us." When we met her, she explained that the disagreement occurred because her husband threatened to remarry if she did not change her attitude toward him. She recounted, "I fought with him because he is irrational, he only thinks of himself and his desires, and not the children who would come out of that. I feel ashamed when I see women and children in town: they look healthy, beautiful, and well dressed."

After a few days, Asha and her sister went to their rural area to inform her father and her paternal uncle (father-in-law) about the dispute and her husband's intention to remarry. Asha said that she made a deal with her father and uncle that if her husband were to remarry, her husband would have to return all the animals that she had given him during the famine. When her husband's animals died during the drought, she had given him her animals (goats and sheep), which were her marriage gift, to sell and thereby start a career in Sinkat. In such a state of destitution, Asha knew that neither her husband nor his father would be able to compensate her for the value of her animals. Later her husband apologized to her and gave up the idea of remarriage. Asha was content vowing to reconsider her attitude toward her husband.

Once, when I was preparing to leave for Khartoum, Asha asked me to bring her a big purse as a gift. My assistant jokingly responded, "But you don't have a lot of money to put in such a big purse." Asha wickedly retorted that if need be she might even move to the *hila* (prostitution area) if it was the only way that women could earn money to fill their purses to buy food and clothes. Her two sisters tensed, as expected, and tried to change the subject. When we were leaving, her oldest sister followed us to apologize for her sister's inappropriate talk, requesting that we not repeat what we had heard in front of other women, especially their aunt Balait. Asha's sister said, "Asha is *halait* [crazy]. My father and uncles know that, so they beg her husband to take care of her because she is his sister. We tried to convince her to go to a *feki* [religious man], but she refused. When I went to the *feki*, he ordered me to put an amulet inside her pillow."

Asha was undoubtedly distressed because of her painful experience, which manifested itself in the ways she questioned her suffering and the meaning of marriage, reproduction, and desire in the context of poverty and destitution. Yet, by turning some of her cultural codes on their heads, Asha was also able to resist, negotiate, and secure her marital status despite her relatives' accusations of mental unfitness. Women perceive mental illness to be caused by spirits that invade the body and affect a person's head, which the Hadendowa associate with wisdom and reason. Protecting the body and the head, especially for women during vulnerable rites of transition and during boundary crossing, helps prevent a spirit from affecting general health and mental abilities. *Halaib* (mentally ill people) are treated by religious practitioners through Qur'anic readings over the head, amulets, and confinement in the residence of the *faqir,* especially if the person is aggressive. However, accusations of mental sickness, as we have seen earlier, are also employed as strategies to undermine a person's honor and social position and to marginalize those who do not conform to cultural codes. It is an exclusionary technique of power to bring in line those who are seen as disruptive to social order (Foucault 1977). Labeling Asha as mentally ill, while she denied that charge, was a disciplinary strategy meant to both silence her resistance and make her actions socially acceptable. Marriage in particular is an arena where such discourses and evaluation of moral behavior receive a greater share in daily conversations and dialogues.

When I went back to visit Asha in 1998, her aunt and oldest sister were still in Sinkat. Her oldest sister told me that Asha, her husband, and their little son had decided to go back to their rural area two years earlier to be near their aging parents and to look after the few animals they own. Although the memories of the last famine still lingered in people's conversation, there had been some good rainy seasons that could sustain the herds and those who had decided to return to the hills.

Embodied Spatiality: The Social Life of the Tent

Besides "breaking the silence of the hills," as our driver Muhammad commented, marriage rituals are places of performing acts of kinship and promoting togetherness through the creation of a new *auqaw* (home) in the *diwab*. They are also sites of demonstrating the identity and *durarit* of *diwab* members through offerings, solidarity, and support. Furthermore, through these celebratory rituals, relatives experience their habitus (Bourdieu 1990), the work of *auslif* and its transformation through time and body space. It is these joyous gatherings of numerous *diwab* members during the vulnerable moments of the life cycle that invite envy and assault by dangerous spirits.

Marriage arrangements, as is the case in many African societies, are comprised of many individual events. For the Hadendowa the two stages of the *iharaw* (proposal) and the *auqaw* (building the home or marriage consummation) are salient. The first category delineates the initial stage of marriage preparation and entails the transfer of small gifts from the groom's family to that of the bride. Customarily, it is the groom's father who shoulders the expense of his son's marriage, especially the nominal contribution for the *ausaf* and the building of the bridal tent. During the proposal period, which can last from a few months to two years, the bride's mother and her female relatives weave the *badab* (seven mats) and the *shamalat* (wool rug), both essential for building the tent.

These marriage practices, however, may vary according to social location and the circumstances of each family. In a wedding that I attended in Sinkat, the bride (Hawwa) was the groom's (Hassan) mother's sister's daughter. Hawwa's mother had died when she was very young and thus she was raised by her maternal grandmother, who lived in Port Sudan. Zainab (age forty-five), Hassan's mother, said, "Because Hawwa is my sister's daughter, I chose her for my son so we can become one family. She is like my daughter." Zainab was divorced, and she worked as a *farasha* (maid) in an NGO office in town. Her son, twenty-five-year-old Hassan, who worked in a shop in the market, also supported her. To prepare the dowry, Zainab noted that her son, her ex-husband, and she all shared the wedding costs and responsibilities. She explained, "We bought seven mats for the tent and three *fautas*: one for the bride, another for her mother [her grandmother], and the third white *fauta* for the newlyweds to cover with during the wedding night. We also bought sugar, coffee, and two cans of *'ajwa* [soft dates], one for the bride's home and another for wedding guests. For the bride's ornamentation, we bought *wadaj* [animal fat], *mahalab,* and *joza* [aromatic herbs] for braiding her hair. We also bought henna, perfumes, three pairs of sandals, and two pieces of fabric to be made into dresses for the bride."

The bride's dowry is determined by her father in agreement with the groom's father. In the case of Hawwa, her father demanded twenty-four goats: four goats for her classificatory mother and the rest to be owned by Hawwa. After the consummation of the marriage, Hassan went to their village to collect the *halaqin* (animal gift) from his relatives. The groom's closest relatives demonstrated their solidarity and support by each contributing a goat or a sheep for the animal gift, which would be reciprocated on similar occasions. The *halaqin* can also be collected in money if animals are unavailable.

Marriage symbolism and ritual practices, especially those of constructing the tent, mirror the division of the gendered social space and labor and the unification of such divisions in the regeneration of the life course. The tent clusters of mothers and their married daughters are spatially separated to mark family boundaries. The open space outside the female domain is characterized as wilderness and is usually inhabited by both benevolent and malevolent spirits. These untamed spirits also reside in trees and mountains on the fringe of the compound. Because of their dissociation from the ambivalent power of reproduction, men are associated with the external domain and are expected to conquer its dangers. The tent therefore represents the domestic space that encompasses female modesty, fertility, and labor while "trees" symbolize external space, danger, and male virility and labor.

The symbolic ritual of combining wood and straw mats in building the bridal tent demonstrates how women use the *halafa* logic to domesticate external elements in order to eliminate their dangers and cultivate their powers to enhance the fertility of the group. Straw mats are made of fronds from the dom tree *(Hyphaene crinita)*, which are procured by men from the

Tents of mother and two daughters

market or cut from the trees outside the domestic space. The wet green leaves, symbol of an external fertility, are dried by women in the domestic space and woven into seven mats, representing the fertility of the Hadendowa ancestral mother and her seven sons. On the wedding day the bride's female relatives gather to build the tent and to enjoy the food brought by the groom's family, which represents the family's generosity, a fundamental quality of *durarit*. The female relatives first erect the wood pillars, the foundation of the tent, and then construct the bed, which is made of wood and covered with straw mats, at the far end of the tent that faces the door. The couple and their young children share the bed, the essential piece of furniture. The husband, however, uses the *imiquad* (right side) of the bed to protect the entrance, while the wife and children occupy the *itriquad* (left side).

After setting the foundation of the tent, the women tie the seven mats together with *whalal* (wooden sticks) and fasten them to the tent structure with goat- or sheep-wool strings. Goats and sheep are domestic animals, and their milk and meat are considered essential to the health of group members, especially children and pregnant women. The wool blanket that the mother gives her daughter as a wedding gift is necessary for protecting the tent during winter. It provides warmth and therefore protects family members, especially women, from *imbarar* (cold diseases) that cause stomach sickness and infertility. In contrast, the Hadendowa consider the products of foreign animals to be dangerous to women's fertility and to group

Women building tent

regeneration. Like the tent, the locus of procreation, the *kalawab* (stomach, literally the "inside"), which includes the *auyam* (womb), is the focal organ that promotes the growth and natural well-being of the human body.

The fact that most marriage rituals, such as building the tent, are undertaken by women emphasizes their central role in physical and social procreation. Women who have many successful children, and particularly if they have more sons than daughters, are the icons of blessed fertility and, therefore, lead its rituals. Such women are considered *masait* (blessed), both for safely navigating their fertility trajectories and for being relatively free from sexuality (by virtue of their old age) and of the polluting dangers of the spirits. Conversely, it is believed that evil spirits haunt childless women and those who suffer fertility traumas. Therefore, the ritual leadership of infertile women, but not their participation, can contaminate the fertility of female initiates.

The bride's relatives erect the tent, which stands as a symbol of fertility and regeneration, near that of the mother. In the case of Hawwa, the bridal *bukar* (wooden room) was constructed near that of Zainab, who was also classified as her mother. The tent opens toward the outside, specifically toward Mecca, the source of utmost blessing, for seven days. The location and direction of the bridal tent can be changed for tactical purposes such as the avoidance of wind or rain or the unavailability of space near the mother's house, as is often the case in town. The tent entrance, however, should always face the direction opposite the bride's mother's tent, as a sign of respect. This custom signifies the concealment of sexuality or desires, especially for men. The tent is completed on the wedding day, when the *sunkab,* a green bundle of dry dom-tree fronds, is transferred to the bride's house. The *sunkab* day also marks the wedding night.

On the *sunkab* day, the groom's female relatives gather at his mother's tent for the *sunkab* ritual and parade. The *sunkab* fronds, like those used for weaving the tent's mats, are handled by son-fertile women. Moreover, the person who cuts the *sunkab* fronds should not be an orphan. Seven women whose firstborns are sons take turns tying and decorating the *sunkab,* while other women sing and ululate during the process, wishing the newlyweds abundant fertility and production. The groom's mother provides *'ajwa,* milk, and *adal awat* for the ceremony. As mentioned earlier, the red powder of *adal awat,* which the Hadendowa procure from the mountains on the fringe of the domestic space, is associated with spirits and is used as a substance of contrast to protect and enhance fertility and kinship ties. Milk, like blood, is also an essential element of fertility and growth. The mixing of the man's semen, synonymous with milk, and the woman's clean blood, after she stops menstruating, denotes the onset of pregnancy. This transformation is also the source of women's breast milk.

Just as milk and blood are essential elements of fertility, soft dates are prized for their nutritional value and blessing power due to their association with prophetic medicine. Mothers and herbalists often prescribe meat (the source of blood), milk, and dates as important dietary components for pregnant women and those who have experienced fertility traumas (see chapter 5). By eating dates and sipping milk during the *sunkab* ritual, women hope to add to the power of the bundle and to enhance its fertility. The positive power of blessed people (*masait* or *masaib;* the term baraka is also used frequently) can be transmitted through direct contact with certain objects or through utterance, such as good wishes for the newlyweds during rituals that communicate good intentions, for example, *daubani masahib* (may your wedding be blessed). Blessing can also be transmitted through the ingestion of blessed substances to promote fertility, health, and success. The same is true for transmitting dangerous power, which is associated with failure and social disruption.[2]

2. See Mary Douglas's (1966) discussion of "failure-biased" power, such as the evil eye, witchcraft, and sorcery, and "success-biased" power, such as baraka.

The *masait* (blessed women), who initiate the *sunkab*, smear the red mixture of *adal awat* and water on the dry leaves. The act of smearing the red substance is said to divert the attention of the spirits and to protect the fertility of the newlyweds. A similar mixture of *adal awat* and blood or either of them is sometimes smeared on hands and stamped on doors and camels for protection (see figure on p. 76). The gathered women then fasten a wooden staff to the *sunkab* bundle with wool strings. Usually women craft two *sunkab*s, one to be fastened at the entrance of the bridal tent and the other to be hung at the groom's mother's tent. The *sunkab* materials are similar to those used in constructing the tent; however, while the tent's shape is enclosed, the *sunkab* is vertical. It resembles a tree, the icon of the outer space, from which men enhance their *durarit* and ability to protect the fertility of the inner domain. Women maintain that the *sunkab* bundle conveys their wishes that the groom's sons be as numerous as its branches. It is worth noting that the Hadendowa refer to their different lineages as *adat* (tree branches). The *sunkab*, therefore, represents fertility linking men to male ancestors. From the day of her marriage, the bride and her fertility are tied to her husband's fertility. This fertility transference is manifested in the ritual of tying the *sunkab* to the bridal tent.

After designing the bundles, the groom's female relatives parade to religious places to bless the *sunkab*. Three senior son-fertile women lead the parade. In Sinkat town, the tomb of Alsharifa Maryam, the granddaughter of the founder of the Khatmiyya religious sect, is the prime site for such blessing rituals. Alsharifa Maryam was married to her *ibn 'am* (father's brother's son), with whom she lived in Sawakin. During her residence in Sawakin, she also commuted to Gabit and Sinkat, especially during summer. She was buried in Sinkat according to the terms of her will. Her tomb is located in the southeastern part of the town, which is also the Khatmiyya residential quarter. As we have seen, although the Hadendowa perceive the Khatmiyya as socially distant because of their non-Beja origin, they also regard them as a source of baraka and Qur'anic knowledge.

The grave of Alsharifa Maryam is a shrine to which many Beja and other groups, especially northern Sudanese, journey to pay homage and to seek blessings. Hadendowa women describe her as a religious woman who was generous to the poor. Haj Hassan Alsafi, a northern Sudanese interviewed in Gabit in 1998, confirmed this view when he maintained:

> Alsharifa Maryam was a religious and virtuous woman. Despite the wealth and fame of her family, she was very humble. She always associated with the poor, and her house in Sinkat was a refuge for orphans and poor people of all ethnic groups. She used to dress in a white *taub* [body wrap] that only showed her face and hands, and she responded to the demands of her male visitors from behind a curtain—*min wara hijab* [according to shari'ah]. She

Seeking blessing inside saint's tomb

built many mosques and established many *khalawi* [religious schools] for men and women in the area. She is famous for her miracles: those who were chronically sick and failed to respond to modern medicine regained their health when they received her baraka. She held the Haulia for her father in the town of Gabit, where people came from different parts of the region to pay homage. She died in the year 1371 of the Hijra.

Although she was childless, Alsharifa was known for her miraculous power to cure the sick and the infertile. In the book of *almanaqib* (life histories), handwritten by Alkhalifa Ibrahim Alsafi (1966), the story of a merchant from Khartoum recounts his agony with son-infertility. The man was married to five women, but he had only one daughter. He traveled to see Alsharifa Maryam, who told him to be patient and to marry again; he would then beget two sons. The prophecy of the saint came true, and the man had two sons whom he named after the saint's two brothers, Taj Alsir and Hashim.

Alsharifa Maryam's virtue and religiosity and her descent from the Prophet are all cited as reasons for her miraculous power. Most Hadendowa women, especially those suffering from infertility, visit the tomb to ask for blessings and good health for themselves and their children. Indeed, stories about Alsharifa Maryam both resemble and contrast with those told about the Hadendowa ancestral mother, Hadat. Although both women derive their blessing from virtue and religiosity, Hadat's power is rooted in her abundant son-fertility and her hybrid Beja/Arab identity. When asked, women often make these comparisons but also assert that Hadat is kin, an ancestral mother, and that their respect for Alsharifa is different. Alsharifa's oppositional fertility—her transcendence over the dangerous effect of pregnancy and childbirth—and her religiosity and foreign descent remain fertile grounds for interpretation.

The *sunkab* then draws more power from the saint's blessing. The parade from the groom's family passes through the Hadendowa residential quarter on the town's periphery to its center, where the saint's tomb is located. The town center, as previously mentioned, is foreign terrain where non-Beja reside and where most Hadendowa men pursue their economic activities during the day. Thus boundary crossing during the ritual requires covering the face and the body as a sign of modesty and as protection from boundary-transgression diseases, especially fertility traumas.

When the parade reaches the shrine, the three female leaders enter the tomb and pray that the saint bestow her blessing on the newlyweds and grant them good health and many good children, especially sons. The three women bless the *sunkab* and the three *fautas* by letting them touch the grave. Each senior woman places a *fauta* over her head during the parade, which again asserts the association of the head with wisdom and blessing. This is true for many cultures in the Sudan and the Muslim world, where kissing an elder's head is a sign of respect. Reading Qur'anic verses over the head also symbolizes transmitting baraka from the healer to the patient. After blessing the *sunkab* and gifts, the parade participants return to the compound and proceed to the bride's confinement tent; they march around the tent seven times to bestow baraka and ancestral blessings. An old woman stands at the door of the confinement tent like a gatekeeper, preventing the crowd from entering. The parade ends at the bride's new tent, where one of the parade leaders fastens the *sunkab* to the tent's entrance.

In town, parading to the bride's family may involve walking a long distance or even renting trucks to transport the groom's family and guests. Instead of marching in front of the parade, the *sunkab* leaders now occupy the front seats of the car or the truck. Today the *sunkab* party is also a marketplace where women and children sell various commodities such as beauty supplies, candy, biscuits, and purses that are often bought in Port Sudan or Sinkat by husbands or sons.

On the *sunkab* day, the bride moves to a confinement tent to be prepared for her wedding. By leaving her mother's tent, the bride enters a liminal

Senior woman (far right doorway) guarding bridal tent

stage at the end of which she becomes a *takat* (married woman). Her confinement is necessary to protect her fertility from the evil eye and evil jinn,
whose danger also resides in the transitional stages of the life cycle. The
bride's married female relatives mark her new status by sartorial symbols
and bodily ornaments, such as braiding her hair and adorning her hands
and feet with henna, seashells, and silver and gold jewelry as protection
from danger. They change her *tatau* hairstyle, representing her *taur* (girlhood status), to the *shadat* style, denoting her marriage. Unlike northern
Sudanese culture, in which women prefer black henna decorations, Hadendowa women favor red and dark green henna, which suggest a close correlation with fertility. The predominance of the color red during marriage
rituals is salient in wedding symbolism and costumes. To mark her transition to womanhood, the bride also changes her old clothes to new, perfumed ones. To further protect her fertility, the bride and one of her friends
stay behind a curtain to avoid contact with exterior dangers. Wooden beds
are covered by curtains that women sometimes decorate with red fabric and
embroider with seashells and beads at the upper ends. A senior Hadendowa
woman maintains that seashells and beads have healing power because they

are procured from the sea (in the case of shells) or bought from the Takarir (West Africans), who sell them in the market and in the streets of Sinkat.

Like the bride, the groom also undergoes similar transitional rituals on *sunkab* day that mark his changing status from *aur* (boyhood) to *rabatak* (manhood). His ritual is performed outside the female domain by old men who are also married and have sons. In a fashion similar to the bride's ritual, the old men replace the groom's old clothes with new, perfumed ones.[3] As a symbol of the groom's status as a guardian of the wife and her fertility, the men cover his head with a *mindil* (long red scarf), which hangs vertically down his back to his hips (see the color photos in this chapter). Women give different explanations for the symbolic meaning of the *mindil* such as, "It is an *auslif* that protects the groom and his wife from spirits," "It is an *auslif* that protects the groom from the evil eye," "It is just an *auslif*," or "It is a *halafa*." The *mindil*, however, evokes the logic of *halafa*, whereby spirit-related objects and substances are used to prevent spirit-caused danger and sicknesses. The red color of the *mindil* recalls the spirits' ability to endanger kinship blood, which the groom can sustain only through his wife's fertility. Among some urban Hadendowa, especially those who maintain close ties with the Khatmiyya, the groom wears a yellow *mindil*, similar to the *shall* or *kufia* worn by men in many Arab countries, especially Yemen. The groom wears the *shall*, like the *mindil*, during this transitional stage only, which indicates its use as a sign of contrast and protection.

Like the bride, the groom wears a *miskit* (golden necklace) and *kulail* (silver bracelet). Gold and silver possess healing power because of their association with the spirit and its domains; they are also manufactured by men or bought from the Rahaida (the Hadendowa's neighbors and competitors over land). This jewelry is also owned by the mother or borrowed from the groom's maternal female relatives, which suggests its association with threatened female fertility and mishaps that are often inherited through the maternal line.

Due to the influence of urbanization and Islamization in towns, some features of these wedding rituals are continuously debated, creating increasing intergenerational tension. After the rise to power of the National Islamic Front (NIF) in 1989, an official discourse about Islam has been propagated via the media and through the preaching of many supporters of the regime, some of whom are Hadendowa elite. Many men and women have also been familiarized with such discourse through voluntary lessons given by local preachers at mosques and *khalawi*. The content of this discourse focuses on the Qur'an and hadith as the main sources of moral guidance

---

3. The standard costume of Hadendowa men is white *sirbadaub* (baggy pants), worn with a white *qamis* (shirt), black *sidari* (jacket), and *shaiqait* (fine white fabric that is wrapped around the waist and tossed over the shoulders).

and proper behavior and on the role of the family as a prime institution in the promotion of Islamic teachings. Women in particular are central to this discourse since their modesty and moral behavior reflect the ways in which they raise new generations of Muslim children. In a *khalwa* lesson I attended, a renowned local preacher reproached women about Islamic rituals of purification after menstruation and childbirth, claiming that certain Hadendowa traditions, such as hair braiding, hinder proper cleanliness. He also attacked female circumcision as harmful and unsanctioned by the Qur'an. Some women who attended the lesson saw it as improper that a man would preach to women about such intimate issues. One commented sarcastically that if one finds water at all, it would be a tough decision whether to use it for washing or for drinking. Some women contest these lessons when they question their *auslif* practices. According to one woman, "The Hadendowa are good Muslims, and their *auslif* practices are not against Islam."

During Hassan's wedding, for example, his mother insisted that he wear the silver and gold jewelry for protection, but Hassan objected that wearing jewelry for men is unsanctioned by Islam. Zainab was very upset over her son's remarks and threatened to discontinue her involvement in the wedding process, arguing that Hassan had no right to object to *auslif* practices. By so doing Hassan was only jeopardizing his well-being during such a vulnerable moment in his life cycle. Fearing to anger his mother further, an act that is also forbidden by both Islam and *auslif,* Hassan agreed to wear the jewelry on the condition that he would take it off in two days instead of seven.

Islamic preachers also advocate the segregation of men and women in many facets of social life, especially during festival and wedding celebrations. In rural areas, for instance, the social space for celebrating the wedding is relatively shared. The groom's veiled female relatives gather outside the domestic space to drum and sing for the groom, his *waridis* (best men), and his male relatives, who show their joy, courage, and talents while dancing. During the weddings I attended in the *khala,* women also formed their own dancing groups under trees away from men's gazes. In town, however, the dancing space becomes exclusively women's space, while men form their own groups under trees outside the domestic area. A senior Hadendowa woman attributed this to both the influence of "government Islam," as she refers to it, and to the fact that people in the shanty settlements are from different *diwab*s and lineages, meaning that they are distant relatives, which makes it less acceptable for men and women to mingle.

Both in the *khala* and in town, however, Hadendowa wedding songs and dances, far from celebrating only the joy over a new union, are dramatizations of the honorable qualities of the men of the different lineages and the sentiment of belonging to the extensive, bounteous land. During wedding ceremonies, the rhythms of the songs and dances shift to describe the beauty and good morality of women, the generosity of the groom and his honorable descent, the strength and beauty of camels, and the "good" rain in the hills. Today wedding songs also direct attention to the Toyota passenger vans and *birnsa* (trucks) that move fast with the wind *(tibirnsa bram tafna)*, the Khawaja *landarober* (Land Rover) that crosses the land, and the trains that move swiftly between Port Sudan and Khartoum. When the rhythms of these songs reach a climax, some people go into a trance. The songs that entrance them can be those whose lyrics pray for bounty and rain in the hills or those that describe *birnsas* and *landarobers*. But as Bahawir, a senior Hadendowa woman from the Garaib group, explains, it is not just the rhythms and songs that entrance people, but the vulnerability and openness of the wedding moment itself, which can make people susceptible to spirits' attacks. During the wedding, the groom, his bride, and their guests are all under the gaze of spirits that are ready to inflict harm on their productive and reproductive capacities. When commenting on *birnsas*, trains, and Land Rovers, Bahawir added that some women become possessed or seek cure for their possession by listening to the click-clack of the passing trains.

The groom's initiation as guardian of the tent and its fertility and honor ends as he is given the *imbad* (sword) and the *kurbadj* (whip), both symbols and means of defending patrimony. Some men beat themselves with the whip while dancing to demonstrate courage and resilience under physical pain. The significance of the *mindil*, the *kurbadj*, and the *imbad* are manifest in these excerpts from wedding songs:

Muhammad waadar mindil awau lila nataiwa	We ululate for Muhammad's [the groom's name] red *mindil*.
Kurbadauk wa habashai qaliltiab	With your whip you expel the Ethiopian [reference to the Beni Amir].
Imbadauk Isankayauk washi hauk tidambityauk	Your sword is on your shoulder and your enemy is under your foot.

Another wedding song includes the following verses:

Hindiwar Aumak sabarwait muharam idabaida riaini	The sons of the Hadendowa, they endure war [and conflicts] because cowardice is unsanctioned [shameful].
Hindiwar Adami saqautaaib bafrai qaubaaib	The sons of the Hadendowa, when very little they are [adorned] with spears, and [in the womb] they have [their battle shields.

Dancing with *sunkab*

Sunkab parade heading toward tomb of Alsharifa Maryam (men celebrating under tree)

Leaders of *sunkab* parade with *fauta* bridal gifts over their heads

Sunkab parade stopping close to tomb

Blessing *sunkabs* at local mosque before heading to tomb

Groom (with one of his best men) wearing *shall*-style yellow *mindil*

Groom and his best men dancing with male relatives to drumming and singing of women (rural area)

Fetching drinking water

Cooking

The groom takes off his *mindil* and jewelry after seven days, by the end of which he is said to have transcended his liminality and gained the blessing of his male ancestors. The bride, on the other hand, continues to wear most of her protective jewelry because of the belief that women are more susceptible to danger. The newlyweds, however, are fully incorporated into their new social status and role after the wedding night.

The bride starts her new life by lighting her own cooking fire, which is placed at the tent's entrance. Women associate the cooking fire with the power of regeneration, nourishment, and protection (see Feldman-Savelsberg 1999). Therefore, the death of a woman marks the death of her tent and the extinguishing of her cooking fire. As the female relatives dismantle the deceased woman's tent, they cover her *aunash* (funeral bed) with a curtain made of her *fauta*s and supported by four wooden pillars fastened at the corners of the bed. They shroud the corpse in a white cloth and wrap it in straw mats before letting down the curtain. The grieving female relatives hand the *aunash*, like the tent that contained the woman's life, to the men at the boundary of the domestic space to carry it to the graveyard, outside the women's sphere. Women associate graveyards with the spiritual domain of the dead, which can also pose danger to women's fertility and procreation (see, e.g., Boddy 1989; Inhorn 1994; Delaney 1991). Like the warmth of a womb, which sustains life, the tent shelters the mother, who transforms her own labor and that of her husband into nour-ishment for children's growth and well-being (see Devisch 1991; Levine and Levine 1991). The tent thus takes its social identity from the mother, who generates its life cycle through the reproductive and productive lives of her daughters and sons. The symbolism and the ritual practices of a person's life cycle, therefore, generate with it the social meanings of gendered iden-tities, embodied spatiality, honor, and group rebirth.

Chapter 4

Gendered Placenta

The Paths to Proper Fertility and Responsible Motherhood

Augaw taur hawi bithaib nadai

[The home in which there is no girl is like an orphan.]

Hadendowa proverb

It was five o'clock one afternoon in 1989. Maryam, my research assistant, and I were going through some interviews we had conducted the previous day, when cheerful ululation disrupted our discussion. Coming from the culture of northern Sudan, where such ululation may announce the happy news of a wedding or a circumcision, I assumed a similar situation was taking place in Sinkat town, where I was doing my master's fieldwork. Not knowing the contents of the songs that merged with the women's ululation, I excitedly asked Maryam, "Are we having a wedding in the neighborhood?" She said with a smile, "No, we are having a new boy." Maryam rushed through the door, urging me to follow her. Not understanding exactly what she meant, I went outside. Approaching us was a crowd of about fifteen women accompanied by children, dressed in colorful clothes and led by a middle-aged woman carrying a tray with an incense burner. Maryam and I joined the parade, which proceeded to an open area across the town's eastern boundaries. At the conclusion of the parade, I learned that the crowd was celebrating the birth of a male child and that the ceremony entailed hanging the placenta that had contained him over a thorny tree outside the female domestic space to symbolize his association with his male ancestors.

Hadat, the Hadendowa ancestral foremother, is buried with her husband and seven sons in Aukar, the original Hadendowa homeland (see chapter 1). Her grave is atop a hill, attesting to her peculiar status, while her husband and sons are buried at the foot. The graves of both parents are adorned with white flags, and fourteen paths engraved in the ground meet at the head of each grave, giving the site the shape of a descent tree. According to Hadendowa women, these paths symbolize the routes that each son took when visiting the graves of his parents to pay homage and pray for them. For women such pilgrimages illustrate the good upbringing of the sons, who continued to respect and care for their parents after their death.

While men associate their *durarit* with their forefathers, women proudly relate the story of their ancestral grandmother, Hadat, as a woman of virtue and ideal fertility and motherhood. Hadat is praised for giving birth to seven male children, who later founded the seven main Hadendowa lineages. She is remembered as a devoted mother whose blessing and attentive care led to her sons' success as gallant fighters and honorable men. Although Hadat had seven daughters, narratives about these daughters associate them with marriage with foreigners and thus with subordinate status (see chapter 1).

Constructions of fertility and motherhood as well as meanings of having sons or daughters are tied to ideas of gender, place, and collective identity. "Wealth in sons" enhances both men's and women's *durarit*. For women it secures their marital status and bestows *hamaustib* on them as expressed in their social value in the eyes of their husbands, in-laws, and community. Although *durarit* is fluid and does not deny infertile women their honor, most women interviewed indicated that sons' mothers are more *masait* and respected than girls' mothers and infertile women. Sons' mothers are often compared to fertile wombs that link men with their forefathers, while son-infertility is seen as a threat to the social order.

The narrative of Hadat and the ritual of "son-birth" *(tamnai aurauk)* present an image of fertility and motherhood that most Hadendowa women aspire to achieve. The son-birth ritual also dramatizes the reverence conferred on mothers of sons and reveals the subordinate status of women with son-infertility. This chapter examines the social tensions among women of different fertility situations and unravels the strategies and practices they employ to negotiate their position in order to be deemed responsible mothers.

Graves of Hadat, Barakawin, and their seven sons

Sons or Daughters: The Many Faces
of Gender Preference

Just as the reproductive careers of some women may be threatened from
the start by a difficult pregnancy or the death of a child, women who deliver
safely face the challenge of the gender of their newly born. Delivering a
child safely is a blessing, but giving birth to a male child is the source of
great respect. *Tamnai aurauk* demonstrates the emphasis the Hadendowa
place on gendering pregnancy outcomes and bestowing honor on mothers
of sons.

The ritual begins with a parade, a joyous drama in which women fill the
town's streets declaring the birth of a male child. Although pregnancy and
giving birth are women's affairs that must be concealed, the birth of a male
child transcends his mother's confinement and unites him with the men's
domain. When a son is born, the women attending his delivery ululate
seven times to announce the happy news. The male placenta is not dis-
carded as waste; rather, it is treated as a symbol of association between the
son and his forefathers. A woman whose reproductive career has ended
with more sons than daughters blesses the placenta and leads the parade.

Before the beginning of the parade, women place the placenta in a straw
basket, which is sewn and placed on a tray with an incense burner. The parade then crosses different alleys and routes, while the ritual leader burns
more incense and the crowd congratulates the boy's mother with songs that
wish her good health and more sons in the future. The kinds of incense used
during the ritual are *bakhaur timan* (twin frankincense), *arad (Acacia etbaica)*, and *qarad (Acacia arabica)*, which are used to ward off the danger of
mobility and boundary crossing. On their way, the participants theatrically
demonstrate their happiness by sitting on the ground, laughing, and then
getting up to continue the parade. The congratulatory song goes as follows:

Tamnai aurauk aumaumi yaki	O son-mother,
	may you complete your rest confine-
	ment safely.
aur imbabyai tirhati iha	You make the son's father happy.
Fatna alzahra, Aumaumi yaki	O son-mother,
Hassan wa Hussain, aumaumi yaki	may Fatima Al-Zahra and Al-Hassan
	and Al-Hussain[1] bestow their bless-
	ing on you during your rest
	confinement.

1. Fatima Al-Zahra was the daughter of Prophet Muhammad, and Al-Hassan and
Al-Hussain were her twin sons.

isalait yaitai, aumaumi yaki

You safely transcended the danger of the rope.[2]

Arau dihaidai, aumaumi yaki

May you have many sons in the future.

Hasab alrasaul, aumaumi yaki

By the Prophet's blessing, end your rest period safely.

While singing, the parade participants leave the domestic space and proceed to an open, tree-covered area. Previously we have seen how the domestic space is associated with femininity, while men's space is often located in the exterior, under trees or in the market. Thus, crossing from the domestic domain into the "wilderness" is the first step in socializing the newly born son into the public space. This boundary transgression, however, is ridden with danger. Therefore burning incense during the crossing process is paramount to mitigating the danger that may befall the mother and her son.

The parade ends under a thorny tree, where the symbolic initiation of the son takes place. Spirits inhabit most wild trees and may harm people who sit under these trees or attempt to collect their wood or leaves without the spirits' permission. Thorny trees, however, are less likely to be inhabited by jinn and thus are safer sites for performing the initiation ritual. When the parade reaches the tree, usually a *shashaut (Balanites aegyptiaca)* or *san-qanib (Acacia tortilis)* tree, each parade participant steps over the incense burner seven times to exorcise the potential danger of boundary crossing.

One parade participant, Raia, explained that since people move around frequently and cross different terrains, it is likely that they transport danger through their feet, especially when the parade returns to the mother's house. This corresponds with women's perceptions that the lower body is more susceptible to spirit assaults than the upper body. After exorcising such danger, a boy or the woman who led the parade throws the placenta to hang over the tree in a symbolic action suggesting the link of the womb with the ancestors and with exteriority. The enclosed straw basket that contained the placenta is made of the same dom-tree leaves that women use to weave the tent mats and to craft the *sunkab* fronds, a fertility symbol, which they fasten to the bridal tent. Women explained that these leaves are used to bring bounty, rain, and fertility and to deter dangerous spirits.

In contrast to son-birth, the birth of a female child is received with indifference, lack of celebrations, yet good wishes for the safety of both mother and female child for surviving the danger of childbirth. Both mother and child are wished the birth of many sons in the future. In

2. The rope refers to an old method of facilitating delivery whereby a woman squatted while holding onto a rope that dangled from the roof.

"Placenta tree"

Part of son-birth ritual under tree

contrast to their treatment of the male placenta, women bury the female placenta near the mother's tent to demonstrate the association of the female child with domesticity, modesty, land, and fertility.

After hanging the male placenta, the women collect green leaves to be thrown over the mother's tent to symbolize fertility, which marks the spatial unity of interiority and exteriority through the birth of a son. Women also make bundles of seven sticks, which they dramatically try to break but soon declare their failure to do so. Malka, another parade participant, explained that this act represents the notion of group solidarity: it is easier to defeat one group but harder to subdue many. The son is thus initiated into the domain of his forefathers, and his future is charted as one that will protect the patrimony and foster the ideology of collective honor.

When the parade participants return to the mother's house, they take different routes in order to reverse any danger that they may have encountered on previous paths. Changing paths conforms to the women's explanation of the *halafa* logic, through which external danger is diverted into positive power to protect the community. Certain routes are said to be less contaminated by the spirits and thus safer than others. For instance, an alley can become very dangerous if a woman throws dirt or hot water into it. This action may immediately irritate jinn, who may retaliate by endangering a passerby. Since spirits reside in the boundaries of the domestic space, however, all alleys are said to be haunted by jinn. Therefore, reversing routes reduces such danger and ensures a successful reproductive trajectory for the mother and her children. To clear the new routes, the parade leader adds more incense to the burner, and the crowd sings songs that wish the mother and her son the blessings and protection of God and his saints, mainly the Khatmiyya of Sinkat.

The main themes of the ritual parade emphasize protection of the health of mother and child during confinement. Central to this is the women's wishes that the Prophet's daughter and her twin sons bless the mother. It is significant to note that these blessings are staged before the blessings of the Prophet himself. It is also worth mentioning that the Prophet had no live sons or daughters except Fatima, the mother of the twin sons. Thus, by bearing a son, a Hadendowa woman not only achieves a position similar to Hadat, her ancestral mother, but she also gains the blessing of the Prophet's family through his grandsons and his daughter, Fatima.

The narrative of Hadat and the ritual of son-birth publicize the significance attributed to male children and bestow honor on mothers of sons. Not surprisingly, the honor enjoyed by mothers of sons also makes them vulnerable to the danger of the evil eye and evil jinn, as well as to the envy of childless women and mothers of girls who aspire to their status. Thus mothers of sons visit the tombs of Alsharifa Maryam and Sidi Ibrahim (also a Khatmiyya saint) in Sinkat to seek, among other things, protection for their living sons and their remaining fecundity. They also visit religious men and women in the area to procure amulets and blessed water. My encounter with sixty-year-old Nafisa illustrates the association that most women make between the concept of danger and wealth in sons.

When I asked Nafisa how many sons she had, she convincingly told me that she had one son and five daughters. When I interviewed her neighbor, she inadvertently told me that Nafisa had six sons. On my next visit to Nafisa, I asked her if all women are suspected of wanting to bewitch mothers of sons. She said, "Mostly women who do not have children, but not all of them bewitch. Nothing harms a person if people's intentions are good and they say *masha Allah* [God is graceful] before praising you or your children, but you do not know people's intentions." Nafisa then asked me, "What about you? Would you tell me how many sons you have without doubting that I will do evil to you?" I said, "If I had six sons, I would tell you, because God is the protector . . . right?" Nafisa nodded, knowing what I was getting at, and said, "Yes, yes, God is the protector." She then uncovered her head and chest to show me the several amulets she was wearing around her neck and in her braided hair. "These are God's words," she explained. "They protect me from the evil of people and jinn." Giving me a half-smile, she said, "My sons, God protect them, they are the ones who are supporting me now. If it were not for them, I may have been dead many years ago."

Nafisa moved to Sinkat after the drought of 1984, which affected most of the Hadendowa rural areas. She decided to settle in Sinkat town to be near her married sons and three daughters-in-law after her husband's marriage to a younger woman in the rural area. She was a respected figure in her community, partly because of her seniority and for transcending her reproductive trajectories safely. Like few women in her community, Nafisa was also endowed with a positive power because of her midwifery practice, a skill she learned from her mother and one that also reflected her fertility blessings. She was often called *masait* or *mabrauka* (Arabic for "blessed"). Although infertile women can become midwives, Nafisa's story illustrates the link that some women make between "blessed" fertility trajectories and accumulation of knowledge. Nafisa, for instance, had extensive knowledge about local histories and medicinal herbs. For this reason women would often refer me to her whenever I needed elaboration on certain issues. We would all then gather in her tent, drink coffee, and listen to her ideas and stories. In such settings women recognized Nafisa's authorship of certain narratives. This is not to preclude women's agency and their frequent interjection of their own personal perspectives during collective interviews.

In a different interview setting, Nafisa elaborated on how wealth in sons may lead to misfortune. She related that one of her relative's sons, who "was very kind to his parents," was once bewitched by a son-infertile woman. The woman, who saw the boy working hard with his father in the sorghum field, commented to the father, "Pity those who do not have sons." She did not say *masha Allah,* and thus the son was suddenly *inqabad* (Arabic for "seized," meaning he fell sick). Persons who experience the evil eye may immediately fall sick, have a concussion, or faint. The son died after a few days.

Nafisa maintained that protection from evil starts with marriage and continues after pregnancy and childbirth. When her children were born (both males and females), she protected them by *kabaun* and *tisaramt aya* (the seven Qur'anic verses) amulets. *Kabaun* amulets contain seven coffee beans, seven grains of sorghum, *lauban timan* (twin frankincense), seven grains of black cumin *(Nigella sativa),* seven thorns, black kohl, and salt. Women explain that coffee beans, sorghum, and frankincense are symbols of growth that are used to reverse the evil that targets child development. Black cumin, black kohl, salt, and thorns also are believed to prevent evil eye and evil jinn, which are perceived to be black and bitter. Nafisa's attempts to protect her fertility and her children's well-being shed light on women's continuous quest for propriety and responsible motherhood.

Hadendowa women's attempts to invest in their health and their children's well-being, however, are situated in a precarious economy that has a direct impact on their ability to bear and raise healthy children. This state of poverty is reflected in cases of poor health and infant mortality among displaced Hadendowa. My statistical data show that fertility mishaps (miscarriages, stillbirths, and child death) represent 22 percent (51 cases) of women's total pregnancies (237), of which 41 percent (98 cases) are living male children, and 37 percent (88 cases) are living female children. Miscarriages of fetuses of unknown gender represent 6 percent (5 cases) out of the 56 cases reported. It is worth noting, however, that most women interviewed expressed their distress in reporting such tragic fertility events, which explains the low percentage reported.

Sinkat Hospital, established in 1962, is staffed with one or two northern Sudanese doctors from Khartoum, Port Sudan, or Kassala, as well as by nurses and midwives. Midwives are mostly urban Hadendowa or non-Hadendowa Beja. Medical consultation in the hospital is free, but patients have to pay additional medical expenses, which many cannot afford. Most Hadendowa migrants interviewed resent hospitals as foreign institutions that, instead of ensuring well-being, threaten it. Such beliefs have substantial grounds in the hegemonic histories of both westernization and *bala-waitization* (northern Sudanese–style urbanization) and in the reality of the deteriorating public health system in the Sudan and its failure to reach the majority of disadvantaged populations and provide them with reliable health services (see Bayoumi 1979; Bell 1999). Thus it is not surprising that women who suffer from infertility and repeated miscarriages, believed to be caused by different forms of foreignness, are advised not to visit hospitals, where they can be contaminated by sickness, bleeding, or death. The location of the hospital in urban centers and its gender hierarchy also renders it difficult for women to consult with doctors without their male relatives' permission. In the few cases I reported, women preferred consulting with midwives instead.

This attitude toward the hospital was voiced in some women's reactions when I told them about the U.S. bombing of an Alshifa medicine factory in Khartoum in 1998. Their response was "thank God we do not use your medicine." Although they were partly joking, the women's comments reveal their attitudes toward what they regard as the Western-*balawait* way of life. For most migrants, therefore, the hospital becomes the last resort for health management. Ethnomedical practices that make use of religious practitioners, fortunetellers, herbalists, and spirit specialists are seen as more effective.

Although the narrative of Hadat and the ritual of son-birth reinforce the meanings of son preference, women's achievement of such a desired goal seems unattainable in practice, for Hadendowa women face biological and social realities that undermine the ideal of having many sons. Few women succeed in bearing and raising many sons. Some have only girls or few sons; others suffer multiple miscarriages, the death of sons, or endure lifelong childlessness. My statistical sample shows that no one had achieved the idealized number of seven sons. Of the eighty-five women interviewed, 40 percent reported no live sons, 47 percent had one to two sons, 11 percent had three to four sons, and only 2 percent had five sons. The comparative youth of married women who have zero to two sons contributes to the high percentage of son-infertility (46 percent). Married women in their late reproductive careers represent 9 percent of those son-infertile, while widows and divorced women in their early to middle reproductive years account for 17 percent. Infertility also seems to be higher among women who have been married for five years or longer (14 cases; 16 percent). Childless women who have been married for less than five years represent 5 percent of the infertility (4 cases). This measure takes into account the women's own perception of "how late they can wait" (Menken 1985), for a childless period of more than five years is considered ominous and a clear indication of infertility even if the woman is still within her childbearing years.

In such situations, which present enormous challenges to successful childbearing, bearing even a few sons is seen as great achievement. However, 31 percent of the eighty-five women interviewed expressed their desire to end their reproductive careers with bearing many more sons than daughters. Most women in this category have either few sons or girls only. Those

Table 3. "Son-infertility" by women's age and marital status

Marital status	Living sons	Women's age						Total	%
		15–24		25–34		35–44			
		(N)	%	(N)	%	(N)	%		
Married									
	0	8	40.0%	13	46.0%	3	27.0%	24	40.7%
	1–2	11	55.0%	8	29.0%	5	46.0%	24	40.7%
	3–4	1	5.0%	7	25.0%	1	9.0%	9	15.3%
	5	0		0		2	18.0%	2	3.4%
Total		20	100.0%	28	100.0%	11	100.0%	59	100.0%
Widow									
	0	1	100.0%	1	17.0%	3	37.5%	5	33.0%
	1–2	0		5	83.0%	5	62.5%	10	67.0%
Total		1	100.0%	6	100.0%	8	100.0%	15	100.0%
Divorced									
	0	1	25.0%	2	67.0%	2	50.0%	5	45.5%
	1–2	3	75.0%	1	33.0%	2	50.0%	6	54.5%
Total		4	100.0%	3	100.0%	4	100.0%	11	100.0%

Data from author's fieldwork, 1998

who wanted more girls than boys (9 percent) were mostly women who have many sons or have no girls at all. Women who wished to have a balanced number of children of both sexes (29 percent) were mostly childless women and those who have daughters only. Those who were too shy to answer the question or responded by saying that they accepted God's will regarding the number and gender of the children they have or wished to have represent 31 percent of those interviewed. A few women attributed their desire not to have more children to the fact that they had grandchildren. Some Hadendowa women consider it shameful to become pregnant simultaneously with one's married daughters or sons' wives. In such cases women may decide to stop childbearing and assume a grandmother's role (see Bledsoe et al. 1994).

Becoming a knowledgeable, respected *hautaun* (grandmother) is a social status that mothers also aspire to achieve. Most Hadendowa grandmothers are fortunetellers, herbalists, or local midwives, a practice inherited from their mothers, as we have seen in Nafisa's case. They also play a central role in managing their daughters' households and their childbearing and child-rearing experiences. Therefore, girls' mothers, unlike childless women, are not seen as completely deprived of social status since they can become grandmothers of their daughters' sons. In fact, many women emphasize that mothers whose daughters marry and have children, especially sons, are also subject to envy and evil eye.

Preference for sons is also grounded in a gendered construction of honor and female sexuality. Women are seen as more sexual than men because of their association with reproduction. Their sexuality can endanger the communal honor if it is not well guarded. In this context female circumcision is cited as a means of curbing female sexuality and thus of constructing a gender difference between male and female children. *Auqashabi* (Pharaonic circumcision) is performed on young girls, usually before they reach age six. In rural areas local midwives use an unhygienic *tishinqil* (local type of razor) to remove the *sharir* (clitoris) and the *ibanon* (labia minora) and part of the *tidafin* (labia majora). Infibulation is then used to cover the excision site. All the women interviewed regarded the practice as necessary to ensure girls' chastity and marriageability (see Gruenbaum 1982; Toubia 1994; Abusharaf 2001). Few women acknowledged the health risks associated with the practice. Rather, they attributed the risks to untrained practitioners and the unavailability of medical treatment when needed. Hibat, one interviewee, asserted that circumcision protects girls' honor and ensures their "cleanliness." Although one of her daughters had bled to death during circumcision, she did not blame the girl's death on the practice itself and claimed that male children also die from bleeding if their circumcision goes wrong. Poverty and local methods of performing circumcision are to be blamed, according to Hibat. The women interviewed also use circumcision as an identity marker to distinguish themselves from the uncircumcised women of neighboring groups. Hibat said, "The women of the Rashaida are *tinkaulit* [a pejorative term, which means the 'uncircumcised']." She grimaced. "They are unclean and unchaste."

Despite most Hadendowa women's support of the practice, there are efforts by non-Hadendowa advocates, such as the Ahafad University women, to eradicate the practice and educate women, through public lectures, about its harmful effects. Although the public debate about circumcision has given these advocates the reputation of being unchaste themselves, they continue to work toward increasing support for integrating development efforts, women's empowerment, and advocacy for the right to health (cf. Shell-Duncan 2001) to provide local women with multiple ways of thinking about their bodies and health. The issue of female circumcision in Sudan, however, has found extensive scholarly and media coverage by both local and international feminists to the extent that other women's health issues have been obscured.

Because of cultural constructions of honor and female sexuality, forty-five-year-old Khadija, a mother of four sons and two daughters, said that mothers of sons "sleep well" as opposed to mothers of girls, who "worry all the time." According to Khadija, a girl's vulnerable sexuality can bring shame to her family. Khadija explained how a mother would be dishonored by her daughter's shame; it is the mother's responsibility to raise her daughters well. This association of honor sheds light on the social obligations of mothers, the guardians of "female honor," and explains why they would prefer to have more sons than daughters.

These social constructions, however, are negotiated in practice, for many women also emphasized their preference for girls despite the cultural emphasis on female vulnerability. Thirty-three-year-old Firdaus said that she was very upset when one of her male relatives commented after the birth of her only daughter:

Inshalla tikati idauba istrit, imimash istrit	I hope that your daughter becomes chaste and gets married. If she does not find a husband, then the grave protects her.

That is, since women are associated with dangerous sexuality, the man expressed a wish that Firdaus's daughter would grow up to be a modest girl who would protect her sexuality (virginity) until she married. Since immodesty can lead to failure to marry, the man preferred that the girl die before bringing shame to her family. Firdaus, who had a successful reproductive career resulting in five sons, wanted a girl. Upset by the old man's comment, she asked her mother, who was sitting near her, "Why would this man wish the grave for my daughter? Didn't he know how much I had waited for her?" Her mother comforted her, saying that she had to put up with such intolerant aspects of the tradition.

Although parents prefer sons, most women interviewed acknowledge that girls benefit their families. Girls are their mothers' friends, and they are the caretakers of their parents, siblings, and old relatives. They also bring bridewealth and husbands to their families (see, e.g., Evans-Pritchard 1960; Cunnison 1966; see also Clark et al. 1995). Sixty-year-old Hadia explained this paradox in the following way: "See, I had two children, a boy and a girl, who died when very little. Look at me now; I look tired and miserable. Halima [her young, married neighbor] is like my daughter. She checks on me every day, but it is not like you have your own daughter." She sadly looked at her torn clothes and said, "If I had a boy or a girl I would not look so miserable."

Moreover, a mother feels empowered by the number of her daughters' tents that surround hers, a vivid representation of how motherhood is central to ideas of group regeneration. On the other hand, mothers who have only sons may feel lonely after their sons' marriages, especially if they have no close relatives nearby. In such cases a son may ask his in-laws' permission for his wife to construct her tent near that of his mother. For all these reasons, girls' mothers seem to be in a better social position than childless women, whose infertility is likened to seedless land (see Delaney 1991).

Polygyny

Infertility is usually blamed on women. Although men's infertility is recognized in practice, it is not openly addressed. A wife's infertility or her failure to bear sons is considered a valid reason for divorce or polygyny. Of the eighty-five women interviewed, nine women in polygynous households said that their husbands married another woman because they wanted more sons, and five (out of eleven divorced women) attributed their divorces to their childlessness. Women's attitudes towards polygyny vary according to their perceptions and experiences. Although women may seek their families' support to resist their husbands' decisions regarding polygyny, especially if they are not infertile, in cases of childlessness and son-infertility, husbands may find it easier to secure their wives' consent before their remarriage. Simrit, from the Gamilab lineage, said that her husband consulted her before his remarriage. She maintained, "My husband told me that the only reason for his marriage was to have more sons to help him with his work. Most of my children are girls, and I have only one son, who is handicapped. My husband asked me to choose a wife for him, but I refused. He chose my mother's brother's daughter. He said he does not want to bring a distant relative to be my co-wife. She is living beside me. She is like my sister, and he treats us equally."

Other women, especially son-fertile women, may see polygyny as an affront to their social status as respected mothers and may resist their husband's decision through divorce or desertion, as in the case of Hadat, another woman from the Gamilab lineage.[3] Hadat, who has many sons, said that her husband did not consult her on his decision to marry a second wife, which she considered a personal assault on her social position. Later her husband bought her a *tisanit* to win her support. She was angry, however, because there was no substantial reason for his second marriage. She maintained that her husband "just wanted a younger woman" because she

3. The Gamilab are known among the Hadendowa for their strict religious observance because of the influence of the renowned Shaikh Ali Bitai, founder of the Hamaush Kaurib *khalawi*. This may explain why most reported cases of polygyny were among the Gamilab. Ali Bitai is a Hadendowa Beja whose religious teachings have influenced many Hadendowa, especially in the eastern borders and the Gash region. He lived from 1930 to 1978. His religious schools in Hamaush Kaurib are renowned educational centers in the region.

Bukars of two co-wives (sorghum sack in middle)

was getting old. "That was a very difficult time for me. I spent the night with my eyes open and felt ashamed when people looked at me and when they inquired about the reasons. The most painful thing for me was that the bride used to tease me by showing off her beauty and youth. When I felt that I could not stay there, I left him and came to Sinkat to be near two of my sons. I did not ask for a divorce because he is my father's brother's son and I have grown sons and daughters by him." Hadat, who was about forty, lived on her own, depending on the mats she sold at the bus terminal and on the assistance of her daughters and sons.

The relationship between the co-wives interviewed, however, is characterized by both tension and friendship. According to Zainab (age thirty-five), polygyny is "difficult for women, it is like being bitten by a snake over and over again, but you have to internalize the anger and jealously so you can show off your *durarit*." She then related this narrative: "Once a woman was invited to her husband's second wedding. Of course, she had to go to show off her *durarit*. She had to dance and everything. I myself can't do it; call me *jabana* [Arabic for 'coward']. But this woman went, and she was chatting with everybody as if nothing was bothering her. A snake came out of its pit and started biting her. Each time the snake bit her, she would bite it back and address it by saying, 'You don't feel what I feel.' At the end the snake died, and she survived its venom."

According to Zainab, the snake died of the woman's overwhelming jealousy and anger, which were more venomous. Yet a woman must conceal her personal feelings in order to establish her *durarit,* which in this context refers to kin support and to the ability to control one's weakening feelings of anger, jealousy, and sexual desire. Relevant to this, women also categorize humor as a quality associated with *durarit,* as in Asha's poem (see chapter 1) when she describes how Barakawin's sons were born with humor and generosity. This is because humor indicates an ability to "laugh difficulties out," to entertain one's guests, and to show tolerance in the face of hardship. *Durarit* therefore is about performing *auslif* in public. In private, however, polygyny can affect the relationship between spouses and co-wives in many ways.

In a dialogue with women at a naming ceremony, some women voiced their views toward polygyny:

M. (about fifty): In the beginning I was angry with my [co-wife], but after a while we became friends. Now she even washes my clothes with hers because I have a back problem. Also whenever I want sugar or coffee, I can ask her.

H. (about thirty): When my husband remarried, I was angry and left him to be near my parents' house. I stayed there until he paid the *tisanit.* Jealousy is subjective, but our relationship [with the co-wife] is good. Why should I blame her? She committed no sin. She is a woman like me. What are we fighting about anyway? A man's [sex] . . . [*she points her finger out; everyone laughs*].

A. (about fifty): My relationship with my [co-wife] is good. But my relationship with my husband is not. Our relationship was greatly affected by his marriage, which also affected our *aumkir* [negotiation and consultation]. Before his marriage we used to consult each other on different matters. [For instance] I gave him the right to take care of my animals. Our money was shared. But after his marriage I took all my animals and gave them to my uncle to look after them for me.

B. (about thirty-five): I really got angry because of my husband's marriage. Sometimes I feel jealous and refuse to sleep with him. He might get angry, but he cannot force me because he can always go and do it with the other wife. It does not matter if he marries two or three. What matters is that he should treat us equally [according to the condition of sanctioned polygyny in the Qur'an]. If he fails to protect us, people will blame him and not us. I don't care since all my needs [are met]. It is shameful to fight over a man.

F. (about thirty): I tried to have children for a long time but to no avail. Then I got pregnant, but I had a stillbirth. I consulted religious people and even

went to the doctor in Sinkat. I also visited the tomb of Alsharifa Maryam
many times and asked her to bestow her blessing on me and to grant me
many sons and daughters. I also asked her to elevate us from poverty, and
I put some money in the box at her tomb [donations to be distributed to
the needy in the name of the saint; people who make such donations are
said to gain blessings]. My husband came to me one day and asked my
permission to marry again in order to have children. I gave him my
permission on the condition that his new wife not live near me. She is in
the *khala* and I am here. I knew that we wouldn't get along very well, and
I did not want troubles.

The story of Bashalit, a childless woman who is about forty, is rather
different. Bashalit maintained that she also gave her husband permission to
marry a second wife because she herself wanted to "see his children and
help raise them." She also chose the bride (her maternal cousin) for him.
Her cousin, who has two sons and two daughters from her marriage, was
present during the interview and commented that her children "like Bashalit a lot; they call her mother, and prefer to stay in her tent because she
spoils them." Bashalit said that her relationship with her husband became
stronger after his second marriage and the birth of his children and that
they treat each other respectfully.

These different voices speak to the wide spectrum of women's attitudes
toward polygyny and their strategies for averting or confronting it. In most
cases the women involved identify with each other, thereby creating a discourse of solidarity, derived from the notions of *auslif*, in order to perform
their *durarit* and secure their marital statuses. Bashalit's case is significant
because it also demonstrates how some women may gain respect through
becoming good mothers to their husband's children by another wife.

Although cases of polygyny are not common among displaced Hadendowa, since most husbands are economically unable to support more
than one family, the majority of reported cases involve childless and son-
infertile women. For this reason childless women, mothers of girls, and
women with reproductive traumas (such as miscarriages and infant death)
represent the majority of women who undertake spirit-possession healing
rituals and other practices that involve visiting tombs, herbalists, and religious practitioners.

Touched by Foreignness: Infertility and Miscarriage

As previously mentioned, women believe that infertility, morbidity, and infant mortality are usually caused by different forms of foreignness, such as
evil spirits, and by the mysterious disease *tisaramt*, both of which threaten
women's fertility and regeneration. Accordingly, infertility and recurrent

miscarriages are seen as evidence of a violation of bodily boundaries and social well-being. Thus, while giving birth to girls only is considered a misfortune, childlessness, repeated miscarriages, and infant mortality are seen as serious, contagious mishaps that can infect new generations of mothers and children. In fact, women who suffer miscarriages and infant death are seen as a separate category (*tibadai ari*, "those whose children die") that is more dangerous than never-pregnant women. Neither *tibadai ari* nor infertile women are allowed to lead marriage and son-birth initiation rituals.

Today an older generation of female herbalists, fortunetellers, and spirit and religious practitioners, who are confronting women's continuous quest for prosperity and motherhood, believes that fertility traumas increased after the Hadendowa migrated to urban centers (cf. Feldman-Savelsberg 1999). When women became mobile, one herbalist said, they were more exposed to new lifestyles and different kinds of foods. Therefore, they become susceptible to attacks by spirits and to the dangers of boundary transgression. According to the female herbalist: "In the *khala*, people are close relatives; thus women were not used to being so mobile. In town women go to visit their relatives in different areas. Mobility is not good for women. It brings evil jinn and *tisaramt*. Also women now eat everything. We are used to a certain diet: milk, butter, and porridge."

Haisha (age thirty-five) confirmed that most problems of infertility and miscarriage are caused by *iqatha* (relief) food, especially dried milk and bottled oil, distributed by foreign and national organizations to famine victims. She maintained that when she came to Sinkat she had two children—a boy and a girl—and since then she had not carried a pregnancy to term.

Besides *tisaramt* and evil spirits, the herbalist enumerated other causes of infertility and miscarriage such as "cold wombs" and *umalsibian* [Arabic, literally "sons' mother," also *tiyaut* or *tinsibiand*). Infertility can be induced by exposure to cold that enters the womb and causes women's fertility blood to thicken and accumulate, resulting in infections and irregular menstrual cycles. Moreover, infertility and miscarriage are also attributed to a mysterious worm that women call *tiyaut* or *umalsibian*, which attacks the womb. This worm is sometimes described as a female jinn who envies pregnant women and thus causes miscarriage. Women, however, do not recount narratives describing the jinn and why she envies pregnant women. Recurrent miscarriages and stomach sicknesses caused by the jinn form of *tiyaut* or *umalsibian* are diagnosed by herbalists and spirit and religious practitioners and are treated with blessed water, amulets, and herbal mixtures extracted from jinn-inhabited trees. An *umalsibian*, however, as is clear from its name, seems to cause women who are pregnant with male children to miscarry. The case of Tyyis illustrates the different practices she undertook to reverse her affliction with an *umalsibian*.

Tyyis, a thirty-four-year-old widow, was the mother of two boys and two girls. She said that she married before menarche and got pregnant two years afterward. Her labor was difficult, and she gave birth to a male child, who died a few minutes after his birth. She said, "That was a painful experience for me; my husband and I wanted a son." This is why Tyyis consulted Halima, a religious woman from the Ashraf family in Sinkat. She continued:

> The religious woman told me that I had an evil eye, which was passed to me from my family, who were bewitched because they were many [members of this family who had succeeded in marriage and in producing many successful sons and daughters]. She also told me that I had the jinn form of *umalsibian*, which killed my son. The *faqiria* [religious woman] gave me blessed water to drink and to massage my breasts and lower body. She also gave me two *auqadat* (knots), which she read the Qur'an over, and told me to wear one and to transfer it later to my child. She also told me to bury the other *auqadat* with the placenta if the child was a girl and to hang it with the afterbirth if the child was a boy. The *faqiria* also told me that I would bear a healthy son and that I should give her some money in return if I did. After a year and a half, I gave birth to a second boy, who is in high school now. When I was pregnant, my relatives made a *nadur* that if I gave birth to a live son they would hold a *shaikhitkaf* [religious party] for me, and they did. They invited women from the Ashraf family, who came and sang religious songs to bestow the blessing of the Khatmiyya saints on my child and me.

Besides seeking the blessings of the Khatmiyya saints, childless and son-infertile women also visit religious people such as Halima, whom Tyyis had consulted. Halima is a renowned religious woman and an herbalist, whose busy schedule made her turn down our request for an interview four times. When we entered her small, two-room mud house at the edge of one of Sinkat's old neighborhoods, Halima was surrounded by many women. There were Hadendowa women, northern Sudanese women, and a Beja woman who had fled the hot summer of Port Sudan, hoping to find a cure for her sickly child. Halima asked the mother to hand the crying child to her. She placed the child comfortably on her lap and began reading Qur'anic verses over his head, ending each verse with a prayer asking God to restore the child's health. Halima then gave the mother some herbs, which were in a jar beneath her bed. "This is fennel seed," she said, addressing the child's mother. "Boil them in water with seven sorghum seeds and give the mixture to the child to drink many times a day. He has appetite loss but he will get better." The child's mother replied, "Yes, since his birth he has not grown substantially, and now he has diarrhea." She then handed Halima some sugar and coffee beans in return for the consultation.

Another woman began telling Halima that she had failed to get pregnant since the birth of her six-year-old daughter. Halima asked her to lie down, checked her lower belly with her trembling hands, and conveyed to her that she was suffering from a "a tilted womb," which had resulted from a forceful move or from carrying a heavy load. Such a condition can only be restored, said Halima, through intensive diet, rest, and herbal medicine. Another woman, who had been married for four years, also complained that she could not get pregnant and that she was suffering from irregular menstrual cycles. Halima told her that she had a "womb infection" resulting from exposure to cold and gave her certain herbs to take with warm milk at the onset of her menstrual cycle.

In the same room where Halima was sitting, there was a bed with a white curtain. When I asked her about it, Halima responded by saying that she was supervising the healing of a patient, a woman in her twenties, who had been in confinement for fourteen days. Some patients asked that they be under Halima's immediate supervision during the healing process to receive her direct baraka and to avoid sexual intercourse with their husbands, essential to healing their womb-related diseases. The young patient had been married for five years, and she had not gotten pregnant. Halima diagnosed her with an *arid* that she had contracted during her wedding. To untie her blockage, Halima ordered her to stay in confinement with restricted mobility. During the first seven days of confinement, the patient was advised to eat porridge with milk for breakfast, drink herbal medicine with pure goat butter at night, and sleep on her left side. During these days she should also remain silent most of the time. In the second half of her treatment period, she would be allowed to move around in the house, have smoke baths, and follow her previous diet (see chapter 5).

At the end of her diagnostic session, Halima turned to me and said, "I know that you are not here to be cured, but you want to write about my healing knowledge so you can tell other people about it. However, I will give you something to protect you." She then tied a piece of plastic into several knots, read Qur'anic verses over them, and then handed it to me. She said, "This will protect you against evil eye across the paths you travel."

Halima, the renowned sixty-year-old Ashraf woman, was married but had no children. She told me that she had baraka because she belonged to the Khatmiyya family, who claim prophetic descent, and also because Sitti Maryam, the Khatmiyya female saint, blessed her when she was little by reading the Qur'an over her head. Like Sitti Maryam, Halima is also infertile. Her baraka healing power may also have stemmed from her transcendence of the jinn-polluting effect on fertility. Because she belongs to the Ashraf family, Halima's infertility cures focus on the Qur'an as an essential power to undo the evil of jinn. Thus she condemns spirit-possession practices and views them as non-Islamic. She either reads the Qur'an over water for women to massage themselves with, or over *auqadat* that are believed to be the source of witchcraft. According to Islamic convention, the Prophet Muhammad was once bewitched by a woman who casts spells over knots to harm him. This Qur'anic verse is always cited by women as a testimony of the Prophet's encounter with witchcraft and recited as protection from evil eye and evil spirits: "Say 'I take refuge with the Lord of the daybreak from the evil of what he has created, from the evil of darkness when it gathers, from the evil of the women who blow on knots, from the evil of an envier when he envies'" (Qur'an 113).

Although many Hadendowa acknowledge witchcraft, I have not found actual cases where witchcraft is intentionally used to cause harm. Some women I interviewed, however, also noted that evil spirits can cast the evil eye on people.

Halima's belief in the Qur'an as the utmost source of healing, however, does not conflict with her belief in biomedicine or even Hadendowa ideas of *halafa* as complementary systems of healing. Despite the ethnic tensions between the Hadendowa and the Ashraf, Halima had succeeded in drawing many Hadendowa women to her practice because of her baraka and her flexibility in incorporating Hadendowa ideas of healing. She said that many women chose to consult with her because they were opposed to "doctors' medicine," and she advised them to consult doctors or other practitioners if she was convinced that their ailments were beyond her knowledge. Pearce (1993) has noted similar integration of ethnomedicine and biomedicine in Nigeria, where new faith healers began to acknowledge the weaknesses and strengths of each medical system and to incorporate ideas from both fields into their medical practices.

Besides Qur'anic treatment, Halima, like many practitioners in the area, also used *nadur* and *halafa* practices as methods of reversing infertility traumas. *Nadur* practices are common in the Muslim world, and they involve promises made by people to God and his saints in exchange for certain favors. Like Tyyis's family, who promised to hold a religious party for her if she bore a son, other women promised to fast or donate food or clothes to poor people to fulfill their pledges. Such offerings are sometimes made to healers who help "unbind" women's infertility. Although it is mostly childless and son-infertile women who make these *nadur* promises, one informant who had sons made a *nadur* to Sitti Maryam to grant her a baby girl. She visited Sitti Maryam's tomb and promised that she would give a white body wrap (worn only by Ashraf women) as a gift to a poor neighbor, a promise she fulfilled when she gave birth to her only daughter. While women believe that infertility and son-infertility can be resolved through the power of the Qur'an, visits to saints' tombs, and *nadur* offerings, the plight of *tibadai ari* and never-pregnant women are often blamed on a combination of ailments caused by the evil eye, spirit possession, and mysterious diseases.

Negotiating Familiarity *(Auslif)*

Because fertility enhances both men's and women's social positions, infertility is seen as a bodily disease that must be redressed. Women who become pregnant one or two years after their marriage are more secure about their marital situation than those who wait longer. Pressures from families and in-laws play major roles in increasing women's feelings of insecurity, even if they receive the support of their husbands. A health visitor in Sinkat Hospital commented that such social pressures are the reason behind the many pseudopregnancy cases she has supervised. Cases such as that of Suaad are examples of how infertility presents a challenge for women, who are usually blamed for it.

Suaad was married for seven years, during which her husband was able to resist his mother's continuous demands that he remarry in order to have children. Suaad's mother too wanted her to have children, and she took her to many herbalists and religious practitioners, to no avail. Finally Suaad's husband submitted to his mother's demands, and he told Suaad that he was going to take another wife. Surprisingly, Suaad began to experience pregnancy symptoms, which delayed her husband's decision to remarry. Suaad discovered her pseudopregnancy when she went into labor. The midwife at Sinkat's hospital informed Suaad's female relatives that she was not pregnant, which annoyed them, and in response, they accused the midwife of jealousy and irresponsibility. The doctor later confirmed the midwife's account, and Suaad was devastated when she woke up from anesthesia. She refused to have a co-wife, however, and asked for a divorce. Later she remarried and gave birth to a baby girl. Her ex-husband married a divorcée and had no children in his second marriage. His second wife also asked for a divorce.

Although infertility is usually blamed on women, cases such as that of Suaad reveal the ways in which issues such as infertility are confronted in reality. In their *sakanab* during coffee gatherings, women often giggle over stories such as that of Suaad's husband, which mock cultural constructions by not withstanding the test of practice. Women relegate such cultural constructions to the realm of *auslif* or *adat*, habitual or familiar norms and beliefs set by the ancestors. To adhere to such beliefs, some women explain, is to follow the ancestral path. To stray from this path is to lose one's identity and self. Yet, because these realms of the habitual guide practice (Bourdieu

1990), the tensions and dynamics inherent in them can undermine the power of the familiar and allow for novel cultural understandings and the accommodation of new rules. As one woman commented, "It is clear that Suaad is not the one to be blamed for infertility." In similar cases some women may fear the stigma of divorce and would otherwise accept a co-wife, while others may refuse and mobilize their male relatives to end their marriages on solid cultural grounds. This negotiation of familiarity gives women opportunities to undertake different strategies to gain the status of responsible motherhood.

An emerging practical strategy that some infertile women have begun to use to fulfill their motherhood desires and to gain acceptance and social status is adoption. Adoption is acknowledged in many Islamic societies since the Prophet Muhammad himself had an adopted son. Yet the status of adopted children is often seen as marginal and associated with illegitimacy. In an interview the doctor at Sinkat Hospital stated that adoption was becoming a common phenomenon; however, it was difficult to discuss it publicly. Adopted children are incorporated into their new families and seldom know that they are adopted.

Although pregnancy out of wedlock is considered damaging to the reputation of both the girl and her parents, cases of premarital pregnancies occur and are sometimes reported to the hospital. A pregnant woman may seek the help of her mother, female friends, or other female relatives to abort her unwanted pregnancy. In some rural areas, midwives insert certain herbs into the vagina to induce abortion. Some of these abortions result in intensive bleeding, which may require medical treatment. In other cases women carry their pregnancy to term and deliver at the hospital, claiming that they are married. In such situations the doctor maintains that it is his ethical duty to help these women deliver and also to protect them from any physical harm that they may face from their male relatives. Women also are given the choice of leaving their babies in the hospital to be transferred to the orphanage in Port Sudan. Some families in Sinkat, who are not necessarily Hadendowa, adopt these children. During my fieldwork the question of adoption was raised many times, but women were unwilling to talk about it openly. Five Hadendowa women I interviewed, however, mentioned that they had adopted children. The stories of these women shed light on how they appropriated existing constructs about "proper" fertility and motherhood to give form to their experiences. The case of Nia provides an example of how some women see adoption as a solution for their infertility.

Nia was twenty-five when she married, which is considered relatively old. Her husband was older than she was, and he had been married before and had grown children. Nia said she agreed to marry him because she was "getting old," and he was also well off. She stayed with him for seven years without getting pregnant. Although she tried many herbal medicines and religious healing, she finally lost hope, and her marriage ended in divorce. While attempting to get pregnant, she also began to inquire about adoption, to which her husband objected. After her divorce, however, Nia thought carefully about her situation: she was the only daughter, and her two brothers from her father's side were in a different town. "I did not want to die alone. I wanted to have children whom I could raise properly and enjoy their company and who could take care of me when I need them," she said. This is when she decided to adopt a boy from an orphanage during one of her rare visits to Khartoum. She continued:

> My application was accepted, and I adopted a one-month-old boy. It was difficult to raise him by myself because I had to work. I sell candy and I also sing in ceremonies to support myself. When I went to work, I used to leave my son with my neighbors. My son's health was good, and after two years I went to Port Sudan and decided to take another boy from the orphanage. I raised the two boys very well. After another year a woman from the Beni Amir came to my house with a pregnant woman. She explained her situation to me and asked me if I wanted to adopt the child after his or her birth. I understood what they were going through and agreed that they stay with me one month until the child was born. The woman gave birth safely and left her baby girl with me. Although I am single, I raised the three children alone, but my neighbors helped. Now my children are grown; they all went to school. The two boys are successful in their jobs in Port Sudan, and they send me money every month. My daughter, who is now eighteen, grew up to be so responsible and polite, and she cares so much about me. When I am busy, she is the one who takes care of the house and of kin obligations. Although they are adopted, my children were raised well. People may talk about the fact that they are adopted, but they can't deny the fact that I raised them well. People refer to my children's behavior and not to the fact that they are adopted.

Nia's story, like the other few reported cases of adoption, exemplifies some women's attempts to venture into culturally contested terrain in order to foster their familial network and fulfill their own mothering desires. In negotiating her situation, Nia appropriated the familiar meanings of propriety to show how her children grew up to be well behaved: they foster kinship relationships, succeed in education and marriage, and finally fulfill their duties and obligations toward her. Her sons already are engaged to *balawait* (northern Sudanese) women in Port Sudan. Yet the question of adoption and how it figures into these children's identities, their social acceptance, and into collective identity merits further research.

On *Halafa* Terms: Nur, the *Balawait* Girl

The contestation of familiarity spans other domains of social practice as a new generation of Hadendowa women channel the realms of the foreign and the familiar by appropriating other cultural logic, such as *halafa*, to negotiate their situations. The case of Zainab is a good example of a *tibadai ari* who engaged different medical practices to cure her fertility misfortune using the *halafa* logic of proximity and distance.

Zainab was married to her mother's brother's son, a police officer in Port Sudan. She was eighteen years old when she married, and her husband was twenty-two. Zainab lived with her mother in Sinkat, and her husband commuted to visit her on the weekends. After two years of marriage, Zainab became pregnant and gave birth to a healthy baby girl, who died on the sixth day after her birth. Zainab was shocked because her baby was born healthy. She noticed, however, a plastic bottle of oil (distributed by a relief organization) with the brand name *Chef* in her room where she delivered her baby. She said that one of her sisters had left the bottle in the room by mistake, and that she had always suspected this brand of oil, especially because of the picture of the chef on the bottle, a foreign representation that did evil to her child. She commented, "I abhor this brand, and I always feel that the chef's eyes are so invasive that he is following me around." Zainab became pregnant again a year after the death of her first child and later gave birth to a baby girl, who died as a result of severe vomiting and diarrhea. Zainab and her husband were very sad over the death of their second daughter; however, Zainab became pregnant a year later and gave birth to a third baby girl, who died suddenly when she was twelve months old.

At this point Zainab and her family began to worry about the consequences of these consecutive deaths on her health and her reproductive future. Her mother urged her to consult an Ashraf *faqir* in the area. The *faqir* gave her blessed water to drink and to massage into her lower body in the mornings and evenings. He also gave her *waisl* (written Qur'anic verses) to burn and inhale and advised her to see him again as soon as she became pregnant. A year and a half after the death of her third child, Zainab became pregnant. She went back to the *faqir*, who gave her more blessed water and *waisl* and told her to come back when she was in her seventh month. When she went back, the *faqir* gave her an amulet to wear and to transfer to her child after birth. He also ordered her to confine herself to her house until she gave birth and her child walked and talked, since mobility and boundary crossing could jeopardize her safety and that of her child. Later Zainab safely gave birth to a male child; however, on his fifth day, a neighbor came to congratulate the mother, and she praised the child without mentioning the name of God. According to Zainab's account, the child cried continuously and died later that day.

Zainab was devastated by her son's death and began to question the credibility of the *faqir*'s cures. Under pressure from her mother and sister-in-law, she went back to the same religious man, who prescribed similar cures. When Zainab gave birth to her fifth child, a girl, she decided to combine religious cures with other *halafa* rituals. Thus she gave her daughter a *balawait* (Arabic, northern Sudanese) name, Raja, which means to request or hope for bounty. Using such signs of *balawait*ness to reverse danger and restore health are common among the Hadendowa. Once I mistook one of my Hadendowa friend's father as a Shaiqi (a northern Sudanese group) because of his backward facial marks. When I asked her if she were half Shaiqia, she laughed and told me that these marks were inscribed on her father's face when he was very little, as reversal signs to guarantee his health and survival because his older siblings had died shortly after birth. Her father was the only child to survive.

According to Zainab's sister-in-law, Raja was healthy, but Zainab neglected the advice of the *faqir* and insisted on going with her mother to Haiya, a nearby town, to visit a sick brother before her daughter began to walk and talk. There Raja became very sick with body ulcers and vomiting, and she died a few days later. Raja's body ulcers made her grandmother suspect that she might have contracted *tisaramt*, which is associated with foreignness. At this stage, however, Zainab decided to move to Port Sudan to be near her husband and to consult a doctor.

After one year of medication, Zainab became pregnant and gave birth, for the sixth time, to a female child. Zainab, who was torn between two realms of medical practices, consequently performed a series of *halafa* reversal rituals to ensure her future health and her daughter's survival. Thus, instead of giving birth near her mother as *auslif* dictates, she gave birth near her sister-in-law. This indicates that if she had contracted evil in her mother's vicinity, delivering near her sister-in-law might reverse such danger. Another implied logic in this reversal reasoning, as some women expressed it, is to outsmart the spirit by changing locations and by adopting its own signs to avert its danger. By facial marking a Hadendowa child as a Shaiqi, for instance, the spirit would mistake the child for a northern Sudanese and would refrain from harming him or her. That is, if external power is targeting *auslif,* then by casting someone as a foreigner (through employment of foreign signs), one can confuse the spirit and distract it from achieving its destructive goal. Zainab also bought an urban-style iron bed for her delivery, as opposed to the familiar wooden bed covered with the *mista* (curtain), to divert external danger. Above all, she insisted on performing the *tamnai aurauk* ritual for her daughter. Her neighbors considered what she said a joke, but in response to her persistence, the women gathered and paraded with the female placenta and hung it over the tree. After all that she had gone through, Zainab considered the joy of giving birth to her daughter equivalent to that of bearing a son. By performing the son-birth ritual, Zainab also attempted to reverse the gender of her child and to unbind the evil that may have entered the domestic domain from without. Furthermore, Zainab altered the duration of the naming ceremony from seven to fourteen days, and again she gave her daughter a *balawait* name, Nur, to ensure her survival. Zainab also told me that she would hold a *sunkab* (the groom's marriage ritual) for her daughter as a form of *halafa*. What is significant about the unbinding power of a *halafa* ritual is that it goes backward and forward in time. It can bind evil that befell someone during past life-cycle transitions and can also prevent such evil in the future.

To protect her female child, Zainab not only altered her baby's gender, but she also intended to reverse any future harm that might befall her daughter's fertility on her wedding day, especially during the transitional stage of her wedding, when the groom's family would transfer the *sunkab* bundle to the bride's tent. Inherent in this reversal logic is also a notion of unbinding danger and normalizing states of health through crossing into unfamiliar domains. This is evident in the case of Halima's aforementioned patient, who was diagnosed with a blockage and was thus confined under Halima's supervision. To unbind her infertility, the patient was taken forward in time into the state of pregnancy and giving birth, when her health could be carefully monitored through dieting, smoke bathing, and confinement. This is because blockage caused by the spirits stunts individual "normal" progression into the different life-cycle stages. The crippling effect of blockage can thus be undone through the deployment of ritual power to assist the patient in crossing forward.

Before I left Sinkat, Zainab's daughter was three months old, and to ensure her safety and well-being, Zainab was taking her regularly to the health center to be weighed and checked. When I asked Zainab why she was more committed to "doctors' treatment," as she calls it, she smilingly responded, "Well, this is Nur, the *balawait* girl," indicating that Nur's survival may well lie in medical treatment, a foreign style that Zainab hopes will reverse her fertility predicament. Although Zainab believes that the doctors' treatment may be the best for her health and that of her child, translating such understanding into the *halafa* logic also eases the tensions between her and her older female relatives, some of whom still contest the efficacy of doctors' medicine. "When you say, 'I am using this as *halafa*,' they leave you alone, for it makes sense to them," said Zainab. "Making sense," or fitting the frame of the familiar, indicates how dangerous spirits are met on *halafa* turf in an attempt to restore women's reproductive health and collective well-being. *Halafa* also sheds light on how processes of identity construction, negotiation, and social change take place. It renders *auslif* flexible and allows women such as Zainab and Halima (see my introduction) to explore different medical views to redress their ailments. In the name of *halafa*, foreign identities can be donned and cast away in order to trick the spirit and deflect its danger. Yet, if these novel paths of healing withstand the test of practice, women may even claim their ownership. *Halafa* as a ritual power of unbinding fertility traumas also manifests itself in the context of spirit possession.

Of Baraka, *Halafa*, and Belligerent Jinn: Nisa's Story

As we have seen, women's beliefs in external danger are central to their interpretation of sickness and fertility traumas. Accordingly, many Hadendowa women attribute their reproductive adversity to spirit attacks that control their blood and render them infertile. Previously we have seen that the popular spirit figures among the Hadendowa are black jinn, representing a male character from the Beni Amir group, neighbors to the Hadendowa. Red jinn characters that represent Europeans and Turks possess few women. In recent years the Islamist government banned possession ceremonies as non-Islamic. Therefore, women resort to a series of small, private rituals to avoid arousing the suspicion of government security. During my fieldwork most of the spirit-possession ceremonies I attended were small, and only one ceremony involved drumming. The latter was surrounded by secrecy, and women sent their children out to inform them of any unexpected surveillance.

Differences among women's fertility cures stem from their personal beliefs and preferences. Unlike women who strongly believe in spirit possession, those who believe in the blessing of Khatmiyya saints denounce *ijar* practices as less effective and prefer to undergo religious cures. In healing fertility traumas, however, women assume that many factors are responsible for their ailments, and thus they try multiple medical strategies, especially if one fails. My statistical data show that spirit-possession practices correspond to women's fertility traumas (infertility, miscarriages, and infant deaths) and the number of their living children. Among the eighty-five women interviewed, fourteen (16 percent) reported never having been pregnant. Of those, four reported engaging in *ijar* (spirit possession) practices. The small number is due to the fact that seven women in the never-pregnant category are in their early reproductive years (ages 15–24), while the other seven women are in their middle to late reproductive years (ages 25–34, 35–44).

Moreover, thirty women out of eighty-five reported having had reproductive traumas, of whom five women (17 percent) had no living children; four of this group reported practicing a spirit-possession ritual. Among the fifteen women (50 percent) who had between one and three living children (thirteen in their early to middle reproductive career, and two in their late reproductive career), eight women had practiced the ritual. Moreover, among women who had between four and seven living children, ten women reported fertility mishaps (33 percent), five in their middle reproductive career, and five in their late reproductive career, of whom three reported spirit-possession practice. Although *ijar* practices seem to correspond to fertility traumas and the number of living children women have, the correlation between reproductive mishaps and spirit-possession practices based on the children's gender produced insignificant results. This indicates the women's understanding that such reproductive misfortune taxes bodily quality and negatively affects a woman's fertility potential and her ability to bear and raise healthy children regardless of their gender.

As emphasized earlier, *ijar* practices among Hadendowa women shift the focus from mere conflict between men and women to the more-powerful level of the body politic, where both men and women are implicated in broader relations of power. Such conflicting power dynamics are resolved through *halafa* logic, whose mimetic magic transforms external danger into positive power to substantiate the power within. While the story of Zainab represents the vulnerable fertility situation of *tibadai ari* and how they employ *halafa* logic to undo their reproductive suffering, the case of Nisa, which follows, shows how *halafa* logic is employed in the context of spirit-possession practice. Both Zainab's and Nisa's examples, however, illustrate how women negotiate their fertility predicament with reference to external dangers. They also shed light on women's attempts to manage and restore their health in order to navigate the path to "proper" fertility and responsible motherhood. Nisa's case is also significant in that it reveals how cases of pseudopregnancies are perceived by some local practitioners.

Nisa, a young Hadendowa woman in her twenties, was married to a close relative who worked in a fishery in Sawakin. Her first child was a boy; however, her story of pregnancy and birth took a dramatic twist. When Nisa was five months pregnant, her mother took her to the health center for a checkup, but to their astonishment, the health visitor told them that Nisa was not pregnant and that she might be suffering from a womb infection or a pseudopregnancy, which would require her to consult a specialist in Port Sudan. Nisa's mother said they could not afford to go to Port Sudan, and they preferred to consult an Ashraf *faqiria* in Sinkat.

The *faqiria* opened the Qur'an and told Nisa that she was touched by a *wali's* (saint's) baraka. Because of this blessing, Nisa would give birth to a male child who himself would carry baraka. For Muslim Hadendowa, ba-raka is a positive power (see Douglas 1966) derived from religious people and places. This blessed child, according to the *faqiria*, appeared in his mother's womb for short periods because he was going to Mecca to per-form the pilgrimage. The *faqiria* suggested that Nisa wait and watch her pregnancy. Nisa's mother maintained that she counted two years from the date of her daughter's pregnancy until the day she went into labor. When Nisa's relative took her to the midwife in Sinkat Hospital, she told her that Nisa was truly in labor, and it was their decision whether to have her give birth at the hospital or at home. Fatna, Nisa's mother, preferred that her daughter give birth at home, and Nisa gave birth to a boy whom they named Sidi Al-Hassan after a famous Khatmiyya saint who was buried in Kassala town in eastern Sudan.[4]

Nisa said that Sidi Al-Hassan was born very frail, and after his birth she went into a phase of depression and refused to breast-feed him. Nisa's mother took care of her daughter's son and fed him boiled goat's milk. Because the child cried continuously, Nisa's mother, who was not breast-feeding then, gave him her breast to suckle. After a few weeks, Nisa's mother noticed that she had breast milk, which she attributed to the child's baraka.

When her sickness worsened, Nisa consulted a doctor in Sinkat Hospi-tal, who diagnosed her with malaria, but her condition did not improve after she took the medication. For this reason her mother decided to take her to a female *shaikha* (spirit-possession specialist) in Sinkat. The *shaikha* told them to bring something that was close to Nisa's body such as a neck-lace, a ring, or a strand of hair so that she could diagnose her ailment. Nisa gave the *shaikha* her ring. The *shaikha* then told them that she would put the ring in a separate room where she kept the spirit paraphernalia and where the jinn would descend on her and inform her about Nisa's sickness. When Nisa and her mother came the next day, the *shaikha* told them that Nisa had been struck by an evil eye after her son's birth. This evil eye gave way to black jinn who entered Nisa's body and caused an *arid*, which prevented her from breast-feeding her child. According to the *shaikha*, this was the reason that "doctors' medicine" did not work on Nisa. Accordingly, the *shaikha* ad-vised Nisa to begin the *fak alarid* (ritual of unbinding her blockage).

Nisa described her *ijar* ceremonies and the *halafa* logic inherent in them as engaging both embodied and spatially constructed cultural contrasts. To perform a *fak alarid* ceremony, Nisa and her family had to buy a flawless black he-goat, which Nisa had to tie near her tent before the ceremony.[5] She

---

4. Al-Hassan was also one of the Prophet's twin grandchildren.
5. A he-goat that is healthy and has no defects such as pierced ears, broken horns, legs, and the like.

also prepared hot spices and fragrant incense, such as sandalwood, and wore a black dress underneath a black *fauta* and black sandals. She also put on a *mikhashash* (a golden necklace with a foreign figure charm), a *walag* (silver ring), and a *kulail* (silver bracelet), all of which are worn as protection during wedding rituals. Nisa described the beginning of her ceremony: "On the day of *fak alarid,* the *shaikha* seated me in the middle of a circle of female guests. She burned the fragrant incenses and the spices and passed them over my body, especially between my legs, and over the body of the he-goat. Then we asked a distant male relative to slaughter the he-goat. After that the *shaikha* soaked the golden necklace, the bracelet, and the ring in the blood of the he-goat. She waited until they were dry; she washed them and put them on me."

During the ceremony of untying her blockage, Nisa was referred to as the *tidauba* (bride), signifying the state of taking her back in time to the liminal stage of her wedding. Although the *shaikha* related Nisa's sickness to an evil eye that struck after her son's birth, Hadendowa women believe that such evil can enter the body during any of the different liminal stages of circumcision, wedding, pregnancy, delivery, confinement, breastfeeding, and child development. Evil attacks are always suspected to first occur during weddings; therefore, ailments caused by red spirits afflict mostly married women and are thus associated with fertility. Therefore, Nisa's return to that pristine stage of her fertility meant the beginning of reversing any evil that might have entered her body at that juncture. Contrary to Boddy's (1989) analysis, it is *halafa*'s temporal backward-forward capacity to undo harm that better describes why *ijar* ceremonies play on wedding metaphors in the Hadendowa context.

To untie Nisa's blockage, a he-goat was brought into the scene as a symbol of foreignness that was the reverse of her world in terms of gender, color, and species. Hadendowa women perceive animals not only as part of the spirit world but also as mediums for transmitting foreign ailments. By rubbing the back of the he-goat at the beginning of her ceremony, Nisa was able to come into proximity with the spirit that endangered her fertility, a crucial stage in reconciling their conflicting powers. The ritual act of killing the animal and shedding its blood that followed signified Nisa's attempt to achieve mastery over the dangerous power that had afflicted her during her wedding. The ritual blood of a foreign reproductive realm, shed by a distant male relative, is contrasted with Nisa's own fertility blood.

This *halafa* logic also manifested itself in the ritual act of soaking the jewelry in the animal's blood. This logic demonstrates that women view gold and silver not only as precious ornaments and a sign of wealth (see Boddy 1989; Inhorn 1994) but also as foreign resources manufactured by men and bought from town centers or from the neighboring "foreign" Rashaida

Ijar silver jewelry with red and black-and-white beads

nomads. Accordingly, most spirit-possession jewelry is characterized by foreign figures such as *katim aljinaiyh almasri* (Arabic for the Egyptian pound's ring), and the most popular one among possessed Hadendowa women is that which represents the figure of King George VI. It is worth noting that King George VI visited Sinkat in 1911 on his way from India to pay homage to the British and Egyptian soldiers killed during the reign of the Mahadia (Ibrahim 1990). It is not far-fetched to suggest that such historical events remain in Hadendowa collective memory and their social imagination of foreignness.

To depollute Nisa's blood, the *shaikha* soaked the spirit jewelry in the animal's blood, the opposite to that of Nisa, and then dried and washed it, in an attempt to reverse Nisa's ailment before Nisa wore the jewelry close to her body. This act of drying also evokes the ritual action of drying the palm fronds for making the tent mats and the *sunkab* during marriage rituals. Wet versus dry here stands in opposition in order to reflect the danger of external influences versus the power of the domestic social space. The *shaikha* followed this healing reversal by marking boundaries on Nisa's vulnerable body parts with the same animal blood. She applied blood to Nisa's forehead, the front boundary of the head and the face that contains the eyes, and to her chin, the lower boundary of the head and the face that contains the nose and the mouth. The *shaikha* also marked Nisa's knees, the boundary between the thigh and the shin, and the big toes, the extremities of the feet or the lower body. The Hadendowa pay close attention to the nose as a medium of transmitting smells that may have a positive or negative impact on the body's well-being (cf. Boddy 1989). While fragrant smells enhance good health, repulsive smells are dangerous to wellness since they irritate and invite jinn. The association of porous boundaries, evil jinn, and misfortune is also expressed with reference to the legs. Hadendowa women believe that the lower body is associated with sexuality, reproduction, and mobility and hence with jinn and boundary crossing. The same danger is related to the mouth, the medium of transforming food into good health. Food, especially milk, is a vital source of growth that can invite the evil eye and evil spirits if consumed in public.

By the end of the *fak alarid* ceremony, Nisa had to change her black clothes, symbols of reconciliation with her foreign black spirit, clean her body and hair, and rebraid her hair; she was then reborn into the normative state of healthy beings. Her transformation was not complete, however, since she had to perform the drumming ceremony to cure her sickness. This, in her view, explained why her discontent spirit attacked again, as manifested in the death of her second son.

Nisa said that she felt much better after her blockage ceremony and began to breast-feed her son. When her son was eighteen months old, she became pregnant again. Her pregnancy went well, and she gave birth to another boy. When he was two years old, her second son became very sick with vomiting and diarrhea, and he died shortly afterward. Nisa fell sick again, and the *shaikha* told her that the evil eye and black jinn were responsible for her second son's death. She advised her to perform the step after *fak alarid,* a similar but more elaborate ceremony called *qaila* (an early afternoon ceremony). Nisa, with the help of her mother, husband, and relatives, was able to collect the money to perform the *qaila.*

The *qaila* is more elaborate in that it includes more expensive and foreign commodities such as cigarettes, incense, spices, and perfumes such as "Soir de Paris," "Fleur D'amour,"[6] sandalwood, *adani* (referring to Aden in Yemen) frankincense, and pepper, which are brought into the healing scene as powerful elements of contrast to ward off exterior evil. Since Hadendowa women perceive jinn as hot spiritual beings associated with and pleased by extravagant commodities and fragrant smells, the healing process plays on signs of proximity and distance to restore communal health.

6. Known in Northern Sudan as *Suwar Paris, filair damaur,* and *alsarawkh* (meaning "the missile," referring to the shape of the container). Some Hadendowa women also refer to it as *alsarawkh.*

Such reverse logic is also evident in eating raw meat versus cooked food, and in drinking an even versus odd number of small *finjan* (cups) of coffee during the *qaila* ceremony. Possessed women smoke cigarettes and eat the raw kidney of the he-goat, while women who are not possessed abstain from smoking and eat only cooked food. Normally, the Hadendowa drink an odd number of *finjan*s of coffee with sugar and spices. In contrast possessed women drink only one *finjan* or a *finjan* and a half during the ceremony. Drinking one *finjan* of coffee bodes ill for one's health and may result in infertility because the number one signals loneliness. Drinking three, five, or seven *finjan*s, however, is used as reverse remedy to protect healthy fertility, symbolized by even numbers.

Nisa, who was cast as a marginal other in this healing scene, had to be brought into the state of normative health not only through what she took in through her body but also through the enactment of cultural contrasts in her spatial surroundings. She was seated in the middle of female guests, surrounded by possessed women in the inner circle and nonpossessed women in the outer circle. While possessed women, including the *shaikha*, were guided by a threatening spirit logic during the ceremony, nonpossessed women were guided by a cultural logic whose presence was meant to counteract danger and restore health.

At the end of the ceremony, Nisa's spirit was also offered a cooked feast as an act of reconciliation between the human and the spirit domains. In the end the *shaikha* advised Nisa not to cross certain boundaries at sunset and not to attend death ceremonies. Death, in contrast to circumcision, marriage, and giving birth, is a transition from human life to a nonearthly domain (e.g., Delaney 1991; Inhorn 1994).

Hadendowa women's anxieties about danger and disease are evident in Nisa's ailments and treatments. Nisa's ill health, which was caused by an evil eye from a socially proximate woman, exposed her to the exterior danger of black jinn. Because of the multiple dangers of evil eye, *tisaramt*, and red jinn, most women protect themselves and their children by wearing several amulets, fish bones (in the case of children), and silver and seashell necklaces. Nisa, for instance, also visited the Khatmiyya tombs in Sinkat with her mother and sister to seek blessings. During these visits they offered money as a *karama* (sacrifice) and asked the saints to protect them and their children from evil. Nisa's mother said that by offering money they were also asking the saints to lift them from poverty.

As constructions of gender and honor articulate meanings of "proper" fertility and responsible motherhood, women's narratives and rituals of fertility and son-birth shift the focus from discriminatory healthcare practices among male and female children (see Croll 2001) to add a new layer of intragender dynamics in which women themselves are differentiated by virtue of their corporeal ability to bear and raise healthy, successful children, especially sons. Such differentiation manifests itself in the social tensions among women of different fertility situations and in the various practices and strategies they use to protect their fertility and to cure their infertility. These practical strategies are means through which women negotiate, contest, and seek empowerment in relation to an ideal fertility. Women's ritual dramas as a technique of power (Foucault 1980; Comaroff and Comaroff 1993) can thus be seen as sites for constructing gender identities and negotiating agency constraints through the experiences of childbearing and child rearing. Just as meanings of interiority and exteriority are deployed through the *halafa* ritual power to maintain physical integrity and social well-being, they also reveal the limit of familiarity and the flexibility of *auslif* practices. Through their spatially embodied practices, women are constructing new meanings of gender and reproduction and engaging novel ideas about a foreign world that is constantly impinging on their ability to fulfill their prescribed gender roles.

Chapter 5

Precarious Trajectories

Managing Reproductive Suffering

And we have charged man concerning his parents—his
mother bore him in weakness upon weakness, and his
weaning was in two years—be thankful to me, and to thy
parents; to me is the homecoming.

Qur'an

Fertility and motherhood are not simple biological matters; they are
contested concepts through which different categories of women strive to
attain social status and security. Women's reproductive practices and discourses are centered mostly around the perception of healthy fertility trajectories to ensure safe pregnancies and births. Bearing live children is not
the only viable outcome of fertility, nor is fertility a linear trajectory bound
by biological concepts of time. Rather, fertility is a "spatially threatened
corporeality" that consists of the precarious episodes of pregnancy, delivery, confinement, breast-feeding, and child rearing, all of which are in-
fused with perceptions of well-timed bodily investments that can affect a
woman's fertility outcome and increase or decrease her chances of achieving the status of responsible motherhood. Since these episodes are inherently precarious, a woman's ultimate fertility outcome is evaluated by
her ability to invest in her health and that of her children in order to transcend the danger embedded in each reproductive stage. Although women's

ultimate fertility outcome is determined by God, who assigns them an
a priori number of potential children (see Bledsoe, Banja, and Hill 1998),
it is also spatially threatened by internal and external forces of danger
that work against God's will to impair women's fertility and render them
marginal.

Accordingly, Hadendowa women gauge fertility by their investment in
the health and success of each pregnancy and later by the productive and
reproductive careers of their children. I first focus on Hadendowa women's
perceptions of reproductive health and their management of bodily traumas. These spatially embodied experiences speak to Hadendowa gender arrangements and to broader concepts of identity and regeneration. I then
analyze two case studies to examine women's fertility strategies and their
continuous efforts to attain the status of "proper" fertility and motherhood
as expressed through the intertwined constructs of childbearing and child
rearing, in a region where maternal and child health are at stake.

Threatened Reproductivity

The path to "proper" fertility and motherhood begins with the onset of
pregnancy within marriage, which is considered the legitimate arena for
initiating a woman's fertility. Fertility, as manifested in pregnancy and its
concomitant episodes, is at risk if not carefully managed through good nutrition and protected from the evil eye, dangerous spirits, and mysterious diseases. Therefore, a woman conceals her pregnancy during the first
months from distant relatives who may cast the evil eye upon her and cause
a miscarriage. The central role of mothers as reproducers of cultural knowledge is reflected in their active role in monitoring their daughter's pregnancies and providing her with the right food, amulets, and herbal medicine
that protect both the daughter and her fetus.

Pregnancy

Resting the body and strengthening the bones of the pregnant woman and
her unborn child are central to Hadendowa ideas of a mother's and her
child's well-being. Therefore, a pregnant woman is not allowed to do taxing
chores that stress her body and may lead to a difficult pregnancy. Meat,
milk, 'ajwa (soft dates), and butter are the basic components of pregnant
women's nutritious diet. Amna (age fifty) commented that before the famine and the current economic situation, husbands used to slaughter sheep
for their pregnant wives. She added, "But we still try to do everything we
can to nourish a pregnant woman."

While milk and meat, especially spleen and kidneys, are considered important for revitalizing the blood of both the pregnant woman and her fetus, butter is necessary for strengthening their bones during the first four months of pregnancy; it also facilitates delivery. Fatna (age sixty) explained that a child whose mother consumes butter during her pregnancy would be delivered easily, emerging clean with "no blood, no scratches or deformities." During the last trimester, butter becomes insignificant and must be replaced with soft dates, taken with milk to continue the revitalization of the body. Due to their healing power, soft dates are taken during the last months of pregnancy, when the bones of the child and the mother are said to be stronger. 'Ajwa are usually imported from Arabia and sold in the market in small packages. A woman's diet during the early months of pregnancy also includes certain herbs, usually extracted from jinn-inhabited trees, to be taken as a precautionary measure against the mysterious disease of *tisaramt* and to prevent miscarriage, sickness, and infant death. As previously mentioned, *tisaramt* is perceived as a foreign disease transmitted through livestock and products that have crossed into Hadendowa territory from neighboring groups. Thus contact with such foreign animals and products can endanger a woman's pregnancy. Because of the danger that boundary transgression poses to procreation, pregnant women are believed to be in a liminal stage, and therefore they must take extra precautions in addition to dieting. Women, especially pregnant women, believe that they are susceptible to *tisaramt* and spirit attacks if they bathe or uncover their heads and breasts during boundary transgression, mainly at sunset (the boundary between day and night), and when they cross dry water streams that divide Hadendowa residences from the town center. The head, containing the porous boundaries of the eyes, the nose, and the mouth, and the breasts, the media of child nourishment, are essential body parts that women should protect and cover during boundary crossing (see chapter 4).

During the third trimester, a pregnant woman uses frequent smoke baths made with certain fragrant woods, such as *talih (Acacia seyal)* and *shaf (Cymbopogon proximus)*, to rest and relax her body. Janice Boddy (1989) has eloquently examined the significance of smoke bathing with reference to notions of beauty and the creation of female persons in northern Sudan. Hadendowa women, however, incorporate ideas of sickness, danger, and well-being into their meaning of smoke bathing. According to the women interviewed, smoke bathing during the first months of pregnancy is dangerous because the fetus is said to be fragile and can be miscarried as a result of excessive heat. Women burn the fragrant wood in a pit dug in the ground while the pregnant woman sits on a stool over the hole, covering her body with a heavy blanket. Sweating heavily as a result of exposure to the smoke signifies the effectiveness of the bath in relaxing her body and freeing it from *imbarar*, which causes infections and ultimately leads to infertility. The women's explanation of hot and cold bodily states resonates well with the classical description of Greco-Islamic humoral medicine and its distinction between hot versus cold essences of health and disease. Cold diseases, for instance, are caused by ingesting cold food and exposing oneself to cold environments and thus can be treated by applying hot media (see Jacobsen 1998). The meanings of such contrasts, however, incorporate a broader realm of ideas about prophetic medicine and interpretations of foreignness and its danger to regeneration.

Not until her third trimester can a pregnant woman take long walks to prepare her body and bones for a safe delivery. The risks surrounding pregnancy are observed with caution and fear. In such a marginal economy, where infant mortality is high, health services are out of reach, and even ethnomedical practices are sometimes unaffordable, Hadendowa women perceive the experience of giving birth as being closer to death than to life. Thus giving birth, like other life-cycle events, entails a symbolic transformation that marks this stage as dangerously liminal. As previously mentioned, women's hairstyles signify the different stages of their life cycle. The *shadat* hairstyle, which denotes a woman's marital status and her childlessness, and the *saulit* hairstyle, which represents marital status and motherhood, are changed into the *maryaub* hairstyle to prepare a pregnant woman for delivery. Unlike her previous hairstyles, which are characterized by tiny braids and meticulous decoration, the *maryaub* consists of big, unembellished braids. The *maryaub* signifies the state of risk during delivery because it is believed that since a woman is closer to death than to life, upon her death one can undo her big braids faster to prepare her for a quick burial according to Islamic convention. This practice indicates that the deceased is a good Muslim who aspires to meet with God sooner. Although such preparation may seem morbid, its explanation must be sought in people's certainties about matters of life and death.

Most women interviewed described giving birth as risky and physically painful. However, they considered a woman' inability to bear the pain of labor as a sign of her incapacity to take the risk of becoming a devoted mother. Social ideas about taking risks and tolerating pain and hardship are inculcated into processes of socialization, meanings of honor and courage, and the struggle for survival. Socializing men and women into adulthood entails inflicting physical pain to test their stoicism and courage. Forty-five-year-old Nafisa explained that by undertaking the pain of labor, a woman demonstrates her courage and ability to shoulder the arduous task of bearing and raising children (cf. Sargent 1990). Although many women adhere to this explanation, others maintain that women should endure the pain of labor because pregnancy and childbirth are related to sexuality and must be concealed.

This association among pain, stoicism, and virtuous womanhood was manifested in the case of a difficult delivery I attended at Sinkat Hospital. The female patient (Fatma) was approximately sixteen years old, and it was her first pregnancy. She and her family lived in the rural area of Arkawait, fifteen miles away from Sinkat town. When Fatma's labor was prolonged, her family decided to bring her to the hospital. After her admission, she had to wait for the doctor to arrive from Port Sudan. Usually there are one or two doctors in Sinkat Hospital during the year who also undertake training in the Port Sudan hospital. When I entered the room, Fatma was lying on a table surrounded by two midwives, who alternated massaging her belly and holding her hands. I was astonished at how a young woman, a child by my standards, could endure such pain and distress without even moaning. The doctor arrived after two hours and decided to perform a Cesarean section. I was later informed that Fatma's child, a boy, had died a few minutes after the operation. Moreover, her prolonged labor had resulted in a fistula that would endanger her reproductive career if not urgently treated in Port Sudan or Khartoum, which seemed unlikely.

Certainly, it was a bad omen for young Fatma to begin her reproductive life with such a crisis, one that might result in her divorce. While I was sitting outside with her family waiting for the doctor, her mother cried and blamed the mother in-law, who was also present, saying that her son, Fatma's husband, had delayed taking her daughter to the hospital. This is not an unusual reaction from husbands and families since trips to the hospital are expensive and can exhaust their resources. Although the attitude of the rural Hadendowa toward the hospital, as a foreign institution, is ambivalent, it is considered a last resort when survival is at stake. While Fatma's mother accused the husband and his mother of negligence, the mother-in-law defended her son, saying that Fatma was struck by an evil eye because of her healthy pregnancy. Such an exchange of accusations is typical when women's reproductive potential is at risk.

Delivery and Confinement

Delivery is another significant reproductive stage that shapes Hadendowa women's fertility outcomes. Delivering a child safely, regardless of its gender, is seen as a blessing. After delivery follows the important stage of mending the wear and tear on the mother's body through rest and good nutrition and by protecting the mother and child from danger. During this fertility stage, both the mother and her child are considered liminal and therefore are separated from others by the *mista* (curtain). Not until seven days after delivery have elapsed can the mother talk to, greet, or see her female neighbors. Women gave different explanations for the relationship between silence and safety. Some emphasized the significance of the mouth as a medium of transforming food, whose susceptibility to external danger, especially during the first days of liminality, may harm the health of the mother and her child. Food is essential to health and regeneration and should be protected and eaten in privacy. Other women related silence to respect and to praising God and the ancestors for a safe delivery.

During the forty-day confinement period, both the mother and her child are said to be susceptible to dangerous spirits. Women perceive the blood of childbirth as reproductive waste associated with uncleanliness and malicious jinn. To protect the mother and child from such danger, the Qur'an is suspended from the roof of the room, a sword is placed behind the mother's bed, and a spear is hung in front of the entrance. Both the sword and the spear are men's fighting weapons that are believed to ward off external danger. Men are the guards of the domestic space (the locus of fertility and growth), which is under assault by external influences. According to the *halafa* logic of social proximity and distance, men's weaponry is brought into the domestic space as a symbol of contrast to normalize the danger of the outside. The husband, however, is not allowed to enter his wife's tent or to touch his baby until the end of the confinement period, when the mother washes and enters her normal social life anew. Since men are associated with the foreign social space, they themselves represent a source of danger to their children and to the fertility of their wives in this liminal stage.

Another powerful protection during the confinement period is the *imidraq,* the wood fire situated in front of the tent's entrance that burns for forty days. Previously I explained how women associated fire with the power of regeneration and the transformation of men's and women's labor into nourishment for growth. Fire is also considered a natural element that is domesticated by women and men to ward off exterior evil. This belief underlies the Hadendowa's symbolic distinction between raw and cooked food. While dangerous spirits can easily contaminate raw substances such as milk, cooked and fermented food is seen as less susceptible to danger. Cooked food such as porridge, for instance, is treated as a domestic product that counteracts external danger as manifested in the custom of spreading porridge over the entrance and exterior of the confinement tent for protection. Porridge is made of dura, which is cultivated by men or bought by them in the market and cooked by women to be eaten with raw or fermented milk. Moreover, the combination of fire and incense is part of most fertility ceremonies, whose focal point is the protection of women's and men's procreative power from dangerous influences.

The *imidraq* derives its power from the fire generated by the red *kamaub* (*Maerua crassifolia*) wood. Women who come to congratulate the mother must stop by the *imidraq* fire before they enter her room and must greet her from behind a curtain in order not to touch her or her baby. The significance of the *imidraq* and its relevance to the Hadendowa conceptualization of fertility and regeneration manifests itself in the many narratives that women relate about external spirits and the threat they pose to Hadendowa mothers and their newly born children, especially sons. A senior Hadendowa woman related this popular narrative:

> Once upon the time there were two men, a Hadendowi and a stranger, who met along the road and decided to travel together. The stranger was riding a horse and the Hadendowi was walking by his side. During their journey they saw an *imidraq* in front of a tent, and they knew there was a woman who had just given birth. The stranger ordered his companion to put out the fire of the *imidraq* so that he could steal the child. The companion agreed reluctantly, and the stranger went in and stole the child. They continued their journey, the stranger and the child on the horse and the companion walking by their side. Along the way the horse tripped and the Hadendowi said *bismillahi* [in the name of God].[1] The man on the horse reprimanded him and ordered him not to mention the name of God in his presence lest he spoil his mission. The horse tripped again, and the Hadendowi mentioned the name of God. When he repeated the name of God for the third time, the stranger and his horse disappeared, leaving the little child behind. The Hadendowa man then raised the child in his village, and after a few years he decided to return him to his family. When the Hadendowi arrived at the child's village, he asked his family if they had a missing son. The father confirmed that they had had a son, a child who was constantly sick, and he had finally died during the time specified by the man. The man then said to the father, "What if I bring your son back?" The family did not believe him at first, but the man told them about the jinn who had deceived him along the road and made him put out the *imidraq* fire so that he could steal the child. The family believed the man and confirmed that the *imidraq* fire had been found extinguished, which resulted in the sickness and death of their son.

The *imidraq* story evokes the notion of external danger as it is mediated by Hadendowa men during travel and boundary transgression. In this story the horse, which is foreign to the Hadendowa, who raise camels, cows, and other domestic animals, is also associated with Turkish and British colonial officers and soldiers who have subjugated the Hadendowa under the rubric of colonial rule. This relationship of dominance is apparent in the senior woman's description of the stranger riding the horse while the Hadendowa

---

1. The name of God is mentioned as protection, especially in situations of unforeseen danger that are believed to be caused by jinn.

man walked by his side. Deceived by his superior, the Hadendowa man re-luctantly accepted the suggestion to extinguish the fire, which resulted in the sickness and death of the child.

Very young children are said to be marginal and not fully socialized into the collectivity. This marginality puts them at the risk of being kidnapped by the spirits or suckled by owls (which represent female spirits) that invade their bodies and result in their handicapping, sickness, and death.

Children undergo various protective rituals at birth to ensure their proper socialization and therefore their survival and future success. They are first socialized into the faith of Islam by calling the *azan* (call for prayers) into their ears. They are then bathed in warm water to rid their bodies of cold diseases that might affect their potential fertility (especially for girls) and future health. The bathing water is mixed with powerful herbs such as frankincense, black cumin, black caraway, and *adal awat* powder.[2] While frankincense and black cumin are believed to purify and protect the child's body from the evil eye and evil jinn, *adal awat* prevents the mysterious disease *tisaramt*. Other protective measures include Qur'anic amulets. Overall, socialization begins in the womb, and Hadendowa male children, as the wedding song in chapter 3 asserts, learn the meanings of courage when very young and even before they are born.

Socializing children into the faith of Islam is significant to the construction of children's identities. The *imidraq* narrative speaks to this question of identity, especially when the Hadendowa man refused to submit to the stranger, who ordered him not to profess his Islamic beliefs. Had the Hadendowa man not mentioned the name of God, the stranger/jinn would have led him astray. The popular narrative affirms the significance of the *imidraq* in protecting fertility, and also highlights the Hadendowa's consciousness of their historic past and their struggle to maintain their identity in the face of different forces of dominance and cultural hegemonies.

The forty days of confinement are also significant for enhancing the health of both the mother and the child. Just as pregnancy taxes bodily energy, Hadendowa women believe that childbirth is an arduous task that weakens women's bones and blood. During delivery women's bodies are also said to be open to attacks by spirits and to cold diseases that cause womb infections. Thus the forty days of confinement are essential for resting the body and releasing it from cold through a nutritious diet and the medicinal mixtures of butter, date juice, *hargal (Solenostemma argel)*, cinnamon, and black pepper. To restore her energy, the mother also eats warm food such as porridge with soup or milk. Such a diet is also important for

---

2. Black cumin is described in prophetic medicine as the black grain *(alhaba alsawda)*.

increasing her breast milk. Good nutrition and protection from evil thus go hand in hand in achieving a healthy reproductive path for both the mother and her children. Her sons' success is measured by their immunity to evil diseases that might hamper their future productive and reproductive careers. The same applies to girls, who can inherit their mother's reproductive mishaps and end up with precarious fertility trajectories.

Although there are no apparent discriminatory health practices for male and female children, women emphasize other gender differentiation specific to the duration of the mother's confinement period. In the case of male children, the rest period can be extended to two months, as opposed to forty days in the case of female infants. According to one woman this is because "giving birth to a boy is more arduous than giving birth to a girl. Boys have heavier bones and it takes more energy to carry and deliver them. Girls, however, are lighter and take less energy to birth. Forty days are, therefore, enough for the mother to regain her health and strengthen her bones."

Such gender differentiation is also evident during pregnancy. A woman who feels heavier and experiences dry skin during pregnancy is believed to be pregnant with a boy, while a woman who feels lighter, looks prettier, and has moist skin is said to be pregnant with a female child. These gender presumptions conform to women's contrasting ideas about the male and female body and about men's and women's assigned gender roles.

Breast-feeding

Investing in children's health continues with breast-feeding. The forty-day confinement period is also a significant fertility stage during which a mother-child bond is established through breast milk. Previously I mentioned how ideas about honor and motherhood are expressed through perceptions of milk and blood as essential substances that signify kinship relations and gender asymmetries. Women often explain concepts of male bravery, generosity, and good manners in terms of honorable qualities transmittable through breast milk. This process of creating honorable persons begins with sexual intercourse, the intermixing of milk and blood in the womb. Since sexual intercourse is a life-creating moment that can be endangered by internal and external forces, touching the wife's breasts during sexual intercourse can jeopardize her potential life-giving breast milk. The interflow of milk and blood inside the woman's womb creates the fetus and later transforms into breast milk to nourish the child after birth.

Although milk is a "feminine" substance that generates life and health, in essence Hadendowa believe that it is a "masculine" product controllable by men. This paradox is evident in the milking taboo, which denotes gender asymmetries and the ambivalent meanings attributed to motherhood.

According to this taboo, women are not allowed to milk animals, a task that is considered exclusively male. The rigorousness of this taboo is expressed in women's comments that they would not milk animals even if their children were to die from hunger. According to Halima (age fifty-five), the taboo is an *auslif*, which is not rooted in Islamic orthodoxy. She maintained, "We all know that Fatima, the daughter of Prophet Muhammad, milked goats." She grimaced. "I do not know how you can drink milk that is milked by women," she added and spat. To reinforce this taboo mothers reprimand their little daughters when they touch a goat's or sheep's udders, an action that is considered shameful.

This milking taboo also evokes the sexual division of labor. Milking animals occurs at sunset when men return to their households. In the absence of the husband, however, sons or other male relatives can milk animals for household consumption. The wife leaves the milk container outside her tent for her husband or male relatives. When the milk is brought home, a child sips from it before the husband and his wife, and the rest of the milk can then be used for household consumption. *Asulif* dictates that the immediate use of the milk prior to its consumption by a child would bring *sa'am* (misfortune) to the household in the form of infertility, children's sickness, and mortality. Women explain the milking taboo with reference to the sacredness of milk and to women's vulnerability because of their susceptibility to spirit attacks that target their fertility blood and render them unclean. This embodied danger is feared to contaminate the milk at the moment of its transfer from the animal's breast to the woman's milking pot, an exchange that evokes the sexual transfer of a man's semen into the woman's womb to create a child. This fear of contamination also persists when the mother's milk leaves her breast to feed her child. If breast milk accidentally drips onto the ground, it is believed to attract dangerous spirits that risk the health of the mother and her child. These symbolic exchanges of milk and blood speak to the dual relationship of power and vulnerability associated with motherhood, and their meanings cannot be disentangled from broader schemes of producing gender and kinship relations.

Breast-feeding is a significant reproductive stage, for mothers must breast-feed their children exclusively for two years. Although some women may breast-feed their children longer, most of the women interviewed specified the maximum of two years as the duration recommended in the Qur'an. After two years mothers can introduce their children to other kinds of food, especially butter, milk, and porridge. As a contraceptive strategy, some women maintain that they refrain from sexual intercourse during the two-year breast-feeding period. Many women, however, stressed that they breast-feed "cleanly," indicating that they are amenorrheic while breast-feeding. They believe that getting pregnant during the two-year breast-feeding period makes the suckling child sick and may lead to infant mortality, for which the mother would be blamed. Therefore, she should refrain from sexual intercourse if her menses have resumed.

In demographic studies, practices such as prolonged breast-feeding or postpartum abstinence are sometimes interpreted as manifestations of "natural fertility" if they are not accompanied by deliberate birth control to limit family size (see Bulatao 1981; Bledsoe et al. 1994). In contrast, Hadendowa women consider breast-feeding a viable strategy by which they can regulate their fertility and manage their health as well as that of their children. Most women adhere to the belief that birth control methods are foreign to their *auslif* practices and may interfere with their bodily capacity by causing infertility and other diseases. Birth control methods, especially the pill, are available at the hospital and are prescribed by doctors and midwives. Forty-one women (out of eighty-five women interviewed) responded to my question, "What kind of birth control are you using?" by saying, "We breast-feed cleanly." Thus I had to rephrase my question to, "What kind of birth control other than 'breast-feeding cleanly' are you using?" For Hadendowa women it is clear that constructing fertility around the ideology of healthy reproductive trajectories has made breast-feeding and other protective measures deliberate acts by which women attempt to improve their chances of having more surviving children, especially sons. Abstaining, prolonging breast-feeding, eating a nutritious diet, resting the body, and protecting the different fertility episodes from evil are significant for ensuring a successful fertility trajectory.

Women thus consciously draw a distinction between breast-feeding and abstinence—contraceptives that do not disrupt their flow of "milk and blood"—and birth control methods, which are engineered techniques that can meddle with their bodily integrity and cause sickness. To take this distinction further, some women draw a fascinating contrast between the color of the birth control pills available at the hospital, white and red, which arouse their doubts about negative effects on their milk and blood. When I inquired about the red tablet, the midwife suggested that the women might be referring to the iron deficiency tablets that are sometimes prescribed, with the pill, for women with menstrual irregularities. Scholars such as Luise White have noted how Western medical practices in colonial Africa have been subject to cultural translation against existing health and disease etiologies (White 2000).

Birth control methods are also associated with the "immodesty" of *balawait* (urban northern Sudanese) and Western lifestyles. Since the famine of the 1980s, migrant Hadendowa women have been targets of educational efforts by many national and international women's groups, which instruct them about income generation, eradication of female circumcision, fertility

Mothering

regulation, and the adoption of "proper" hygiene and childcare practices. These groups include NGOs, Ahafad College for Women in Khartoum, and health visitors (senior midwives) at Sinkat Hospital, whose educational program is sponsored by the Ministry of Health.

In the face of such an ideational influx, Hadendowa women carefully listen to and observe these educators with mixed feelings of acceptance and mistrust. During one of the education sessions given by some female graduates from Khartoum about circumcision and family planning, women expressed their perplexity by giggling and covering their faces modestly. Fatumab (age fifty-five), whom I talked to after the session, exclaimed that "Khartoum girls" found no shame in preaching to them about issues considered taboo to discuss in public spaces. Issues concerning circumcision and birth control involve sexuality and should not be addressed openly. To justify her argument, Fatumab maintained that "Khartoum girls" are against circumcision and for contraceptives because they are "sexually lax, and they use contraceptives to prevent pregnancy in order to engage in premarital affairs." Fatumab's comments, however, do not represent the views of all women, because ideas about social change and alternative systems of health and medicine are constantly challenged and debated by both the old and the new generations.

Two Reproductive Trajectories

The following stories of Adraut and Kauata further explain the concept of "healthy fertility trajectories" and women's continuous efforts to manage their reproductive suffering in order to bear and raise successful children, especially sons.

Tired of Childbirth: Adraut's Story

Forty-seven-year-old Adraut was from the Imairab lineage, which assumes ownership of the Sinkat area. Adraut was born and raised in a poor household in one of the old shanty settlements at the outskirts of the town's center. Her father was a *faqir,* and her mother was known to be possessed by *ijar.* The fact that Adraut's mother had ended her reproductive career with three daughters and no sons seems to underlie the belief that she is possessed by *ijar.* As the oldest daughter, Adraut married her mother's father's brother's son (classified as a paternal cousin), who was working as an *askari* (soldier) in Port Sudan. He was twenty-five when he married Adraut. Working as a government employee in the city gave him a social status different from that of his father and grandfathers, who were predominantly pastoralists. Thus Adraut was promised a social status different from that of her mother's generation. She described how happy her mother was that by her marriage she had also gained a son-in-law who would be like her own son. A good husband, as we have seen, is one whose responsibility goes beyond his immediate family to include his in-laws as well. Since Adraut's mother had no sons, her joy over her daughter's marriage was ineffable.

When she married, Adraut had not reached menarche. According to *auslif* she had to stay one year (two years for other Hadendowa lineages) with her mother before she moved to her own house.[3] After the year had passed, she moved to her own *bukar* near her mother. One year after her first menstrual cycle, she became pregnant with her first child. Adraut reported having been very scared but happy that she was having a child, which would please her husband and family. Her pregnancy was well monitored, and she safely gave birth to a female child. Although she wished to

---

3. The logic behind this customary practice is to allow the bride to gain more training and knowledge about her wifely duties and to ease the transition to her new marital life. Some women also maintain that the bride may become pregnant during this transition, which necessitates her stay with her mother, who would help manage her first pregnancy. Moreover, a woman's pregnancy is also proof of her fertility, which would strengthen her marital position in her new household.

begin her reproductive career with the birth of a son, Adraut said she had to accept God's will. She also maintained that she loved girls herself and that she cherished their companionship and care. She did not wish, however, to inherit her mother's *ijar* and end her reproductive career with daughters only.

After the birth of her first daughter, Adraut commuted between Sinkat and Port Sudan, where her husband worked. In Port Sudan she lived in her own *bukar*, located in Daim Al'Arab, a poor residential area occupied by Beja and other lower-income classes. When her daughter was two years old, Adraut became pregnant again and immediately stopped breast-feeding, as breast-feeding during pregnancy is considered harmful to the health of the mother and her fetus. Shortly before Adraut returned home to give birth near her mother, her daughter died of smallpox. Adraut said that she took her daughter to the hospital in Port Sudan but that did not save her. She returned to Sinkat with a broken heart to deliver her second child.

Adraut's sadness over her daughter's death was soon overcome by the birth of her first son, Muhammad, who filled the family with joy. They celebrated his birth with all possible means, slaughtering animals and dancing the *bibaub*. Adraut said that she received more gifts from her husband and family than she had when she gave birth to her late daughter. She commented that the economy was much better in the sixties and seventies, and therefore giving birth to a male child was well celebrated.

The oldest son is a source of support for his parents, especially in raising his younger siblings. Thus Adraut tailored her dreams and expectations around her son's future. Since urban jobs are more prosperous than nomadism, Adraut hoped that Muhammad would advance in education and compete with the *balawait* in securing a good job in the city. She expressed her hopes in this lullaby, which she sang for her little son (the song is phrased in both Arabic and Tu-Badawie):

Ya qalbi inta alsabab ya qalbi laih	O my heart, you are agonizing [She is longing for her son, who moved to work in Port Sudan.]
Sinkatai dahaia katau ana Muhammad daiatau	I traveled from Sinkat to see Muhammad in Port Sudan.
Bawarsib ifaslib sana taltha irhininhaib, ya qalbi	[In the city] he is seen [by his relatives] studying in high school. He is in third grade, O my heart.
Muhammad shaqamia banki rais ikwasinain, ya qalbi	Muhammad is appointed a bank manager, O my heart.

Waira sauqi bijamaib silaili irhininhaib, ya qalbi	He is seen praying in the grand mosque [in Port Sudan].
Muhammad shagamia telephonjib ik-wasinain, ya qalbi	Muhammad is appointed to work in the telephone company, O my heart.
Muhammad shaqamia caumaundan ik-wasinain, ya qalbi	Muhammad is appointed [police or army] commander, O my heart.
Muhammad shaqamia baladi kintin ik-wasinain, ya qalbi	Muhammad is working in a grocery store [owned by *balawait*].

In this song Adraut revealed her hopes that her infant son would take a good job in the city to honor her and his relatives. Presenting a contrast to the values of rural areas, where honor is measured by wealth in sons, livestock, and land, Adraut's song directs attention to the changing perceptions of urban Hadendowa. Although modernity in its Western–northern Sudanese blend is received halfheartedly, the Hadendowa are not unaware of its resourcefulness and power hierarchies. Education, especially for boys, is perceived by most displaced Hadendowa as a means to access power and compete for better economic conditions. Muhammad, however, still had far to go.

When Muhammad was one year old, his father was sent to serve in southern Sudan. Muhammad thus breast-fed for more than two years. When Muhammad was three, Adraut became pregnant and bore another son, Omar. When she was breast-feeding Omar, her husband retired, returned to Sinkat, and took an irregular job in the market. Adraut soon became pregnant, and as a result, Omar breast-fed for less than two years. She explained the leap to her fourth pregnancy by saying: "I was very careful. I do not know how it happened. It was a big mistake, but I thought because I always breast-fed cleanly I was safe from becoming pregnant, but I guess I was wrong."

When she discovered she was pregnant for the fourth time, Adraut said that she immediately stopped breast-feeding Omar and started to feed him butter and milk to compensate his loss of her breast milk. She maintained that her mother and sisters reprimanded her and were very afraid that Omar might get sick or die. But with their help, she said, she was able to take care of her son and manage her new pregnancy. Adraut then gave birth to a female child, Sitta, whose birth, after the two sons, was joyfully welcomed. After another two years, Adraut bore another daughter, who died of whooping cough when she was six months old. Adraut describes the time of her third daughter's death as a miserable time (around 1973–74), during which her mother died and there was an outbreak of disease due to drought and famine in rural areas, which made Sinkat a center for drought victims.

After this crisis Adraut did not get pregnant immediately because, as she said, she was *aufrai dairsnat* (tired of childbirth). She wanted to rest her body and invest in her health. A year and a half after her daughter's death, she became pregnant again. Her health stabilized thereafter, and she successively gave birth to Hausain (male), Amna (female), Hassan (male), and Ali (male), each born after a two-year breast-feeding interval. After these four children, Adraut said she was exhausted, but she was happy that her pregnancies proceeded with fewer mishaps than did those of other women. At this juncture in her reproductive career, she said that she was continuously thinking of her children's health and future. Her boys were growing, and she wanted to send them to school in Sinkat. This is when she decided to stop childbearing in order to focus on her children's careers. She was also ashamed that she would still be having children when her oldest sons were "becoming men," denoting the sense of shame associated with pregnancy and sexuality, which would embarrass her sons. While she was having these thoughts, she became pregnant again a year after her last pregnancy. This pregnancy, however, ended with a miscarriage during the first two months. Adraut described this pregnancy as another mistake that she was not expecting. She ended her reproductive career in her late thirties with five living sons and two daughters.

Adraut's description of her fertility trajectories did not end by counting her pregnancies; rather it unfolded in a biographical account of her children's success and failure and their sickness and health. She reflected on how her children's experiences had shaped her social and emotional experiences and her own role as a mother.

Muhammad, Adraut's oldest son, went to elementary school in Sinkat and quit when he did not pass the requisite intermediary school exams. Although he dashed his mother's dreams of becoming a bank manager, he made it to the city. At the time of Adraut's interview, he was working as a car mechanic in Port Sudan and earning a relatively good income. It was readily apparent to any observer that Muhammad was his mother's pride and joy. She hardly missed any chance to express her gratitude that he had grown up to be a responsible man who was taking good care of his parents and siblings. One day when I visited Adraut, she was very happy because Muhammad had sent her a new body wrap, as well as some money for their household management. She told me that she usually saved part of the money to prepare to pay for his wedding, which was planned to take place in February 1999, after I left Sinkat. Muhammad was engaged to the only daughter of his mother's youngest sister. He was about thirty years old, while his bride was about eighteen years old. She had attended high school for a time but quit to prepare for her wedding.

The story of Omar (Audraut's second son) presents a rupture in his mother's career following his birth. He was healthy until he was six years old, when he became ill a year after his admission to elementary school. According to his mother, Omar suffered from periodic seizures. She attributed her son's illness to an evil eye that attacked him because of his good health and humor. She maintained that when Omar was drinking his milk one evening, a female neighbor touched his skin and said, "Oh, my God, you have smooth skin! Tell me, where did you get the milk that you drink?" Adraut continued to describe how the evil eye worked on her son in the following way:

> Omar immediately threw up, and since then he has been sick. It is hard to cure evil eye; however, we took him to see many religious people. Whenever we heard that there was a good religious man somewhere, we would go to him. The last time Omar's father and oldest brother took him to see two religious men, one in Kosti [a town in central Sudan] and the other in Port Sudan. Finally, we tried a medical doctor's medicine. His brother took him to this doctor in Port Sudan, who put him on medication. He is much better now, but he still faints. Anytime I see that woman, I read verses from the Qur'an to protect my children and myself from her evil eye.

Omar quit school, and despite his sickness, he attempted to take irregular jobs at coffee shops in the Sinkat market. He was approximately twenty-seven years old at that time, and Adraut said that she would arrange for his marriage when he regained his health.

Sitta, Adraut's oldest daughter, lived near her mother. She was approximately twenty-five years old. She had attended elementary school in Sinkat and quit after third grade. Adraut maintained that Sitta was not interested in school and that she wanted her to help with the overwhelming household chores and to attend to her brothers. When she was eighteen, Sitta married her father's nephew (a classificatory cousin). After a year of marriage, she gave birth to a daughter, who at the time of the interview was in the second grade of elementary school. Four years later, Sitta bore a male child (now four years old). Sitta, who was present during her mother's narration, explained the long intervals between the birth of her two children as the result of her husband's long absence (her husband worked as a tailor in Khartoum). He came to visit once or twice a year.

Hausain was about twenty-one. He had attended elementary school and quit after the eighth grade. At the time of the interview, he had recently started trading animals between rural areas and Port Sudan with some of his relatives. He was engaged to his mother's middle sister's daughter. His mother described him as a quiet, responsible man.

Amna, according to her mother, showed special interest in school. She was one of the top ten in her class. She was told by her father and older brothers, however, that she could not continue on to college because she had to begin her marital career. At school Amna also showed talent for singing and the theater. During a school performance, however, one of her brother's friends saw her acting and singing. He was angered by such behavior, which he viewed as entirely against the Hadendowa concept of female modesty. The friend reported her activities to the oldest brother, who felt offended by his sister's behavior and forbade her going to school. Thus Amna's dream of continuing school was shattered. Her teachers tried to talk her family into letting her continue her education but to no avail. Although Adraut wanted Amna to get some education, she was not sure that she would accept the idea of sending her to college. She commented that she wished one of her sons had Amna's strong interest in school. During this dialogue with Adraut, Amna was busy singing while washing her brothers' clothes. Amna is approximately eighteen years old, and she is engaged to her mother's sister's son (her cousin).

Hassan was then about fifteen years old. He was in the eighth grade of elementary school. Ali was about twelve years old and in the seventh grade of elementary school. Although Hassan and Ali expressed their desire to work in the market, their older brothers insisted that they stay in school.

With a reproductive history of ten pregnancies, five sons alive (though one was chronically ill), two daughters alive, two daughters who died, and one miscarriage, Adraut seemed to have endured fewer traumatic fertility episodes than do many Hadendowa women. The fact that she had more sons than daughters made her more successful than those with fewer sons or no sons at all. Her fertility, however, was not trouble-free since she had also experienced precarious periods during her reproductive career. Adraut gave an intriguing explanation of her few reproductive mishaps. Although she explained the death of her daughters, the sickness of her son, and her miscarriage with reference to infectious diseases, a successive pregnancy, a tired body, and the evil eye, she also included jinn as a powerful factor. To explain her success and partial failure, Adraut claimed that her jinn were Muslims. Unlike black and red jinn, which can haunt and impair women's reproductive careers, Muslim jinn are less dangerous.

Due to the power of her socially proximate Muslim jinn, Adraut endured less taxing bodily misfortune. Consequently, she could tell women's fortunes and treat their troubled fertility by reading a rosary and seashells. Moreover, she was endowed with the power of finding lost property with her jinn's assistance. This power made Adraut very popular among her neighbors, who referred to her as *masait,* and therefore they requested her presence during delivery to bestow her blessings on mother and child.

When I asked Adraut if she had felt this power immediately after her first daughter's death, she explained that such power is inherited through one's parents. She maintained that usually *ijar* are passed through the maternal line (which confirms the association of *ijar* with fertility), while Muslim jinn are inherited both paternally and maternally. Adraut also stated that she inherited her Muslim jinn from her father, a religious practitioner, who employed Muslim jinn to cure people. Adraut's two sisters seemed to have inherited their mother's *ijar*. Her youngest sister ended her fertility trajectory with three miscarriages and one girl, while the other sister had two miscarriages, two girls, and one son. Adraut's reproductive career was thus not much damaged, and her precarious trajectory was finally blessed with more sons than daughters.

Sons for the Aumaudia *(Leadership): Kauata's Story*

Unlike that of Adraut, Kauata's story presents a different setting within which to explain the precariousness inherent in a woman's fertility trajectory. Kauata was about forty-eight years old. Like most women of her generation, she had expected to marry early and start her reproductive career. However, she waited longer than she had expected and went through a stressful time watching as her peers married and started their own families.[4] Consequently, she was moody, secluded herself, and would sometimes refuse to eat. Her mother feared for her life and took her to an *ijar* (spirit possession) specialist, who diagnosed Kauata with an *arid* caused by black jinn, who prevented her from getting married. Since unmarried women are not allowed to perform the elaborate spirit-possession ceremony accompanied by drumming and dancing, the specialist suggested that Kauata only undergo the initial *fak alarid*. Kauata could only undergo the elaborate spirit-possession ceremony if she suffered future blockage after her marriage.

Kauata married one of her father's brother's sons shortly after she untied her blockage. She was about twenty, and her spouse was about thirty. One year after her wedding, Kauata became pregnant and gave birth to her first son, Salih. Salih was born healthy and his delivery was smooth, thus Kauata thought she was free from her jinn-induced blockage. When Salih was one year old, his father decided to move to Sawakin, because of the drought in their rural area, to find a stable job, and he wanted Kauata to accompany him. Kauata, however, thought it was too early for her and her child to travel, and that she would lack the care of her mother and family.

---

4. Kauata did not comment on why she married later than her peers.

Therefore she preferred not to accompany him. This disagreement resulted in her divorce.

When Salih was four years old, Kauata married again, to the *aumda* of her lineage, who was in his fifties. Although Kauata was aware that the *aumda*, who had married three times before her, wanted her to grant him male heirs, to marry a tribal leader was prestigious. The *aumda*'s first wife had had only one girl. Then he had married another woman, who did not give birth for five years, and then divorced her. His third wife, too, did not bear children and they divorced after four years of marriage. Then he married Kauata. During that time (in the seventies), drought was taking its toll in rural areas, and the *aumda* decided to move with his new wife and her son to Sinkat.

Kauata's reproductive career with the *aumda* started with the birth of a female child only two years after their marriage. That was not what she had anticipated, for she wanted to be the one who would have the *aumda*'s first son. Further escalating her tension was the *aumda*'s decision to marry another wife. Although Kauata had a son from her previous husband, she described the *aumda*'s decision to marry another wife as a personal affront or a response to her inability to provide him with a male heir. She said, "When I married the *aumda*, he was already married to three women. He divorced two, and he was still married to one. But I considered these marriages prior to mine; thus I was not as angry as when he married again after me. If he was happy about his daughter's birth, he would have waited longer before marrying again."

Accordingly, Kauata stopped breast-feeding her daughter after only one year and got pregnant again. But she gave birth to another female child. At this point Kauata started to worry about her blockage and the influence of black jinn on her reproductive outcomes and thus decided to consult a spirit-possession specialist. The specialist diagnosed Kauata with a European male spirit, rather than the black jinn that had caused her previous blockage. Kauata described her spirit as *kustani*, referring to the costume that her male European spirit wore, a full suit with a hat and black shoes. Kauata thus had to execute the demands of her red spirit by hosting a three-day ceremony that included drumming, singing, and dancing. Although this kind of ceremony was expensive, Kauata, the *aumda*'s wife, could afford it.

When Kauata described her *ijar* ceremony to me, her two daughters were present and were following the dialogue. After she finished the description of her ceremony, Kauata's youngest daughter said sarcastically, "And after the ceremony, my mother became pregnant with my brothers, the twins. They were healthy, but they had such big heads you could tell they were conceived by jinn." They all laughed.

Ijar costume of European, *kustani* (left), and Beni Amir, *jibali* (right)

Kauata breast-fed her second daughter for one year and became pregnant with the twins. When she gave birth to the twins, she was simultaneously happy and scared because of the Hadendowa fear of multiple births. Having twin boys or girls is seen as excess fertility that can easily invite envy. Accordingly, one of the twins or their parents may die. Kauata's fear came true, for one year after their birth, one of the boys died of smallpox. During this time the *aumda* divorced his fifth wife, who had not had children by then, and married another woman four months after his son's death.

Kauata said that she felt uncomfortable after his sixth marriage, but she understood that the *aumda* was getting old and he wanted to have more than one son to bear his name and inherit his *aumaudia*. The *aumda*, however, died one year after his wedding before his new wife had borne a child. Since the *aumda*'s son was very young at the time of his father's death, the *aumudia* was transferred to his father's brother's son with the condition that it would be transferred to the previous *aumda*'s son when he was old enough to claim his father's position. Let us now read Kauata's marital history and her biography of pregnancies and births as she unfolded it.

Kauata's oldest son, Salih, from her first marriage, was around twenty-seven. He had attended elementary school in Sinkat, quit after sixth grade, and decided to open a small grocery shop in his neighborhood. He married a distant relative and convinced her family that she should reside near his family so that he could take care of his mother. As the oldest son, he was also expected to be the guardian of his mother's tent after her husband's death. Salih's wife, who was in her late twenties, had two daughters and two sons. Although Salih was the only son from his mother's first marriage, he counted as a continuation for her entire reproductive career. When I first interviewed Kauata, she told me that she had been married twice, but she did not specify that Salih was her son from her first marriage. Rather, she counted him among the children from the second marriage. Not until she elaborated on her marital history did she make the distinction clear. Kauata commented that they were all the children of her womb. When it came to her second marriage, however, Salih would not be called the *aumda*'s son, denoting the social and political status of her second husband and disjoining her reproductive career. According to his mother, however, Salih was a well-raised son who was taking complete responsibility for her and his siblings while attending to his family's affairs.

Kauata's oldest daughter, Iylat, from her second marriage, was about twenty-three. When she was seventeen, Iylat quit high school to marry her mother's sister's son. When she was eighteen, she gave birth to her first daughter. Iylat was sick during her pregnancy and continuously depressed. Her mother related her depression to an evil eye that attacked her because of her healthy pregnancy. Iylat's failure came during delivery, when she was weakened by the pain of labor and fainted at the sight of childbirth blood. This association between childbirth blood and weakness during delivery made Iylat's mother believe that she had transmitted her red jinn to her daughter. Jinn malevolence involving blood renders women susceptible to their attacks during menstruation, giving birth, or contact with other bloody scenes.

Kauata was sad over her daughter's sickness, and she took her to many herbalists and *ijar* specialists, who attempted to cure her with amulets, incense, and herbal mixtures. Iylat felt much better but got sick again after the birth of her twin boys. She had breast-fed her first daughter for just six months when she became pregnant with the twins. Her mother wished that Iylat had waited longer before her second pregnancy just to regain her health and energy, but Iylat and her husband wanted a son. Iylat's sickness became severe when one of her twins died after the naming ceremony. "He was born weaker than his brother," she said. Iylat then had to continue the same process of cure and medication. She felt better but became pregnant again eighteen months after her last pregnancy. Her pregnancy was very difficult, and she experienced heavy bleeding during delivery and fell sick again. She gave birth to a healthy boy, but she had to endure trips to different healers, herbalists, and religious people to cure her depression.

During my interview with Kauata, my assistant conveyed to me Kauata's agony over the sickness of her daughter and asked me to approach the issue sensitively if Kauata brought it up during her narration. Before I left Sinkat, Iylat's mother convinced her to continue breast-feeding her son for two years before becoming pregnant again. She undertook an intensive health regime consisting of a diet of warm porridge, milk, and soft dates mixed with herbs accompanied by smoke baths. According to Kauata, the *ijar* specialist suggested that Iylat undertake the elaborate spirit-possession ceremony, but her family could not afford it. As an alternative, however, she took the *ijar* medicine, which included herbs, amulets, and incense to be burned and inhaled. Her brothers were also thinking of taking her to a psychiatrist in Port Sudan. Iylat's husband had an irregular income from petty jobs in the market.

Kauata's second daughter, Saba, was about twenty-two. She had quit elementary school in the fifth grade when she was fifteen to marry one of her father's relatives, a twenty-year-old. She gave birth to her first and only son two years after her marriage. After that, she experienced irregular menstrual cycles, bloating, and back pain and did not give birth until her husband's death from malaria two years later. Before Saba's husband died, Kauata said that she had advised her daughter to use herbal medicine to cure her condition, but Saba was not motivated to follow her mother's advice. Saba interjected, "My relatives would call me careless, but I was very young and really did not care."[5]

Three years prior to the interview, Saba had married her mother's sister's son (her sister's husband's brother), who had one daughter from his divorced wife. She said that her husband wanted more children, especially sons, and he always reprimanded her for not following her mother's advice to cure her illness. Although she believed in jinn, Saba thought that only God has the power to help or harm a human being. Thus, she always debated her mother's claims that she inherited her *ijar* and that she had to be treated for it. Saba's views were influenced by the Islamic trends spreading across the country and by the *khalwa* education she was then pursuing under the supervision of a religious woman in town. She had decided to wear a veil and to open her own *khalwa* near her *bukar* to teach her female

---

5. Saba, who was present during her mother's narration, interrupted often to confirm or debate her mother's narrative. This is a style of *sakanab,* which characterizes women's narratives.

neighbors the Qur'an and hadith. Thus she only agreed to go with her mother to a female herbalist, who diagnosed her with *imbarar* and gave her herbal mixtures to take with warm food accompanied by smoke baths.

Saba's friends, however, were not taking her new religiosity seriously and commented that she was only using it as strategy to escape her infertility and her anxiety that her husband might take back his previous wife or marry another one. But Saba thought otherwise, as her husband, who had recently became interested in religious education himself, considered children to be God's endowment and said that he did not blame Saba for her infertility. Before I left Sinkat, Saba was also considering consulting a doctor in Sinkat Hospital.

Kauata's youngest son, Aunur, was about twenty years old. He had finished high school and was accepted at a college in Khartoum. Although he was interested in higher education, his mother thought that he should soon be ready to claim his father's *aumaudia*. His father had agricultural land in their rural area that was taken care of by his brother's sons and cousins. The previous *aumda* was also a leader of a *kala*, a dockworkers' organization, each of which is monopolized by a tribal leader who recruits people from his own group. Moreover, the *aumda* was an auctioneer in the *dikhaulia*, a market where tribal leaders auction livestock for people from their own tribes in Port Sudan. Kauata also made her son get involved, during his school breaks, with his father's brother's sons in managing his father's business. Aunur may still rely on his relatives to look after his father's business if he decides to go to college. Saba, his sister, maintained that if Aunur went to college and got his degree, he would be the first *aumda* with a college degree from his lineage.

The reading of these converging reproductive trajectories yields different discourses through which women explain their contingent situations with reference to metaphors of social proximity and distance. Women who transcend reproductive dangers with less fertility misfortune and bear and raise many successful sons and daughters are seen as *masait*, whereas women who experience more reproductive traumas are often seen as haunted by the evil eye, foreign spirits, and diseases.

Unlike Adraut, Kauata's reproductive trajectory was shaped by her own circumstances. Unlike Adraut, she married late, got divorced, and then remarried to a lineage leader older than herself. Her husband died when she was in her thirties. Moreover, one of her twin sons died, and her two daughters inherited her evil eye– and jinn-infested fertility trajectories. Faced with such misfortunes, Kauata offered a different explanation for her situation. Unlike Adraut, whose Muslim jinn salvaged her reproductive career from complete mischief, Kauata attributed her traumas to European red jinn and to black jinn, which are both socially distant from her own world. They harmed her reproductive career and blocked the path to her desired fertility outcomes.

The contrasting stories of Adraut and Kauata provide vivid examples of how women's strategies and fertility decisions are determined not only by cultural constructions but also by the specificity and precariousness of their life events. We have seen how women's preference for sons or daughters is shaped by their social positions in particular conjugal settings and by the economic transformation of their social world within which meanings of identity, gender, and honor are negotiated in pursuit of reproductive propriety and social well-being.

Hadendowa construction of reproductive trajectories thus posits a health model that engages meanings of threatened corporality in the interpretation of fertility practices and outcomes. By monitoring bodily quality through regimes of diet, rest, prolonged breast-feeding, and protection from the evil eye and spirits, Hadendowa women strive to achieve a desired fertility outcome leading to social security and responsible motherhood. Practices such as breast-feeding, far from being an extemporaneous behavior, are vital strategies that women use to manage their bodily traumas and to enhance their children's survival in the absence of prevalent contraception use. Although my statistical data do not support the predominance of discriminatory health practices favoring male over female children, five women in my sample, including Kauata and her daughter Iylat, shed light on their subtle attempts to breast-feed their daughters for shorter periods (less than two years) in order to bear sons.

Moreover, a thick ethnographic analysis of women's reproductive histories illustrates the significance of demographic events, such as miscarriages, stillbirths, and "sick children," to the evaluation of women's fertility trajectories (see Bledsoe, Banja, and Hill 1998). While miscarriages and infant mortality negatively affect a woman's fertility trajectory, her children's success in health, marriage, work, and reproduction is considered part of her success in bearing and raising "true" Hadendowa children. The construction of healthy fertility trajectories therefore asserts women's centrality in regeneration and signifies the social processes through which ideas of collective identity are produced and negotiated through embodied meanings and practices.

Chapter 6

Whose Modernity?

Negotiating Social Change

First you will raise the island of the Sirens,
those creatures who spellbind any man alive,
whoever comes their way. Whoever draws too close,
off guard, and catches the Sirens' voices in the air—
no sailing home for him, no wife rising to meet him,
no happy children beaming up at their father's face.
The high, thrilling song of the Sirens will transfix him.
Homer, "The Cattle of the Sun," The Odyssey

The Hadendowa move between two realities, two constructed spatialities. The first is composed of scattered tent clusters made of worn-out mats or small rooms built of timber and scrap metals, in which women and children spend most of their day. The second is an urban setting dominated by *hishan* architecture (enclosed cement, brick, or mud houses) and the official government institutions such as schools, courts, and hospitals that are culturally maintained by Muslim, Arabic-speaking northern Sudanese. It has long been the role of pastoral Hadendowa men to mediate between these rural and urban social spaces through their frequent camel trips to exchange their livestock products for other consumer goods in town. Recently, due to extensive migration and displacement, Hadendowa men and women have become entirely dependent for their living on the urban market economies, on the NGOs, and on their employers.

In Port Sudan the social distance between the Hadendowa who live in *daims* (working-class residential areas) and the different classes of northern

Sudanese, Sawakinese merchants, and other Beja elites is even more pronounced than in Sinkat town. Along the shore the ships' sirens mix with the work songs of *kala* workers, many of whom have left their families behind in search of work in the harbor. In the city they confront new realities of poverty and marginalization that prevent them from sustaining their household economies back home. In response displaced Hadendowa women are facing the dual responsibility of working both inside and outside their homes. In Sinkat town many women squat along the highway for long hours to sell mats, eggs, and candies for pennies to the passengers traveling to large urban centers. Right before their eyes, the "time-space" continuum compresses (Harvey 1989) through the extensions of railways, roads, and ports that bring more "foreign" people and commodities across their land, creating an imaginary world of desires and a reality of poverty and destitution they must confront. A few Hadendowa men manage to travel these "constructed routes" seeking education and better jobs, a journey that may take them as far as the Gulf or the West. In Sinkat town women such as Halima, whom we encountered in the introduction, still enter the *hishan* houses as housemaids and receive less in wages than their physical efforts warrant. The Hadendowa are thus part of these rural-urban social realities that have long influenced their economic lives and physical well-being and their conceptualization of danger, foreignness, and regeneration.

Within the Hadendowa honor economy in both rural and urban settings, women experience the changing realities of their worlds through their bodies, as they struggle to maintain *auslif* relations through their modesty and regenerative power. Wealth in sons and daughters is the definitive source of honor for regenerating the social and economic foundation of patrilineality and maintaining collective identity. Like the ancestral land, women's fertile bodies, as the icons of regeneration, can be "colonized" as well. Yet "colonization" in this sense can be both manifest, as in threats from external groups to the ancestral land, or implicit, as in marriage to outsiders as well as in dangerous diseases transmitted through "unfamiliar" people, commodities, and livestock that endanger the productive and reproductive capacities of lineage members.

Because both men and women occupy a precarious location within the community, we have come to realize that both are situated on the margins of a larger political nexus. Although men struggle to ensure that the power within remains intact and external power is defeated, women too must defend their bodies from being lost to the transfixing effects of an external power. Homer's narrative of the Sirens, the creatures on the horizon who entice people and threaten their identities with their singing, evokes women's narratives about the "deceptive" foreign spirits that target their modesty and responsible motherhood. In this context social distance communicates meanings of power and danger that can transfix, harm, and transform. The increasing porousness of the Hadendowa world, however, renders their contact with foreignness inevitable. Both men and women are becoming more mobile and subject to more subordination and external influence. Although men can protect against foreignness, they can also endanger procreation through their frequent travels, especially through camel trips, which are deemed responsible for many ailments, including sexually transmitted diseases that threaten women's fertility and children's well-being.

From women's narratives of sickness and health, we learned that perceptions of danger and disease intensify with proximity to towns and exposure to unfamiliar commodities and medicine. Before I left Sinkat, a widespread sense of fear surrounded a vaccination campaign for children in town. Many women refused to vaccinate their children on the premise that the injected medicine was dangerous to their health. Those who accepted the vaccination claimed that their children contracted a lingering fever and advised other women not to accept the treatment. Although a feverish reaction to vaccination is common, women used it to question the efficacy of a medication that was purported to maintain health. This anxiety coincided with the construction of a Chinese-Canadian oil pipeline company in Sinkat that attracted laborers from different ethnic groups. Fear that these foreigners would kidnap children was very strong among many families. Mothers keenly watched their children play in the *khaur,* and they advised them not to go to the town center after sunset. Rumors also had it that the town dogs had disappeared, as Asian and Canadian strangers were consuming them.

The Hadendowa construction of foreignness, therefore, reflects their concern over the danger of boundary transgression to fertility and regeneration. Such anxieties direct attention to the notion of embodied spatiality as a significant concept to understanding Hadendowa constructions of gender and fertility. This condensed body-space relationship highlights the materiality of power and the historicity and politicization of spatiality as it was overtly eclipsed by anthropological emphasis on embodied time (Foucault 1980; Ong 1987; Pellow 1996; Gupta and Ferguson 1997).

Hadendowa cultural complexes of fertility, honor, and gender preference are thus interwoven with their lineage and kinship politics and their vision of the world beyond their boundaries. The value attributed to male children stems from ideas about regenerating patrilineality and protecting collective honor. Sons also bridge the inner community and its morally antithetical exterior. Meanings of honor and gender preference, however, are not merely symbolic reflections of social structures; rather, they are manifested in actual practices of fertility and infertility through which women seek agency, propriety, and social status. Just as chronically sick children, for instance, may demographically count as family members, many women explain fertility traumas, including children's chronic sicknesses, as representing major setbacks for their fertility trajectories, their emotional well-being, and their ability to achieve "proper" fertility and responsible motherhood.

Unlike Asian examples, where poor families may take extreme measures that go as far as female infanticide or "high-tech sexism" (Sen 2001) to control the number and the gender of their children, Hadendowa kinship and gender logic offers a different configuration of the ideology of son preference in which absence of female children signals "social orphanage." Yet, since many couples favor large families, sonless women may continue childbearing to a later age in order to bear a son.

This aspect of son-infertility draws attention to the issue of women's reproductive health. Despite cultural practices that emphasize investment in prenatal and postnatal health for mothers, the current economic situation of extreme poverty prevents most families from fully providing for pregnant women. The senior midwife at Sinkat Hospital related the cases of women who consulted her for pregnancy checkups to their previous experiences of successive miscarriages and infant mortality. She maintained that most of these women experienced repetitive pregnancies in a quest for sons, and they suffered from infections, malnutrition, and iron deficiency.

In the 1990s the senior midwife, in collaboration with a team from the Ministry of Health, funded by the United Nations Population Fund, launched a maternal and children's health program counter to other NGO programs, which focused on women's income-generating activities in the Sinkat area. According to her, the program enabled them to initiate a woman's health unit situated outside the hospital to encourage women to consult senior midwives in order to ease the cultural restrictions associated with consulting male doctors inside the hospital. The program offered regular checkups for pregnant women, family-planning services, and training for local midwives. Local midwives, who are central figures in their communities, were trained to practice hygienic procedures during childbirth and to report difficult pregnancies. The senior midwife, however, blamed the subsequent lack of funds and the hospital's male hierarchy, which gave doctors priority to use available equipment, such as cars, for hampering her training efforts.

Rayha, one of the local midwives recruited for this training from one of Sinkat's shanty settlements, commented that the program was "generally good," but they expected more from it. After the training each midwife received a metal box containing scissors, cotton wool, and antiseptics as part of her midwifery paraphernalia. Moreover, each midwife was given money to buy a donkey to facilitate her mobility and a white *taub* as a work uniform in conformity with professional midwifery practice in Sudan. Rayha complained that the quality of the *taub*s was very cheap compared to what "urban" midwives used to wear. She also maintained that local midwives did not receive salaries to supplement their income. Before the famine, she continued, midwives usually received gifts such as baby goats or money, especially if the newly born was a boy. At the time of the interview, however, such payments were unaffordable for many families. As a result local midwives enlisted in the training program expecting that they would receive salaries like their hospital counterparts. Rayha commented, however, that this sort of discrimination was also evident in the way that "urban" midwives looked down on them as "Arab midwives." She said, "I was once in the hospital and a *balawait* woman was in labor. The urban midwife prevented me from helping her deliver by telling me, 'You are responsible for your women [rural women] only.'" Rayha said that this incident discouraged her from following up with the health center. These efforts of development, despite their paucity, are grounded in global, national, and local power hierarchies that exacerbate gender, ethnic, and class inequalities and divisions.

Cultural meanings associated with fertility, gender preference, and honor, however, are being transformed in urban contexts, allowing for greater flexibility and negotiations. In these settings meanings of male honor extend to incorporate success in other domains. Education, working with NGOs, in government jobs, and as dockers in Port Sudan, or traveling to Gulf countries for work enhance men's honor and the value attributed to male children. With the increasing influence of national and international development organizations working in eastern Sudan, many Hadendowa youth are recruited as permanent employees, which gives them a status similar to that of *shaikh*s and respected senior men. They become key figures in consultation processes regarding their tribal affairs. Although they gain power in a foreign domain, their honorable qualities continue to be evaluated against *auslif* practices. Aunur, a Hadendowa *shaikh* interviewed in Sinkat, related the case of one of his nephews, Mohamed, who held a government job in town. During a land ownership conflict between his lineage and a neighboring group, Mohamed was called upon to be part of the consultation process. When Mohamed failed to be present, his armed cousins showed up at his office door denouncing him as a man of no *durarit*. One of his cousins would have struck him with his sword had it not been for the intervention of Mohamed's colleagues.

Moreover, some migrant Hadendowa who have resided longer in town manage to transform the *bidaiqaw* (tent) into a *bukar* (timber room) or mudrooms with wood or low mud enclosures. As the terms of these permanent settlements are negotiated among the leaders of the guests and the host lineages, most families are fearful that the government might destroy their homes at any time on the grounds that they are constructed in unplanned residential areas. This is a legitimate concern of residents in shanty settlements since urban planning is authorized by the government, which considers such peripheral zones as 'ashwai (literally "random") settlements. Some women, however, lamented the loss of the tent, which was previously owned by the wife. Today it is the male head of household who owns the bukar and mudrooms, which require more labor and monetary investment and are constructed by hired men.

In the same vein, a new generation of Hadendowa women and men is negotiating the constructions of honor and gender preference, blaming these constructions for most problems of divorce, polygyny, and the health risks associated with successive pregnancies. Some of these women were born in town and have either primary or high school education and/or are married to government employees, including teachers, health workers, NGO workers, or soldiers, as in the cases of Zainab (chapter 4) and Saba (chapter 5). Zainab, who experienced miscarriages after her seven pregnancies, questioned herbal and religious cures and decided to consult a doctor in Port Sudan despite her mother's disapproval. Although Zainab may have used a "doctor's treatment," a form of foreignness, to undo her infertility predicament, she celebrated its "contradictory power" by giving her daughter a balawait name as halafa.

Saba, on the other hand, who was influenced by the country's new Islamic trend, decided to take Qur'anic and hadith lessons in town and denounced her mother's beliefs in zar and halafa methods of healing as non-Islamic. She also decided to consult a doctor in Port Sudan for her infertility problem. Both Zainab and Saba represent a generation of women who also see in education a means of accessing a new domain of knowledge about women's and children's health. Some of these women were supported by their husbands, who espoused similar views. Ali, a Hadendowa man, who had a primary school education and was employed by an NGO in town, was able to move with his wife and children from one of Sinkat's shanty settlements to a rented three-room mud house in the town center. He attributed his divorce from his first wife to "her carelessness as she did not pay close attention to her house and kid," who died of fever and vomiting when he was two years old. His second wife was also a close cousin, and they had three children. Ali asserted that he wanted a balanced number of male and female children but "not at the expense of his wife's health." Hence, he encouraged the use of contraceptives, confirming that it is sanctioned by Islam (see Musallam 1983). Through family planning, Ali maintained, they could space pregnancies to take care of the health of the mother and the children, as well as to invest in their children's future education.

Although most Hadendowa perceive formal education as foreign to their auslif practices, especially those emphasizing women's modesty, some families have accepted the idea that girls, as well as boys, need an education, yet they object to sending their daughters to college. The influence of the late *shaikh* Mohamed Badri Abu-Hadia, a Hadendowa Beja activist, who advocated inclusion in broader nation-state building projects, is greatly felt in town. He advocated women's education, which he supported through his personal efforts and contacts with larger development and educational institutions in Khartoum, Port Sudan, and other larger cities. Abu Hadia Center in Sinkat is one example of his personal efforts to raise literacy rates among Beja women and train them in income-generating activities, such as weaving and sewing. Although none of the women interviewed reported enrollment in the center, Abu Hadia had been a personal contact for a few families that were enthusiastic about sending their children, especially daughters, to college in Port Sudan or Khartoum. Nafisa, who had seven girls and no son, was married to a close cousin who was a teacher in Sinkat. She maintained that the moral codes regarding the danger of mobility to women's honor were so great that families fear sending them to nonlocal schools and colleges. She had contacted Abu-Hadia, however, to facilitate sending her eldest daughter to college in Port Sudan regardless of some familial objections. She confirmed that her daughters were "modest because they [were] well raised, and education would only substantiate their modesty and enhance their social status."

Educated Hadendowa women also take social status into consideration when deciding to marry. Hence, some of them object to marrying their uneducated cousins and prefer to wed educated suitors from other lineages. One Hadendowa high school graduate remarked that "educated Hadendowa women are confronting a dilemma," because their uneducated cousins perceive of them as too *balawai*tized, and schooled Hadendowa men would rather choose uneducated female cousins "who would not argue with them." Because of this dilemma of being "betwixt and between," she continued, "many educated Hadendowa women remain unmarried though they are in their thirties."

The aspirations of this generation, however, are reflected in the various girls' songs that compare urban and rural lifestyles. These songs also comment on the transformation of Sinkat town in the wake of foreign investments sweeping the country, such as the Chinese-Canadian oil pipeline company established in Port Sudan and Sinkat, Syrian travel businesses, and Arab soap operas shown on Sudanese television. Although electricity is a problem in Sinkat town, a few elite families own TVs that are operated through personal oil generators. The boundaries between elite Hadendowa families who live in the town center and their relatives in shanty settlements are fluid, as they exchange visits and participate in ceremonies and other kinship obligations. Many Hadendowa who live in the *daims* of Port Sudan also move near their relatives in Sinkat during the city's hot summer. Thus information about urban lifestyles is also exchanged through these relational contacts. The following song, which young girls sing during weddings and leisure time and is composed in both Arabic and Tu-Badawie, comments on perceptions of a new generation in town:

Inta qamar fi alsma ya awa taqa fi Alkhala ya	You are a handsome man; do not end up in *khala*.
Lila ailwai fi alkala ya salimauni awraqa	I want to own a Lila 'alwai (land cruiser) that landed in the *khala*.[1]
Thalt abka polyster irishala naur baubin	I sing for the pretty girl with long eyelashes, who is wearing a polyester body wrap.
Ihaya taun Sinkat tisharika naur baubin	I love Sinkat and the company's light.
Dafari kiwihirair tisifinji maqisihaib	I like to wear these sandals; they make me hate my rubber slippers.
Swarti saurimihaib tidiqaiq shaukinyaib	I will travel to visit you by Sawrti bus,[2] which is express and punctual.

As efforts of development are increasingly welcomed and "modernity" halfheartedly celebrated despite its "discriminatory tactics" (Comaroff and Comaroff 1993), Hadendowa men and women in urban settings negotiate issues of power and marginality differently. In this regard the *halafa* reverse logic, which signals relations of power and domination, renders women's continuous attempts to make sense of their murky social location logical. *Halafa* thus signifies attempts to reconcile conflicting powers to serve the interests of those who paradoxically embody honor and experience marginality. Although *halafa* acknowledges the positive effect of external power, it deflects attention from it by pointing to its danger and by revealing the mastery of the power within by highlighting the potency of its commodities, spatial organization, and regenerative practices. In this sense *halafa* is an empowerment technique by which women, who bear the brunt of economic and social marginality, claim modernity's benefits without losing their identities and selves. In other words, *halafa* reverse ritual can be viewed as a "scale of power" that ensures its fair distribution (Foucault 1980) among those who are often denied access to it.

1. Land cruisers are owned by national and international NGOs and affluent classes in towns. Lila 'alwai, the nickname given to the van, is a famous Egyptian actress, who appears in many series on Sudanese television.

2. Sawarti Nassar, owner of a Syrian express bus company, which began service recently in Sudan.

I left Sinkat via Port Sudan on my way to Khartoum and then to the United States, taking the historically and politically constructed routes that connected globally and differentiated locally. Three memorable voices remained with me throughout my journey. Two were Fatima's voice implying that I should "write fairly" and Asha's wish that when I return to Sinkat I visit her in a large cement house. I said teasingly, "And what would you do with this USA can-door?" (see figure on bottom of p. 28). She responded, "It may become a *halafa* story." She giggled as she hugged me good-bye. The third voice was of a gathering of male and female children playing in the *khaur* before sunset; they were divided into two groups, as they chanted in Tu-Badawie–accented Arabic:

Lih mabtajauna? ashan amalna dish   Why did you stop visiting? Is it because
                                       we installed a satellite dish?

The second group responded,

Ayi mabnajikum ashan khaifin natish   Yes, we stopped visiting because we are
                                       afraid to stray.

The strength of these voices merged with the amplified sounds of escalators, carts, and other foreign accents at the New York airport. I handed my blue Sudanese passport to the white officer, who reviewed it carefully and directed me to a different office crowded with arriving passengers from the East. The African American officer who rechecked my passport sensed my tension and fatigue and said with a grim face, "Don't bother. You will become an American soon." I could not help but smile. He frowned. My fingerprints were taken over and over again. My luggage was thoroughly searched by a white American woman who apologized, "Sorry, it's my job." The airport was relatively quiet. It was late at night. The voices of the "nomads" are forced to settle. I am now allowed to reenter.

Glossary
of Tu-Badawie and Arabic Words

Bibliography

Index

Glossary of Tu-Badawie and Arabic Words

adal awat: red stone
adarawb: red
adat: maximal lineages (Tu-Badawie for tree branches)
aib: (Arabic) shameful, dishonor
Aid Aladaha: (Arabic) sacrifice fete
Aid Alfitr: (Arabic) post-Ramadan fete
'ajwa: soft dates
alhishan/hishan: (Arabic) urban-style housing with enclosed walls
almanaqib: (Arabic) virtues, feats
altusa': (Arabic) one-ninth
amara: temporary land rights
arad: herb *(acacia etbaica)*
arid: fertility blockage
ashraf: (Arabic) descendants of the Prophet (sing. *sharif,* honorable)
'ashwai: (Arabic) unplanned residential areas
askari: (Arabic) soldier
asl: (Arabic) original

audimim aubrinau: disappearance of rain

audrar: evening meal

aufrai dairsnat: tired of childbirth

aukam: camel

aulib: hinterland region

aumaudia: (Arabic) leadership

aumda: maximal lineage leader

aumkir: consultation; council; wise men

aunash: funeral bed

auqadat: knots

auqashabi: Pharaonic circumcision

auqaw: home

auqunub: coastal region

aur: boy; boyhood

ausaf: bridewealth

aushar: evil

auslif: the familiar and habitual

auyam: womb

azan: (Arabic) call for prayer

Badawait: Bedouin

badab: seven mats for building the tent

bahai natu: loosely means neglected children (motherless)

bakhaur timan: (Arabic) twin frankincense, also *lauban timan*

bala: (Arabic) misfortune or catastrophe

balawait: northern Sudanese; also implies foreigner, intruder, superior

baraka: (Arabic) blessing

bibaub: a male dance

bidaiqaw: tent

birnsa: appropriation of the English word "princess." It is used satirically to refer to the (small) Toyota trucks, introduced in the 1980s and locally accessorized to serve as public transport vehicles.

bukar: timber room

bura: spinster

dabalaub: little ones (mainly children)

daims: (Arabic) an old term that refers to working-class neighborhoods

dairwawut: seven-herb mixture

dawrib: good, nice, beautiful

dikhaulia: livestock market

diwab: minimal lineage

dura: sorghum; also durra

durarit: loosely translates as "honor"

duriatuaur: maternal cousin

duriaur: paternal cousin

fak alarid: (Arabic) ceremony for untying the blockage

faqiria: (Arabic) religious woman (masc. *faqir;* plural masc. *fuqara;* plural fem. *faqiriat*)

farasha: (Arabic) maid
fauta: the Beja female body wrap
feki: (Arabic) religious man
finjan: (Arabic) coffee cup
Halab: (Arabic) Aleppo in Syria, believed to be the original homeland of Gypsies
halafa: reverse logic
halaib: mentally ill (fem. *halait*)
halaqat: deserted
halaqin: animal or money gift for the groom from his relatives
hamaustib: respect
haram: religiously unsanctioned
hargal: herb *(solenostemma argel)*
hasbib: refugee
hasham: respect (modesty)
hashaw: refers to spirits (jinn)
Haulia: annual memorial of Alsharifa Maryam, the granddaughter of the founder
    of the Khatmiyya brotherhood
hautaun: grandmother
hila: (Arabic) neighborhood
hisra: measles; also *hisba*
ibanon: labia minora
iblis: (Arabic) devil; also *shaitan*
ibn 'am: (Arabic) father's brother's son
iharaw: proposal
ijar: red spirits; spirit possession synonymous with *zar* in northern Sudan
imbad: sword
imbarar: cold disease
imidraq: wood fire situated in front of the tent's entrance indicating childbirth
imiquad: right-hand side
indiwab: family or sub-lineage
inqabad: (Arabic) seized
iqatha: (Arabic) relief food
italaw: lightning
itriquad: left-hand side
jabana: coffee; also coffee pot
jallaba: (Arabic) northern Sudanese traders
jantaib: spirits; (Arabic) jinn
jantaib adarawb: red spirits
jantaib ailab: white spirits
jantaib hadal: black spirits
jibali: (Arabic) mountains
joza: aromatic herb
kabaun: a kind of amulet that contains several herbs and is worn for protection; it
    may also contain black cumin *(kamaun)* or black grain *(alhaba alsawda* in Arabic)
kala: Beja cargo dockworkers' organization
kalawab: stomach

kamaub: red wood
karama: (Arabic) sacrifice
katkauta: whooping cough
khala: (Arabic) desert, rural area
khalawi: (Arabic) religious schools (sing. *khalwa*)
kharaba: (Arabic) ruins
khasa: slaves; used to refer to the Beni Amir
khaur: seasonal stream
Khawada: European; also Khawaja
khumra: (Arabic) a mix of oil perfumes, cloves, and musk
kishab: black of slave descent
kiyaus: half *fauta* worn by pubescent girls
kohl: black substance used to color the edges of the eyelids
kufia: (Arabic) head cover for men; it can also be tossed over shoulders, also *shall*
kulail: silver bracelet
kulausai: suspicious
kulup: hairstyle for boys
kurbadj: (Arabic) a whip
kustani: costume for a European spirit
lailit: evil eye
mabrauka: (Arabic) blessed
mahalab: aromatic herb
maryaub: hairstyle characterized by big braids that prepares a pregnant woman for
    delivery
masait: blessed (masc. *masaib*)
mihaya: (Arabic) blessed water
mikhashash: golden necklace with a foreign figure charm
mindil: long red head scarf similar to the *shall* or *kufia* worn by men in many Middle
    Eastern countries
miskit: golden necklace
mista: bed curtain
mutwai: winter
muzawria: dock laborers
nadur: a binding promise to God and his saints
nazir: tribal leader
qabilat: tribe
qafir: (Arabic) guard
qaila: an early afternoon spirit-possession ceremony
qalad: council of consultation that includes the *shaikh* and other male elders whose
    role is the observance of customary regulations
qamis: (Arabic) shirt
qaraa: (Arabic) gourd container
qarad: herb *(Acacia arabica)*
qaudab: animal or money gift given in recognition of land rights
rababa: lute-like musical instrument
rabatak: man; manhood

rakauba: (Arabic) wooden verandah-like dwelling
sa'am: poverty and misfortune
sahir: (Arabic) evil eye
sakanab: chatting while exchanging information
samin: (Arabic) butter
sanqanib: tree *(Acacia tortilis)*
saulit: hairstyle denoting motherhood
saulit wahalit: children's hairstyle
shadat: hairstyle for married women
shade: camels used for travel and other common purposes
shaf: wood used for smoke bathing
shafats: small, rectangular wooden houses for pubescent boys
shaikh: minimal lineage leader
shaikhat: (Arabic) religious women (fem. sing. *shaikha;* masc. sing. *shaikh*)
shaikhitkaf: religious party
shaiqait: fabric that men wrap around the waist and toss over their shoulders, part
    of Hadendowa men's costume
shamalat: wool rug
shari'ah: Islamic law
sharir: clitoris
shashaut: tree *(Balanites aegyptiaca)*
sidairi: jacket (usually black) worn by men
sijin: prison
simrit: brown skin color
sirbadaub: baggy pants worn by men
sunkab: bundle of dried dom-tree fronds, used as a symbol of fertility
taikam silail: camel prayers or blessing
Takarir: West African
takat: married woman
talih: wood used for smoke bathing
tamhasa: morning meal
tamnai aurauk: the ritual of "son birth"
taqar: retribution for declaring a woman's honor
tarha: (Arabic) loose head cover for pubescent girls
tatau: descending braids for pubescent girls
taub: northern Sudanese term for female body wrap
taur: girl; girlhood
tibadai ari: women whose children die
tidafin: labia majora
tidauba: bride
tihalifa: council of oath
tihibi: summer
tinkaulit: an uncircumcised girl, used pejoratively
tisanit: a gift of gratification to win a woman's consent after moral accusation
tisaramt: mysterious disease; also refers to syphilis; also *tifgid*
Tu-Badawie: Hadendowa Cushitic language (unwritten)

umalsibian: (Arabic) sons' mother; mysterious worm; also *tiyaut* or *tinsibiand*
wadaj: animal fat used as hair butter and conditioner
waisl: written Qur'anic verses
walag: silver ring
wali: saint
waridis: best men
whalal: wooden sticks used for fastening
yawaib: locust
zar: (Arabic) used in northern Sudan to mean spirit possession; synonymous with *ijar* (Tu-Badawie); literally means to appear or descend upon someone

For writing the Tu-Badawie terms and verses used in this book, I relied on my interviewees' and assistants' direct pronunciation of the words. This style, however, may not conform to proper pronunciation of Tu-Badawie in every instance. For Arabic-Tu-Badawie, I relied on simple Arabic transliteration, forgoing the use of stressed Arabic consonants, since they might not conform to Hadendowa pronunciation of Arabic (see Hans Wehr's *Dictionary of Modern Written Arabic* edited by Milton Cowan [London: MacDonald and Evans, 1980] for comparison).

Bibliography

Abdel-Ati, Hassan. 1988. The Process of Famine: Causes and Consequences in Sudan. *Development and Change* 19:267–300.

——. 1990. The Developmental Impact of Small Towns in Regions under Conditions of Environmental Stress: The Case of Sinkat–Eastern Sudan. Paper presented at the Red Sea Area Program Annual Workshop, Sinkat, Sudan.

——. 1996. Beyond the Locality: Urban Centers, Agricultural Schemes, the State and NGOs. In *Survival on Meager Resources: Hadendowa Pastoralism in the Red Sea Hills*, ed. Leif Manger, 103–19. Uppsala: Nordiska.

Abou-Zeid, Ahmed. 1965. Honour and Shame among the Bedouins of Egypt. In *Honour and Shame: The Values of Mediterranean Society*, ed. John Peristiany, 243–60. London: Weidenfeld and Nicolson.

Abu-Lughod, Lila. 1986. *Veiled Sentiments: Honor and Poetry in a Bedouin Society*. Berkeley: University of California Press.

——. 1990. The Romance of Resistance: Tracing Transformations of Power through Bedouin Women. *American Ethnologist* 17:41–55.

——. 1993. *Writing Women's Worlds: Bedouin Stories*. Berkeley: University of California Press.

Abusharaf, Rogaia. 2001. Virtuous Cuts: Female Genital Excision in an African On-
tology. *Differences: Journal for Feminist Cultural Studies* 12 (1): 112–40.

Abu Sin, Mohamed. 1990. Urbanization and Environmental Change in the Red Sea
Province. Unpublished RESAP workshop report, January. Khartoum, Sudan.

Abu-Zahra, Nadia. 1971. On the Modesty of Women in Arab Muslim Villages: A
Reply. *American Anthropologist* 72:1079 –87.

———. 1974. Material Power, Honour, Friendship, and the Etiquette of Visiting.
Anthropological Quarterly 47:120–38.

Ahmed, Abdel Ghafar. 1980. Planning and the Neglect of Pastoral Nomads in the
Sudan. In *Problems of Savannah Development: The Sudan Case,* ed. Gunnar
Haaland, 39 –54. Bergen: Dept. of Social Anthropology, University of Bergen,
Norway.

Ahmed, Hassan A. Aziz. 1974. Aspects of Sudan's Foreign Trade during the 19th
Century. *Sudan Notes and Records* 55:16 –32.

Ahmed, Leila. 1982. Western Ethnocentrism and Perceptions of the Harem. *Feminist Studies* 8 (3): 521–34.

———. 1992. *Women and Gender in Islam.* New Haven, Conn.: Yale University Press.

al-Guindi, Fadwa. 1978. The Angles in the Nile: A Theme in Nubian Ritual. In *Nubian Ceremonial Life,* ed. John Kennedy, 104 –13. Berkeley: University of California Press.

Alnagar, Samia Alhadi. 1975. Spirit Possession and Change in Omdurman. Master's
thesis, University of Khartoum, Sudan.

Alsafi, Ibrahim Alkhalifa. 1966. Almanaqib. Unpublished manuscript, private col-
lection of Alsafi family. Gabit, Sudan.

Altorki, Soraya. 1980. Milk Kinship in Arab Society: An Unexplored Problem in the
Ethnography of Marriage. *Ethnology* 19:233 –44.

Asad, Talal, ed. 1973. *Anthropology and the Colonial Encounter.* New York: Ithaca
Press.

———. 1993. *Genealogies of Religion: Discipline and Reasons of Power in Christianity
and Islam.* Baltimore: Johns Hopkins University Press.

Auslander, Mark. 1993. "Open the Wombs!" The Symbolic Politics of Modern
Ngoni Witchfinding. In *Modernity and Its Malcontents: Ritual and Power in Postcolonial Africa,* ed. Jean Comaroff and John Comaroff, 167 –92. Chicago: University of Chicago Press.

Barth, Frederik. 1969. *Ethnic Groups and Boundaries.* Boston: Little, Brown.

Basu, Alaka, and Peter Aaby, eds. 1998. *The Methods and Uses of Anthropological Demography.* Oxford: Clarendon Press.

Bayoumi, Ahmed. 1979. *The History of Sudan Health Services.* Nairobi: Kenya Literature Bureau.

Bell, Heather. 1999. *Frontiers of Medicine in the Anglo-Egyptian Sudan, 1899–1940.*
Oxford: Clarendon.

Berlant, Lauren, ed. 2004. *Compassion: The Culture and Politics of an Emotion.* New
York. Routledge.

Bledsoe, Caroline. 2002. *Contingent Lives: Fertility, Time, and Aging in West Africa.*
Chicago: University of Chicago Press.

Bledsoe, Caroline, Fatoumatta Banja, and Allan Hill. 1998. Reproductive Mishaps and Western Contraception: An African Challenge to Fertility Theory. *Population and Development Studies* 24 (1): 15–57.

Bledsoe, Caroline, Allan Hill, Umberto D'Alessandro, and Patricia Langerock. 1994. Constructing Natural Fertility: The Use of Western Contraceptive Technologies in Rural Gambia. *Population and Development Review* 20 (1): 81–113.

Boddy, Janice. 1989. *Wombs and Alien Spirits: Women, Men, and the Zar Cult in Northern Sudan.* Madison: University of Wisconsin Press.

Boissevain, Jeremy. 1979. Towards a Social Anthropology of the Mediterranean. *Current Anthropology* 20 (1): 81–93.

Bouhdiba, Abdelwahab. 1985. *Sexuality in Islam.* London: Routledge and Kegan Paul.

Bourdieu, Pierre. 1965. The Sentiment of Honour in Kabyle Society. In *Honor and Shame: The Values of Mediterranean Society,* ed. John Peristiany, 191–242. London: Weidenfeld and Nicolson.

——. 1990. *The Logic of Practice.* Stanford, Calif.: Stanford University Press.

Bowen, John. 1993. *Muslims through Discourse.* Princeton, N.J.: Princeton University Press.

Bulatao, Rodolfo. 1981. Values and Disvalues of Children in Successive Childbearing Decisions. *Demography* 18 (1): 1–25.

Cain, Mead. 1983. Fertility as Adjustment to Risk. *Population and Development Review* 9 (4): 688–702.

——. 1991. Widows, Sons, and Old-Age Security in Rural Maharashtra: A Comment on Vlassoff. *Population Studies* 45:519–28.

Caldwell, John, and Pat Caldwell. 1987. The Cultural Context of High Fertility in Sub-Saharan Africa. *Population and Development Review* 13 (3): 409–35.

Campbell, J. K. 1965. Honour and the Devil. In *Honour and Shame: The Values of Mediterranean Society,* ed. John Peristiany, 139–70. London: Weidenfeld and Nicolson.

Carter, Anthony. 1995. Agency and Fertility: For an Ethnography of Practice. In *Situating Fertility: Anthropology and Demographic Inquiry,* ed. Susan Greenhalgh, 55–86. Cambridge: Cambridge University Press.

Clark, Sam, Elizabeth Colson, James Lee, and Thayer Scudder. 1995. Ten Thousand Tonga: A Longitudinal Anthropological Study from Southern Zambia, 1956–1991. *Population Studies* 49:91–109.

Clifford, James. 1986. On Ethnographic Allegory. In *Writing Culture: The Poetics and Politics of Ethnography,* ed. James Clifford and George Marcus, 98–121. Berkeley: University of California Press.

Collier, Jane, and Michelle Rosaldo. 1981. Politics and Gender in Simple Societies. In *Sexual Meanings: The Cultural Construction of Gender and Sexuality,* ed. Sherry Ortner and Harriet Whitehead, 275–329. Cambridge: Cambridge University Press.

Comaroff, Jean. 1985. *Body of Power, Spirit of Resistance.* Chicago: University of Chicago Press.

Comaroff, Jean, and John Comaroff. 1993. Introduction. In *Modernity and Its Malcontents: Ritual and Power in Postcolonial Africa,* ed. Jean Comaroff and John Comaroff. Chicago: University of Chicago Press.

Constantinides, Pamela. 1979. Women's Spirit Possession and Urban Adaptation in the Muslim Northern Sudan. In *Women United, Women Divided: Comparative Studies of Ten Contemporary Cultures,* ed. Patricia Caplan and Janet Burja, 185–207. London: Tavistock.

——. 1991. The History of Zar in the Sudan: Theories of Origin, Recorded Observation and Oral Tradition. In *Women's Medicine: The Zar-Bori Cult in Africa and Beyond,* ed. Ioan M. Lewis, Ahmed Al-Safi, and Sayyid Hurreiz, 100–117. Edinburgh: Edinburgh University Press.

Croll, Elisabeth. 2000. *Endangered Daughters: Discrimination and Development in Asia.* London: Routledge.

Cunnison, Ian. 1966. *The Baggara Arabs: Power and the Lineage in a Sudanese Nomad Tribe.* Oxford: Clarendon Press.

Dahl, Gudrun. 1988. Who Can Be Blamed? Interpreting the Beja Drought. Paper presented at the International Conference on Environmental Stress and Security, December 13–15, Royal Swedish Academy of Sciences, Stockholm, Sweden.

Daly, Martin. 1991. *Imperial Sudan: The Anglo-Egyptian Condominium, 1934–1956.* Cambridge: Cambridge University Press.

Das Gupta, Monica. 1987. Selective Discrimination against Female Children in Rural Punjab, India. *Population and Development Review* 13 (1): 77–100.

Davis, John. 1977. *People of the Mediterranean: An Essay in Comparative Social Anthropology.* London: Routledge and Kegan Paul.

Delaney, Carol. 1991. *The Seed and the Soil: Gender and Cosmology in Turkish Village Society.* Berkeley: University of California Press.

Deng, Francis, and Larry Minear. 1992. *The Challenges of Famine Relief: Emergency Operations in the Sudan.* Washington, D.C.: Brookings Institution.

Devisch, René. 1991. Symbol and Symptom among the Yaka of Zaire. In *Body and Space: Symbolic Models of Unity and Division in African Cosmology and Experience,* ed. Anita Jacobson-Widding, 283–302. Stockholm: Almqvist and Wiksell International.

——. 1993. *Weaving the Threads of Life: The Khita Gyn-Eco-Logical Healing Cult among the Yaka.* Chicago: University of Chicago Press.

De Waal, Alex. 1989. *Famine That Kills: Darfur, Sudan, 1984–1985.* Oxford Studies in African Affairs. New York: Oxford University Press.

di Leonardo, Micaela. 1991. Gender, Culture, and Political Economy: Feminist Anthropology in Historical Perspective. In *Gender at the Crossroads of Knowledge: Feminist Anthropology in the Postmodern Era,* ed. Micaela di Leonardo, 1–48. Berkeley: University of California Press.

——. 1998. *Exotics at Home: Anthropology, Others, American Modernity.* Chicago: University of Chicago Press.

Dirar, Mohamed Salih. 1991. *The History of Suakin and the Red Sea* [in Arabic]. Khartoum: Aldar Alsudania Lilkutub.

——. 1992. *The History of Eastern Sudan: Beja Tribes and Kingdoms* [in Arabic]. Cairo: Dar Al-Itihad Al-Arbi Liltibaa.

Douglas, Mary. 1966. *Purity and Danger.* Middlesex: Penguin Books.

——. 1970. *Natural Symbols: Explorations in Cosmology.* New York: Pantheon Books.

Drewal, Margaret. 1992. *Yoruba Ritual: Performers, Play, Agency*. Bloomington: Indiana University Press.

Dundes, Alan, ed. 1981. *The Evil Eye: A Folklore Casebook*. New York: Garland.

Edkins, Jenny. 2000. *Whose Hunger? Concepts of Famine, Practices of Aid*. Minneapolis: University of Minnesota Press.

Egeimi, Omer. 1994. The Political Ecology of Subsistence Crisis in the Red Sea Hills, Sudan. Ph.D. diss., Department of Geography, University of Bergen, Norway.

El Harbi, Abbas, and Mohamed Osman Ziad. 1990. Beja Traditional Methods of Famine Prediction and Response Strategies: A Case Study of Sinkat District. Paper presented at the Red Sea Area Program Annual Workshop, Sinkat, Sudan.

El Hassan, Idris Salim. 1990. Khalwa as a Religious Institution. Paper presented at the Red Sea Area Program Annual Workshop, Sinkat, Sudan.

El Nour, Abdel Hamid Balla. 1991. Demographic Characteristics and Population Dynamics of the Red Sea Area: An Appraisal. Paper presented at the Red Sea Area Program Annual Workshop, Sinkat, Sudan.

Evans-Pritchard, Edward. 1956. *Nuer Religion*. Oxford: Oxford University Press.

———. 1960. *Kinship and Marriage among the Nuer*. Oxford: Clarendon Press.

Fadlalla, Amal Hassan. 2005. Modest Women, Deceptive *Jinn*: Identity, Alterity, and Disease in Eastern Sudan. *Identities* 12 (2): 143–74.

Farmer, Paul. 1992. *AIDS and Accusation: Haiti and the Geography of Blame*. Berkeley: University of California Press.

———. 1996. Women, Poverty, and Aids. In *Women, Poverty, and AIDS: Sex, Drugs, and Structural Violence*, ed. Paul Farmer, Margaret Connors, and Janie Simmons, 1–39. Monroe, Maine: Common Courage Press.

Featherstone, Mike, Mike Hepworth, and Bryan Turner, eds. 1991. *The Body: The Social Process and Cultural Theory*. London: Sage.

Feldman-Savelsberg, Pamela. 1999. *Plundered Kitchens, Empty Wombs: Threatened Reproduction and Identity in Cameroon Grassfields*. Ann Arbor: University of Michigan Press.

Fortes, Meyer. 1970. *Time and Social Structure and Other Essays*. New York: Humanities Press.

Foucault, Michel. 1977. *Discipline and Punish: The Birth of the Prison*. New York: Vintage Books.

———. 1980. *Power/Knowledge: Selected Interviews and Other Writings, 1972–1977*. Ed. Colin Gordon. New York: Pantheon.

———. 1991. Governmentality. In *The Foucault Effect: Studies in Governmentality*, ed. Graham Burchell, Colin Gordon, and Peter Miller, 87–104. Chicago: University of Chicago Press.

Gadalla, Saad, James McCarthy, and Oona Campbell. 1985. How the Number of Living Sons Influences Contraceptive Use in Menoufia Governorate, Egypt. *Studies in Family Planning* 16:164–69.

Gal, Susan. 1991. Between Speech and Silence: The Problematics of Research on Language and Gender. In *Gender at the Crossroads of Knowledge: Feminist Anthropology in the Postmodern Era*, ed. Micaela di Leonardo, 175–203. Berkeley: University of California Press.

Gellner, Ernest. 1969. *Saints of the Atlas*. London: Weidenfeld and Nicolson.

Gennep, Arnold van. 1960. *The Rites of Passage*. Chicago: University of Chicago Press.

Gilmore, David, ed. 1987. *Honor and Shame and the Unity of the Mediterranean*. Washington, D.C.: American Anthropological Association.

Ginsburg, Faye, and Rayna Rapp, eds. 1995. *Conceiving the New World Order: The Global Politics of Reproduction*. Berkeley: University of California Press.

Goffman, Erving. 1959. *The Presentation of Self in Everyday Life*. New York: Anchor Books.

———. 1963. *Stigma*. Englewood Cliffs, N.J.: Prentice-Hall.

Goody, Jack. 1976. *Production and Reproduction*. Cambridge: Cambridge University Press.

Gottlieb, Alma, ed. 1988. *Blood Magic: The Anthropology of Menstruation*. Berkeley: University of California Press.

Graham, G. W. 1927. Water Supply in the Gash Delta. Unpublished report, Sinkat Council Archives.

Grauer, Armgard, and John Kennedy. 1978. The Dogri: Evil Beings of the Nile. In *Nubian Ceremonial Life*, ed. John Kennedy, 114–24. Berkeley: University of California Press.

Gravel, Pierre. 1995. *The Malevolent Eye: An Essay on the Evil Eye, Fertility, and the Concept of Mana*. New York: P. Lang

Greenhalgh, Susan. 1994. Controlling Births and Bodies in Village China. *American Ethnologist* 21 (1): 3–30.

———, ed. 1995. *Situating Fertility: Anthropology and Demographic Inquiry*. Cambridge: Cambridge University Press.

Gruenbaum, Ellen. 1982. The Movement against Clitoridectomy and Infibulation in Sudan: Public Health Policy and the Women's Movement. *Medical Anthropology Quarterly* 13:4–12.

———. 2001. *The Female Circumcision Controversy: An Anthropological Perspective*. Philadelphia: University of Pennsylvania Press.

Gupta, Akhil, and James Ferguson. 1997. Beyond "Culture": Space, Identity, and the Politics of Difference. In *Culture, Power, Place: Explorations in Critical Anthropology*, ed. Akhil Gupta and James Ferguson, 33–51. Durham, N.C.: Duke University Press.

Guyer, Jane. 1995. Wealth in People, Wealth in Things. *Journal of African History* 36: 83–90.

———. 1996. Traditions of Inventions in Equatorial Africa. *African Studies Review* 39 (3): 1–28.

Hale, Sondra. 1997. *Gender Politics in Sudan: Islamism, Socialism, and the State*. Boulder, Colo.: Westview Press.

Hamadi, A. Hamadi. n.d. *Suakin: The Port of Good Tidings*. Khartoum: Ministry of Information.

Hamid, Gamal. 1996. *Population Displacement in the Sudan: Patterns, Responses, Coping Strategies*. New York: Center for Migration Studies.

Hammel, Eugene A. 1990. A Theory of Culture for Demography. *Population and Development Review* 16 (3): 455–85.

Handwerker, W. Penn, ed. 1990. *Births and Power: Social Change and the Politics of Reproduction.* Boulder, Colo.: Westview Press.

Harfouche, Jamal Karam. 1980. The Evil Eye and Infant Health in Lebanon. In *The Evil Eye: A Folklore Casebook,* ed. Alan Dundes, 86 –106. New York: Garland.

Harvey, David. 1989. *The Condition of Postmodernity: An Inquiry into the Origin of Cultural Change.* Cambridge, Mass.: Blackwell.

Helms, Mary. 1988. *Ulysses' Sail: An Ethnographic Odyssey of Power, Knowledge, and Geographical Distance.* Princeton, N.J.: Princeton University Press.

Herzfeld, Michael. 1980. Honor and Shame: Problems in the Comparative Analysis of Moral Systems. *Man,* n.s., 15 (2): 339 –51.

———. 1981. Meaning and Morality: A Semiotic Approach to Evil Eye Accusations in a Greek Village. *American Ethnologist* 8:560 –74.

Hill, Jane, and Judith Irvine, eds. 1992. *Responsibility and Evidence in Oral Discourse.* Cambridge: Cambridge University Press.

Hjort, Anders, and Gudrun Dahl. 1991. *Responsible Man: The Atmaan Beja of North-Eastern Sudan.* Uppsala: Nordiska Afrikainstitutet.

Holt, Peter Malcolm, and Martin Daly. 1979. *The History of the Sudan from the Coming of Islam to the Present Day.* Boulder, Colo.: Westview Press.

Hornborg, Alf, and Mikael Kurkiala, eds. 1998. *Voices of the Land: Identity and Ecology in the Margins.* Lund: Lund University Press.

Hughes, Diane, and Thomas Trautmann, eds. 1995. *Time: Histories and Ethnologies.* Ann Arbor: University of Michigan Press.

Hunt, Nancy Rose. 1999. *A Colonial Lexicon: Of Birth Ritual, Medicalization, and Mobility in the Congo.* Durham, N.C.: Duke University Press.

Ibrahim, Abdullahi. 1990. Beja Scholars and the Creativity of Powerlessness. Proceedings of the Red Sea Area Program, Third Annual Workshop, University of Khartoum, Sudan, and University of Bergen, Norway.

———. 1994. *Assaulting with Words: Popular Discourse and the Bridle of Shariah.* Evanston, Ill.: Northwestern University Press.

Inhorn, Marcia. 1994. *Quest for Conception: Gender, Infertility, and Egyptian Medical Traditions.* Philadelphia: University of Pennsylvania Press.

Jacobsen, Frode. 1998. *Theories of Sickness and Misfortune amongst the Hadendowa Beja: Narratives as Points of Entry into Beja Cultural Knowledge.* London: Kegan Paul International.

Jacobson-Widding, Anita, ed. 1991. *Body and Space: Symbolic Models of Unity and Division in African Cosmology and Experience.* Uppsala Studies in Cultural Anthropology 16. Stockholm: Almqvist and Wiksell International.

James, Wendy, ed. 1995. *The Pursuit of Certainty: Religions and Cultural Formulations.* London: Routledge.

Janzen, John. 1982. *Lemba, 1950–1930: A Drum of Affliction in Africa and the New World.* New York: Garland.

———. 1992. *Nagoma: Discourses of Healing in Central and Southern Africa.* Berkeley: University of California Press.

Keesing, Roger. 1992. *Custom and Confrontation: The Kwaio Struggle for Cultural Autonomy.* Chicago: University of Chicago Press.

Kenyon, Susan. 1995. Zar as Modernization in Contemporary Sudan. *Anthropological Quarterly* 68 (2): 107–20.

Kertzer, David, and Tom Fricke. 1997. Toward an Anthropological Demography. In *Anthropological Demography: Toward a New Synthesis,* ed. David Kertzer and Tom Fricke, 1–35. Chicago: University of Chicago Press.

Khalifa, Muna. 1984. Mortality in North Sudan. *Sudan Journal of Population Studies* 2:57–74.

Kleinman, Arthur, and Joan Kleinman. 1991. Suffering and Its Professional Transformation: Toward an Ethnography of Interpersonal Experience. *Culture, Medicine, and Psychiatry* 15 (3): 275–301.

Kopytoff, Igor. 1991. "Medicines" and the Sexual Transmission of Disease among the Suku of Zaire. In *Body and Space: Symbolic Models of Unity and Division in African Cosmology and Experience,* ed. Anita Jacobson-Widding, 303–14. Stockholm: Almqvist and Wiksell International.

Kramer, Fritz. 1993. *The Red Fez: Art and Spirit Possession in Africa.* Trans. Malcolm Green. London: Verso.

Kurkiala, Mikael. 1998. Modernity, Culture, and the Construction of Identity. In *Voices of the Land: Identity and Ecology in the Margins,* ed. Alf Hornborg and Mikael Kurkiala, 35–48. Lund: Lund University Press.

Lambek, Michael. 1990. Certain Knowledge, Contestable Authority: Power and Practice on the Islamic Periphery. *American Ethnologist* 17 (1): 23–40.

Launy, Robert. 1995. The Power of Names: Illegitimacy in a Muslim Community in Côte d'Ivoire. In *Situating Fertility: Anthropology and Demographic Inquiry,* ed. Susan Greenhalgh, 108–29. Cambridge: Cambridge University Press.

Leach, Edmund. 1954. *Political Systems of Highland Burma: A Study of Kachin Social Structure.* Cambridge, Mass.: Harvard University Press.

Levine, Nancy. 1987. Differential Childcare in Three Tibetan Communities: Beyond Son Preference. *Population and Development Review* 13 (2): 281–304.

Levine, Robert, and Sarah Levine. 1991. House Design and the Self in an African Culture. In *Body and Space: Symbolic Models of Unity and Division in African Cosmology and Experience,* ed. Anita Jacobson-Widding, 155–76. Stockholm: Almqvist and Wiksell International.

Lewis, Ioan M. 1989. *Ecstatic Religion: A Study of Shamanism and Spirit Possession.* London: Routledge.

Lock, Margaret, and Nancy Scheper-Hughes. 1990. A Critical-Interpretive Approach in Medical Anthropology: Rituals and Routines of Discipline and Dissent. In *Medical Anthropology: A Handbook of Theory and Method,* ed. Thomas Johnson and Carolyn Sargent, 47–73. New York: Greenwood.

MacCormack, Carol. 1982. *Ethnography of Fertility and Birth.* London: Academic Press.

Malkki, Liisa. 1996. Speechless Emissaries: Refugees, Humanitarianism, and Dehistoricization. *Cultural Anthropology* 11 (3): 377–404.

Maloney, Clarence, ed. 1976. *The Evil Eye.* New York: Columbia University Press.

Manger, Leif. 1994. *From the Mountains to the Plains: The Integration of the Lafofa Nuba into Sudanese Society.* Uppsala: Nordiska Afrikainstitutet.

———. 1996. Making Ends Meet: Some Viability Problems among Hadendowa

Households. In *Survival on Meagre Resources: Hadendowa Pastoralism in the Red Sea Hills*, ed. Leif Manger, 120–38. Uppsala: Nordiska Afrikainstitutet.

Marcus, Michael. 1987. Horsemen Are the Fence of the Land: Honor and History among the Ghiyata of Eastern Morocco. In *Honor and Shame and the Unity of the Mediterranean*, ed. David Gilmore, 49–60. Washington, D.C.: American Anthropological Association.

Martin, Emily. 1987. *The Woman in the Body: A Cultural Analysis of Reproduction.* Boston: Beacon Press.

Menken, Jane. 1985. Age and Fertility: How Late Can You Wait? *Demography* 22 (4): 469–83.

Mernissi, Fatima. 1977. Women, Saints, and Sanctuaries. *Signs* 3:101–12.

Messick, Brinkley. 1987. Subordinate Discourse: Women, Weaving, and Gender Relations in North Africa. *American Ethnologist* 14 (2): 210–23.

Mohamed Salih, Hassan. 1976. The Hadendowa: Pastoralism and Problems of Sedentarization. Ph.D. diss. in social anthropology, University of Hull, England.

Mohanram, Radhika. 1999. *Black Body: Women, Colonialism, and Space.* Minneapolis: University of Minnesota Press.

Morgan, Kathryn. 1994. Women and the Knife: Cosmetic Surgery and the Colonization of Women's Bodies. In *Living with Contradictions: Controversies in Feminist Social Ethics*, ed. Alison M. Jagger, 239–56. Boulder, Colo.: Westview Press.

Morinis, Alan, ed. 1992. *Sacred Journeys: The Anthropology of Pilgrimage.* Westport, Conn.: Greenwood Press.

Morsy, Soheir. 1990. Political Economy in Medical Anthropology. In *Medical Anthropology: A Handbook of Theory and Method*, ed. Thomas Johnson and Carolyn Sargent, 26–47. New York: Greenwood.

Morton, J., and Z. Fre. 1986. Red Sea Province and the Beja: A Preliminary Report to Oxfam. Port Sudan, Sudan.

Musallam, Basim. 1983. *Sex and Society in Islam: Birth Control before the Nineteenth Century.* Cambridge: Cambridge University Press.

Nadel, Siegfried Frederick. 1952. Witchcraft in Four African Societies: An Essay in Comparison. *American Anthropologist* 54:18–29.

Newbold, D. 1935. The Beja Tribes of the Red Sea Hinterland. In *The Anglo-Egyptian Sudan from Within*, ed. John Hamilton, 140–64. London: Faber and Faber.

Obermeyer, Carla, ed. 1995. *Family, Gender, and Population in the Middle East.* Cairo: American University Press.

——. 1996. Fertility Norms and Son Preference in Morocco and Tunisia: Does Women's Status Matter? *Journal of Biosocial Science* 28:57–72.

O'Brien, Jay. 1985. Sowing the Seeds of Famine: The Political Economy of Food Deficits in Sudan. *Review of African Political Economy* 33:23–101.

Ong, Aihwa. 1987. *Spirits of Resistance and Capitalist Discipline: Factory Women in Malaysia.* Albany: State University of New York Press.

Ortner, Sherry. 1978. The Virgin and the State. *Feminist Studies* 4 (3): 19–35.

Ortner, Sherry, and Harriet Whitehead, eds. 1981. *Sexual Meanings: The Cultural Construction of Gender and Sexuality.* Cambridge: Cambridge University Press.

Oxfam Nutritional Surveillance Team. 1985–1986. Port Sudan Office, Sudan.

Palmisano, Antonio. 1991. *Ethnicity: The Beja as Representation.* Berlin: Das Arabi-sche Buch.

Parkin, David, ed. 1985. *The Anthropology of Evil.* Oxford: Basil Blackwell.

Paul, Andrew. 1954. *A History of the Beja Tribes of the Sudan.* London: Frank Cass.

Pearce, Tola Olu. 1993. Lay Medical Practice in an African Context. In *Knowledge, Power, and Practice: The Anthropology of Medicine and Everyday Life,* ed. Shirley Lindenbaum and Margaret Lock, 150–65. Berkeley: University of California Press.

Pellow, Deborah, ed. 1996. *Setting Boundaries: The Anthropology of Spatial and Social Organization.* Westport, Conn.: Bergen and Garvey.

Perkins, Kenneth. 1993. *Port Sudan: The Evolution of a Colonial City.* Boulder, Colo.: Westview Press.

Pitt-Rivers, Julian. 1965. Honour and Social Status. In *Honour and Shame: The Values of Mediterranean Society,* ed. John Peristiany, 19 –78. London: Weidenfeld and Nicolson.

———. 1977. *The Fate of Shechem or the Politics of Sex: Essays in the Anthropology of the Mediterranean.* Cambridge: Cambridge University Press.

Pong, Suet-Ling. 1994. Sex Preference and Fertility in Peninsular Malaysia. *Studies in Family Planning* 25 (3): 137 –48.

Rapp, Rayna. 1991. Moral Pioneers: Women, Men, and Fetuses on a Frontier of Reproductive Technology. In *Gender at the Crossroads of Knowledge: Feminist Anthropology in the Postmodern Era,* ed. Micaela di Leonardo, 383 –95. Berkeley: University of California Press.

Rasmussen, Susan. 1995. *Spirit Possession and Personhood among the Kel Ewey Tuareg.* Cambridge: Cambridge University Press.

Reminick, Ronald. 1976. The Evil Eye Belief among the Amhara. In *The Evil Eye,* ed. Clarence Maloney, 85 –101. New York: Columbia University Press.

Rene, Elisha. 1996. Perceptions of Population Policy, Development, and Family Planning Programs in Northern Nigeria. *Studies in Family Planning* 27 (3): 127 –36.

Riesman, Paul. 1986. The Person and the Life Cycle in African Social Life and Thought. *African Studies Review* 29:71–138.

———. 1992. *First Find Your Child a Good Mother: The Construction of Self in Two African Communities.* New Brunswick, N.J.: Rutgers University Press.

Robson, Brian. 1993. *Fuzzy-Wuzzy: The Campaigns in Eastern Sudan, 1884–85.* Tun-bridge Wells: Spellmount.

Roden, David. 1970. *The Twentieth Century Decline of Suakin.* Khartoum: Univer-sity of Khartoum, Sudan Research Unit.

Rosaldo, Michelle, and Louise Lamphere, eds. 1974. *Women, Culture, and Society.* Stanford, Calif.: Stanford University Press.

Saghayroun, Atif A. 1983. Values and Cost of Children in Rural Sudan. *Sudan Jour-nal of Population Studies* 1 (1): 29 –59.

Saghayroun, Atif A., and Muna A. Khalifa. 1984. Fertility and Islam in the Sudan. *Sudan Journal of Population Studies* 1 (2): 1–28.

Said, Edward. 1978. *Orientalism.* New York: Pantheon.

Sargent, Carolyn. 1990. The Politics of Birth: Cultural Dimensions of Pain, Virtue, and Control among the Bariba of Benin. In *Births and Power: Social Change and the Politics of Reproduction,* ed. W. Penn Handwerker, 69 –80. Boulder, Colo.: Westview Press.

Scheper-Hughes, Nancy. 1997. Demography without Numbers. In *Anthropological Demography: Toward a New Synthesis,* ed. David Kertzer and Tom Fricke, 201–22. Chicago: University of Chicago Press.

Schneider, Jane. 1971. Of Vigilance and Virgins: Honor, Shame, and Access to Resources in Mediterranean Societies. *Ethnology* 10:1–24.

Scott, James. 1990. *Domination and the Arts of Resistance: Hidden Transcripts.* New Haven, Conn.: Yale University Press.

Sen, Amartya. 1981. *Poverty and Famines: An Essay on Entitlement and Deprivation.* Oxford: Clarendon Press.

———. 2001. The Many Faces of Gender Inequality. *The New Republic,* September 17, 35 –40.

Shell-Duncan, Bettina. 2001. The Medicalization of Female "Circumcision": Harm Reduction or Promotion of a Dangerous Practice. *Social Science and Medicine* 52: 1013 –28.

Sikainga, Ahmad. 1996. *Slaves into Workers: Emancipation and Labor in Colonial Sudan.* Austin: University of Texas Press.

Sinkat Council. 1993. Statistical data.

Skinner, William. 1997. Family Systems and Demographic Processes. In *Anthropological Demography: Toward a New Synthesis,* ed. David Kertzer and Tom Fricke, 53 –95. Chicago: University of Chicago Press.

Sobo, Elisa. 1993a. Bodies, Kin and Flow: Family Planning in Rural Jamaica. *Medical Anthropology Quarterly* 7 (1): 50–73.

———. 1993b. *One Blood: The Jamaican Body.* Albany: State University of New York.

Spooner, Brian. 1976. Anthropology and the Evil Eye. In *The Evil Eye,* ed. Clarence Maloney, 279 –86. New York: Columbia University Press.

Stewart, Frank. 1994. *Honor.* Chicago: University of Chicago Press.

Stoler, Ann Laura. 1991. Carnal Knowledge and Imperial Power: Gender, Race, and Morality in Colonial Asia. In *Gender at the Crossroads of Knowledge: Feminist Anthropology in the Postmodern Era,* ed. Micaela di Leonardo, 51–101. Berkeley: University of California Press.

Stoller, Paul. 1995. *Embodying Colonial Memories: Spirit Possession, Power and the Hauka in West Africa.* New York: Routledge.

Strathern, Marilyn. 1992. *Reproducing the Future: Essays on Anthropology, Kinship and the New Reproductive Technologies.* New York: Routledge.

Sudan Demographic and Health Survey. 1991. Khartoum: Department of Statistics, Ministry of Economics and National Planning; Columbia, Md.: Demographic and Health Surveys, Institute for Resource Development/Macro International.

Sudan News Agency (SUNA). 2001. Media reports.

Taussig, Michael. 1993. *Mimesis and Alterity: A Particular History of the Senses.* New York: Routledge

Toubia, Nahid, ed. 1988. *Women of the Arab World: The Coming Challenge.* London: Zed Press.

———. 1994. Female Circumcision as a Public Health Issue. *New England Journal of Medicine* 331:712–16.

Turner, Victor. 1974. *Dramas, Fields, and Metaphors: Symbolic Action in Human So-ciety*. Ithaca, N.Y.: Cornell University Press.

———. 1975. *Revelation and Divination in Ndembu Ritual: Symbol, Myth and Ritual*. Ithaca, N.Y.: Cornell University Press.

Umbada, Siddiq. 1989. Economic Crises in Sudan: Impact and Response. ISER paper presented at the University of West Indies.

Vermeulen, Hans, and Cora Govers, eds. 1994. *The Anthropology of Ethnicity: Be-yond Ethnic Groups and Boundaries*. Amsterdam: Spinhuis.

Voll, John. 1969. A History of the Khatmiyyah Tariqah in the Sudan. Ph.D. diss., Harvard University.

White, Luise. 2000. *Speaking with Vampires: Rumor and History in Colonial Africa*. Berkeley: University of California Press.

Whyte, Susan. 1997. *Questioning Misfortune: The Pragmatics of Uncertainty in East-ern Uganda*. Cambridge: Cambridge University Press.

Wikan, Unni. 1984. Shame and Honour: A Contestable Pair. *Man* 19:635–52.

Yanagisako, Sylvia, and Jane Collier. 1994. Gender and Kinship Reconsidered: To-ward a Unified Analysis. In *Assessing Cultural Anthropology*, ed. Robert Borofsky, 190–203. New York: McGraw-Hill.

Young, William. 1996. *The Rashaayda Bedouin: Arab Pastoralists of Eastern Sudan*. Fort Worth, Tex.: Harcourt Brace.

Index

Page numbers in italics refer to figures and tables.

199